SOUTHEAST ASIA IN THE GLOBAL ECONOMY

The **S. Rajaratnam School of International Studies (RSIS)** was inaugurated on 1 January 2007 as an autonomous School within the Nanyang Technological University (NTU), upgraded from its previous incarnation as the Institute of Defence and Strategic Studies (IDSS), which was established in 1996.

The School exists to develop a community of scholars and policy analysts at the forefront of Asia-Pacific security studies and international affairs. Its three core functions are research, graduate teaching and networking activities in the Asia-Pacific region. It produces cutting-edge security related research in Asia-Pacific Security, Conflict and Non-Traditional Security, International Political Economy, and Country and Area Studies.

The School's activities are aimed at assisting policymakers to develop comprehensive approaches to strategic thinking on issues related to security and stability in the Asia-Pacific and their implications for Singapore.

The **Institute of Southeast Asian Studies (ISEAS)** was established as an autonomous organization in 1968. It is a regional centre dedicated to the study of socio-political, security and economic trends and developments in Southeast Asia and its wider geostrategic and economic environment. The Institute's research programmes are the Regional Economic Studies (RES, including ASEAN and APEC), Regional Strategic and Political Studies (RSPS), and Regional Social and Cultural Studies (RSCS).

ISEAS Publishing, an established academic press, has issued almost 2,000 books and journals. It is the largest scholarly publisher of research about Southeast Asia from within the region. ISEAS Publishing works with many other academic and trade publishers and distributors to disseminate important research and analyses from and about Southeast Asia to the rest of the world.

SOUTHEAST ASIA IN THE GLOBAL ECONOMY

SECURING COMPETITIVENESS AND SOCIAL PROTECTION

EDITED BY
Helen E.S. Nesadurai
and **J. Soedradjad Djiwandono**

**S. RAJARATNAM SCHOOL
OF INTERNATIONAL STUDIES**
A Graduate School of Nanyang Technological University

I5EA5
INSTITUTE OF SOUTHEAST ASIAN STUDIES
Singapore

First published in Singapore in 2009 by
ISEAS Publishing
Institute of Southeast Asian Studies
30 Heng Mui Keng Terrace, Pasir Panjang
Singapore 119614

E-mail: publish@iseas.edu.sg
Website: bookshop.iseas.edu.sg

jointly with
S. Rajaratnam School of International Studies
Nanyang Technological University
Blk S4, Level B4,
Nanyang Avenue,
Singapore 639798

E-mail: wwwrsis@ntu.edu.sg

The responsibility for facts and opinions in this publication rests exclusively with the authors and their interpretations do not necessarily reflect the views or the policy of the publishers or their supporters.

ISEAS Library Cataloguing-in-Publication Data

Southeast Asia in the global economy : securing competitiveness and social protection / edited by Helen E.S. Nesadurai and J. Soedradjad Djiwandono.
   1. Competition—Southeast Asia—Congresses.
   2. Competition—Government policy—Southeast Asia—Congresses.
   3. Industrial policy—Southeast Asia—Congresses.
   I. Nesadurai, Helen Sharmini.
   II. Djiwandono, Joseph Soedradjad, 1938-
   III. S. Rajaratnam School of International Studies.
   IV. Workshop on Southeast Asia in the Global Economy: Avoiding the Problem of Globalisation's 'Missing Middle' (2005 : Singapore)
HD3616 A9S82   2009

ISBN   978-981-230-823-8 (hard cover)
ISBN   978-981-230-824-5 (PDF)

Typeset by International Typesetters Pte Ltd
Printed in Singapore by Mainland Press Pte Ltd

CONTENTS

PART 1:
SOUTHEAST ASIA/ASEAN AND THE ASIAN "GIANTS"

PART 2:
SECURING INTERNATIONAL COMPETITIVENESS

PART 3:
COMPETITIVENESS AND THE SOCIAL DIMENSION

LIST OF TABLES AND APPENDICES

Tables

Tables

Tables

Appendices

LIST OF FIGURES

CONTRIBUTORS

Mukul G. Asher is Professor in the Lee Kuan Yew School of Public Policy at the National University of Singapore.

Chew Soon Beng is Professor of Economics and Industrial Relations in the Division of Economics, School of Humanities and Social Sciences, Nanyang Technological University, Singapore.

Rosalind Chew is Associate Professor in the Division of Economics, School of Humanities and Social Sciences, Nanyang Technological University, Singapore.

Heribert Dieter is Senior Research Associate at the German Institute for International and Security Affairs, Berlin, and an Associate Fellow of the Centre for the Study of Globalisation and Regionalisation, University of Warwick, U.K.

J. Soedradjad Djiwandono is Emeritus Professor of Economics at University Indonesia and Professor at the S. Rajaratnam School of International Studies (RSIS, formerly the Institute of Defence and Strategic Studies), a research graduate school of the Nanyang Technological University, Singapore.

Carolina S. Guina is an independent consultant working on a variety of social development and regional integration issues for international organizations.

Liu Yunhua is Associate Professor of Economics in the School of Humanities and Social Sciences, Nanyang Technological University, Singapore.

Amarendu Nandy is a doctoral student in the Lee Kuan Yew School of Public Policy, National University of Singapore.

Helen E. S. Nesadurai is Senior Lecturer in International Studies at the School of Arts and Social Sciences, Monash University (Sunway Campus, Malaysia). Previously, she was Assistant Professor at the S. Rajaratnam School of International Studies (RSIS, formerly the Institute of Defence and Strategic Studies), a research graduate school of the Nanyang Technological University, Singapore.

Bala Ramasamy is Professor of Economics at the China-Europe International Business School (CEIBS) in Shanghai, China.

Rajah Rasiah is Professor of Technology and Innovation Policy in the Faculty of Economics and Administration, Universiti Malaya, Kuala Lumpur, Malaysia.

Rahul Sen was a Fellow in the Regional Economic Studies Programme at the Institute of Southeast Asian Studies (ISEAS) in Singapore at the time of this project. He is now Lecturer in Economics at the AUT Business School in Auckland, New Zealand.

Sadhana Srivastava was a Research Scholar in the South Asian Studies Programme at the National University of Singapore. She is now Lecturer in Economics at the AUT Business School in Auckland, New Zealand.

ACKNOWLEDGEMENTS

Many people have been involved in the completion of this edited book, not least the book's contributors. Their patience as we editors put together this volume, delayed by the move by one of us from Singapore to Malaysia, is highly appreciated. Their insights have made possible this collaborative contribution to ongoing debates about the fate of Southeast Asia in a highly competitive world economy.

Special thanks are due to Ambassador Barry Desker, Dean of the S. Rajaratnam School of International Studies (RSIS, formerly, the Institute of Defence and Strategic Studies), a research graduate school of the Nanyang Technological University, Singapore, who generously allocated the funding that made possible the November 2005 Workshop in Singapore at which the various chapters in this book were first presented and debated. We are also grateful to the participants at that workshop whose active and lively participation helped the authors clarify many points of contention that emerged during the course of our deliberations.

We are also indebted to Ambassador Kesavapany of the Institute of Southeast Asian Studies for supporting the publication of this edited volume under the joint imprint of the Institute of Southeast Asian Studies (ISEAS) and the S. Rajaratnam School of International Studies. Mrs Triena Ong, Managing Editor and Head of ISEAS Publications, deserves special mention for her unwavering support for this book project. The support of the staff of ISEAS Publishing is also deeply appreciated.

Our final thanks go to the administrative staff at RSIS/IDSS who deserve special mention for their hard work, cheerful good humour and willingness to go the extra mile to ensure the successful completion of the workshop and the production of this book. Regina Arokiasamy's excellent administrative support before, during and well after the workshop has been invaluable to the editors, Peter Ee went out of his way to ensure the smooth running of the workshop, ably supported by Ben Ng, Adeline Lim and Yvonne Lee, while Caroline Ng made sure the project progressed smoothly and its financial needs efficiently addressed. Without the help and support of these and many others at RSIS, we, the editors, would not have been able to complete this book project.

Helen E. S. Nesadurai and J. Soedradjad Djiwandono
November 2007

ABBREVIATIONS

ACCA   Association of Certified Chartered Accountants
ADB   Asian Development Bank
AEC   ASEAN Economic Community
AFTA   ASEAN Free Trade Area
ASCC   ASEAN Socio-Cultural Community
ASEAN   Association of Southeast Asian Nations
AUSFTA   Australia-United States Free Trade Agreement
BBC   Brand-to-Brand Complementation Scheme (of ASEAN)
BI   Basic Infrastructure
BPO   Business Process Outsourcing
CECA   Comprehensive Economic Cooperation Agreement
            (between India and ASEAN)
CEO   Chief Executive Officer
CPF   Central Provident Fund (of Singapore)
CSR   Corporate Social Responsibility
EFTA   European Free Trade Area
EPF   Employees' Provident Fund (of Malaysia)
EU   European Union
FDI   Foreign Direct Investment
FSPSI   All Indonesia Workers Union Federation
FTA   Free Trade Agreements
G-21   Group of 21
GATT   General Agreement on Tariffs and Trade
GCF   Gross Capital Formation
GDCF   Gross Domestic Capital Formation
GDP   Gross Domestic Product
GIC   Government Investment Corporation (of Singapore)
GLC   Government Linked Company

GNI	Gross National Investment
GPF	Government Pension Fund (of Thailand)
GSIS	Government Service Insurance System (of the Philippines)
HR	Human Resources
HS	Harmonized System
HTI	High Technology Infrastructure
ICT	Information and Communication Technology
ILO	International Labour Organization
IMF	International Monetary Fund
IPR	Intellectual Property Rights
ISO	International Standards Organization
IT	Information Technology
JSEPA	Japan-Singapore Economic Partnership Agreement
KPO	Knowledge Process Outsourcing
MES	Minimum Efficiency Scale
MFN	Most Favoured Nation
MNCs/MNEs	Multinational Corporations/Multinational Enterprises
MSC	Multimedia Super Corridor (of Malaysia)
MTUC	Malaysian Trade Union Congress
NAFTA	North American Free Trade Area
NC	Network Cohesion
NEP	New Economic Policy (Malaysia)
NIS	National Innovation System
NS	Network Strength
NTUC	National Trades Union Congress (of Singapore)
OECD	Organization for Economic Cooperation and Development
PANEURO	Pan European Cumulation of Origin
PAP	People's Action Party (of Singapore)
PRC	People's Republic of China
PSA	Port of Singapore Authority
PT	Process Technology
R&D	Research and Development
SAP	Structural Adjustment Programme
SITC	Standard International Trade Classification
SME	Small and Medium-Scale Enterprises
SSO	Social Security Organization (of Thailand)
SSS	Social Security System (of the Philippines)
TI	Technological Intensity
UMNO	United Malays National Organization (of Malaysia)
UNCTAD	United Nations Conference on Trade and Development

USA/US	United States of America
USSFTA	United States-Singapore Free Trade Agreement
WEF	World Economic Forum
WTO	World Trade Organization

Currencies

AU$	Australian Dollar
Baht	Thai Baht
P	Philippine Peso
RM	Malaysian Ringgit
Rp	Indonesian Rupiah
S$	Singapore Dollar
US$	United States Dollar

1

INTRODUCTION
Southeast Asia in the Global Economy

Helen E. S. Nesadurai and
J. Soedradjad Djiwandono

In a 2004 article in the journal *Foreign Affairs*, Professor Geoffrey Garret of the University of California in Los Angeles highlighted a problem increasingly identified as a key feature of globalization — what he called globalization's "missing middle". Garret (2004) argued that that while globalization has clearly benefited many, it has also squeezed those in the middle — certain middle-income countries in the international system as well as middle-income groups within states, particularly in the industrial world. Although Garret directed much of his remarks at Latin American and Eastern European countries, this issue is relevant to Southeast Asia as well. There is a growing sense that while globalization certainly benefited this region, especially from the 1990s' boom until the 1997 Asian financial crisis, Southeast Asia may be in danger of becoming globalization's "missing middle" if it is unable to maintain its attractiveness to global capital in an increasingly competitive world economy.

It was once believed that countries could avoid such a predicament and enhance their international competitiveness by leveraging lower labour and other costs, and/or become conversant in the knowledge economy. In fact, the region's development story showcases how both approaches have brought success to Southeast Asia. Today, both strategies seem fraught with potential problems and pitfalls, not least because of the looming presence of India and China, which seem to have "cornered" the market in both sets of activities. With both these Asian "giants" seemingly able to appropriate the entire range of economic activities that span the value chain, the worry is that Southeast Asia is in danger of becoming globalization's casualty, its "missing middle".

How Southeast Asia fares in the global economy will depend a great deal on what its leaders and policymakers do to ensure their respective economies adjust to the Chinese and Indian economic presence. That both these giants will need to be factored into governments' economic planning remains certain. In a recent World Bank study on the global implications of India's and China's economic rise, the Bank emphasized that despite the problems and challenges faced by these two countries, China and India will continue to grow at roughly twice the rate of the global economy over the next fifteen years.[1] Thus, while Bank officials point to the considerable opportunities that will be created by China's and India's economic dynamism and their integration into world markets, they also advise other governments to identify "niche" areas safe from the competition that these two Asian juggernauts will pose to virtually every country in the years to come.[2]

The importance of identifying economic niches in which countries have clear comparative or competitive advantage has been raised by scholars of Southeast Asia as well, including authors in this volume — Rahul Sen and Sadhana Srivastava writing on India in Chapter 2, and Liu Yunhua discussing China in Chapter 3. Half a decade ago, in reviewing Southeast Asia's traditional approach to growth and development following the 1997 Asian financial crisis, Freeman and Hew called on the region to move away from its preoccupation with cost competitiveness and to "make the transition from a conventional production-based economy to a knowledge-based one" (Freeman and Hew 2002, p. 4). They also advised governments to focus on niche areas of economic activity — specific areas where their countries' comparative advantage was greatest. This point on niche areas was also emphasized by Garret.

Garret (2004) suggested that globalization had been disappointing for many countries because they had not managed to find their particular niche in world markets. In particular, Garret called on countries to find ways to "tech-up" — to build up a large pool of skilled, creative labour that will, in turn, foster a climate of innovation and creativity. Winters and Yusuf, editors of the World Bank study mentioned previously, similarly emphasize skilled and innovative human resources and technological capability as vital for countries wishing to adjust to competition from China and India, and to sustain their own growth performances in the future. For these two writers, countries can only hope to avoid being hurt by competition posed by the Chinese and Indian powerhouses if they "invest heavily in the skills and technological capabilities of firms" (Winters and Yusuf 2007, p. 33).

STRIVING FOR COMPETITIVENESS

Despite Krugman's (1994) admonishment that competitiveness is a "dangerous obsession" for countries, we find governments, business firms, and international organizations such as the World Trade Organization (WTO), the World Bank, and the International Monetary Fund (IMF), continuing to emphasize the critical importance of competitiveness for countries. Likewise, the World Economic Forum (WEF),[3] a private, not-for-profit foundation that engages the world's leaders, captains of industry, leading opinion makers, and scholars, has been producing an annual Global Competitiveness Report since 1979,[4] with national governments each year eagerly waiting to see how their respective countries have fared in this annual "beauty" pageant. In the latest 2006–07 report, countries have been ranked according to their performance in nine pillars or areas identified to be critical in driving productivity and competitiveness (Lopez-Claros 2006, p. xiv). This approach, in fact, is an innovation in methodology for the WEF, developed by Professor Xavier Salai-i-Martin, and was adopted for the first time in compiling the 2006 index (Lopez-Claros 2006, p.xiv). The nine areas identified as critical for competitiveness have, in turn, been subdivided into three sub-indexes — basic requirements, efficiency enhancers, and innovation factors (see Table 1.1).

A closer look at the sub-indexes reveals the crucial role of technology and innovation in determining a country's productivity and competitiveness worldwide. In identifying Singapore, Japan, Hong Kong, and Taiwan as high performers in Asia, the Competitiveness Report emphasized their excellent basic infrastructure as well as their well-educated and well-trained workforce. The Report additionally pointed out that these countries were "operating on the outer boundaries of the technology frontier, both at the firm and consumer level" (Lopez-Claros 2006, p. xvi). In particular, the Report regards the capacity for innovation by firms and the sophistication of firm operations as key factors in determining national competitiveness.

Unfortunately, the sub-indexes also reveal that Southeast Asian countries need to take serious steps to enhance their technological readiness and innovation. Rajah Rasiah's findings in Chapter 5 of this volume — that firms in Southeast Asia lag behind those in Northeast Asia in terms of research and development (R&D) and technological enhancement activities — further confirms the need for governments and firms in Southeast Asia

TABLE 1.1
Global Competitiveness Rankings, 2006

Country	Overall Index of Competitiveness Score (Rank)	Basic Requirements Score (Rank)	Efficiency Enhancers Score (Rank)	Innovation Factors Score (Rank)
India	4.44 (43)	4.51 (60)	4.32 (41)	4.60 (26)
China	4.24 (54)	4.80 (44)	3.66 (71)	3.75 (57)
Singapore	5.63 (5)	6.13 (2)	5.63 (3)	5.11 (15)
Malaysia	5.11 (26)	5.44 (24)	4.89 (26)	4.91 (22)
Thailand	4.58 (35)	4.98 (38)	4.29 (43)	4.15 (36)
Indonesia	4.26 (50)	4.41 (68)	4.12 (50)	4.07 (41)
Philippines	4.00 (71)	4.19 (84)	3.85 (63)	3.63 (66)
Vietnam	3.89 (77)	4.37 (71)	3.45 (83)	3.32 (81)
Cambodia	3.39 (103)	3.83 (100)	2.94 (110)	3.05 (102)

Notes:

a. The maximum score possible is 7. A total of 125 countries were ranked.

b. Basic requirements cover four pillars or areas: institutions, infrastructure, macro-economic management, and health and primary education.

c. Efficiency enhancers include three pillars: higher education and training, market efficiency, and technological readiness.

d. Innovation factors cover two pillars: business sophistication, and innovation capacity.

Source: Compiled from *The Global Competitiveness Report 2006–2007* of the World Economic Forum.

to rethink their policies and strategies for technology and innovation. This point, surprisingly, seems to apply to Singapore as well. Despite its status as a high performer (ranked third) in the WEF's Global Competitiveness Index, Singapore was ranked at fifteenth position in the innovation sub-index with a score of 5.11 compared with an overall competitiveness score of 5.63 (see Table 1.1).

In fact, all nine pillars identified in the *Global Competitiveness Report* work in interconnected ways to drive overall productivity improvements in countries (Lopez-Claros 2006, p. xiv). This seems theoretical common sense. Firm-level technological capabilities are likely to depend not merely on what is done at the firm level, but also on the overall economic climate in which the firm is located. Whether a firm adopts new technologies or engages in firm-level innovative activities will depend, for instance, on the prevailing investment policy in the country, which helps determine whether firms engage in productive networks and relationships with other firms domestically and abroad. In an environment where there are local research and development (R&D) agencies and universities engaging in high quality scientific research, the relationships of films with such local bodies in the area of research and technology development are deemed to be crucial in helping them enhance their own technological and innovative capabilities. A separate Business Competitiveness Index from the WEF reiterates these points, emphasizing that the productivity firms can achieve depends a great deal on a range of macroeconomic, political, legal, and institutional features found in a country, particularly, its competition policy, the sophistication of its financial and equity markets, as well as the quality of its scientific research institutions (Lopez-Claros 2006, p. xxiv).

The theoretical case for a comprehensive treatment of the various factors that contribute to the competitiveness and productivity enhancements of firms, and the economy, more generally, is clear. In reality, however, it may be rather difficult to achieve, given the often weak capacity of many developing countries' governments in policy design, review, and implementation.[5] Many developing countries scored poorly in the overall competitiveness ranking because of this weakness. Nevertheless, Indonesia's rise of twenty-four rungs in the 2006 Business Competitiveness Index from its position in 2005 has been attributed to key improvements in government functions. In contrast, Vietnam fell in the rankings, which also illustrates the fluid nature of a country's competitiveness standing, and the continuous improvements that governments and firms need to make to sustain their competitive edge (Lopez-Claros 2006, p. xxvi). Such efforts clearly require so much more from policymakers who may opt for other, seemingly easier, policy options.

The continued use of low exchange rates in many parts of Southeast Asia to maintain cheap exports suggests that governments will continue to use other tools to manage their export competitiveness, even if such acts are criticized by the international community as ultimately destabilizing (Bowring 2006). What is needed, instead, is for governments and firms to engage in long-term productivity enhancements, particularly in the area of technological upgrading and innovation, as well as labour productivity, two areas in which Southeast Asia, with the exception of Singapore, displays weaknesses. Governments in the region are also beginning to embrace yet another strategy to boost their ability to access markets and foreign capital — bilateral free trade arrangements. Although these are seen as instruments to help firms compete on world markets by securing for them preferential access to the market of the bilateral partner, the anti-competitive effects of bilateral FTAs have yet to be acknowledged by policymakers.

Although trade economists theoretically regard regional cooperation schemes as second best policies of trade liberalization, compared with unilateral or multilateral liberalization, and, consequently, a potential stumbling block to global liberalization, the "new regionalism" of the 1990s tends to be supportive of globalization rather than being a form of resistance to it (Nesadurai 2003, p. 178). Both the ASEAN Free Trade Area (AFTA) and the ASEAN Economic Community, which are cooperative projects to enhance the integration of the Southeast Asian countries collectively into world markets, and to attract global capital to the region, are well known.

However, *bilateral* arrangements are now mushrooming in the region, a response to both the stalemate at the WTO since the abortive 1999 Seattle Ministerial Meeting and the slow pace of regional liberalization in ASEAN (Desker 2004). While bilateral arrangements are usually defended on grounds that they secure access to markets and capital in an uncertain trading environment, critics point to the market fragmentation to which bilateral arrangements can lead (Scollay and Gilbert 2001). Far more than the case of regionwide arrangements, it is the bilateral FTA that gives rise to what Bhagwati et al. (1998) have called the "spaghetti bowl" effect. Given the growing regionalization of production and the growth of intraregional trade in parts and components within Southeast Asia, regional liberalization makes more economic sense than bilateral FTAs, which cut across existing regional production networks in ways that also raise costs for firms already engaged in such relationships (Nesadurai 2003, pp. 182–84).

Heribert Dieter writing in Chapter 4 of this volume argues that not only do *bilateral* FTAs make poor economic sense, but unlike *regional* or plurilateral trading agreements, bilaterals are also suboptimal from the *political* point of view, particularly for developing countries that tend to be in a weaker negotiating position compared with their industrial country negotiating partner. Thus, Dieter also questions the common wisdom that bilateral FTAs tend to be adopted more for their political worth than their economic benefits. More than that, Dieter carefully traces the burden that bilateral FTAs pose for firms because of their complex rules of origin, and the complications such arrangements raise for transnational production in which firms participate. Thus, in assessing the value of bilateral FTAs, we need to consider not only their potential for securing market access — which Dieter argues has been oversold in any case — but we must also evaluate their implications for the cost competitiveness of firms.

While criticizing protectionist strategies as inappropriate responses by governments to the pressures of global competition, Garret (2004) also cautioned governments against rushing to sign more free trade agreements (whether bilateral, regional, or multilateral), which he argued are misguided efforts to ensure countries stay competitive globally. As already noted, Garret advocated instead an emphasis on a more fundamental task — enhancing the technological and innovative capacity of firms and people so that an innate, long-term capacity to respond to all manner of competitive challenges can be built up. For Garret, trade liberalization alone, in whatever form, is insufficient. Moreover, liberalization taking place through bilateral FTAs could inadvertently undermine competitiveness, as Dieter persuasively argues.

One key reason Paul Krugman (1994) criticized the growing obsession with international competitiveness was his concern that it might lead governments to adopt inappropriate and possibly self-defeating policies. If bilateral FTAs and the deliberate preference for undervalued exchange rates are policies that governments have adopted because of their perceived utility in enhancing their countries' international competitiveness, then Krugman was right to be concerned. These policies may be helpful in the short- to medium-term, but their long-run effects are unclear. Economists doubt that such policies can result in a sustained capacity by countries and firms to remain competitive internationally. These policies may be attractive to governments because they may be the "easier" option. Maintaining low exchange rates may yield immediate gains while a bilateral FTA clearly shows that the government in question has, at least formally, secured market opening for its domestic firms.

Yet, as the preceding discussion has shown, productivity and competitiveness are best enhanced through continuous efforts in upgrading human resources, and enhancing the technological and innovative capacities of firms. Governments have a key role in this regard. While the days of interventionist governments may be over, governments, nonetheless, are vital as providers of basic and high technology infrastructure, which firms then draw on to improve their own technological and innovative capacity.

IS COMPETITIVENESS EVERYTHING?
SECURING SOCIAL PROTECTION

Krugman's (1994) point that an obsession with international competitiveness might well result in the adoption of inappropriate or misguided policies, also applies to the sphere of social protection, including labour standards. The common assumption has been that social protection policies will invariably raise firms' operating costs as well as reduce their ability to respond flexibly to the pressures of competition. Consequently, social protection in general, and pro-labour policies in particular, have been rejected by governments and firms as likely to undermine competitiveness. The financial crisis, however, coupled with ongoing domestic economic and social transformations in many parts of Southeast Asia, have brought concerns with economic security to the forefront of policy debates in the region (Nesadurai 2006). Even in China, the socio-economic insecurities arising from rapid industrialization and economic change have prompted the authorities to take the issue of social welfare and social protection seriously (Wang 2006).

Market integration, whether regionally or globally, carries with it both risk and uncertainty under conditions of globalization, which has also made it difficult for governments virtually everywhere to "achieve distributive compromises that accommodate and attenuate class, communal and regional conflicts" (Thakur 1997, p. 58). It is now increasingly recognized that deep and extensive global market integration — globalization — creates both winners and losers, thereby resulting in considerable dislocations between and within states even as global trade and investment increases (Kapstein 2000; Thomas 2002). Even strong proponents of free trade such as Jagdish Bhagwati acknowledge the downside of globalization, including its distributional effects (Cooper 2004).

Latin America in the new millennium best reveals the political consequences of globalization's distributional effects as many countries in that region embrace leftist politics (Castanda 2006). This tendency is viewed as an unsurprising legacy of a decade or more of neoliberal market reforms that have produced much social dislocation in the region. Fortunately, the leftist shift in countries such as Chile, Uruguay, and Brazil largely involves a stronger emphasis on social policy, albeit within a broad market framework, and is regarded as a wise and necessary policy shift after decades of the neoliberal economic message that simply liberalizing markets and making them more efficient and competitive would ultimately take care of the distribution question through the trickle-down effect. Unfortunately, countries such as Venezuela, Bolivia, and Argentina have embraced a far more strident, populist, nationalism that has so far seen a wave of nationalizations in the oil and gas and minerals sectors (Louth 2006) as the rising tide of discontent amongst groups suffering the worst effects of global capitalism are then exploited by politicians seeking power (Castanda 2006).

If the socio-economic and political consequences of participating and competing in the global capitalist economy are not adequately addressed by both firms and governments, then a backlash might well result as different groups in society challenge those who seek overall benefits for the economy from greater integration with global markets. The worry is that policymakers might be tempted to use the easiest or most visible policy instruments to address, or be seen by voters to address, such pressures — trade protectionism, the use of low exchange rates, and negotiating unending bilateral trade agreements. Miles Kahler (2006) identifies how the right kinds of institutions at the domestic, regional, and global levels can mitigate the economic insecurities associated with globalization. In particular, he argues that economic liberalization and the imperatives of competitiveness do not automatically imply shrinkage of the public sector and a shift to a stark form of the "night watchman" state. Instead, Kahler draws from a range of studies to point out that the "insurance functions of governments may increase under conditions of increasing economic openness" (Kahler 2006, p. 32). At the regional level, ASEAN's push for the ASEAN Socio-Cultural Community (ASCC) reflects growing concern among regional policymakers, as well as the region's civil society, that some form of regional mechanism to address issues of social protection for the losers of market integration is necessary. While such moves by the region's policymakers might have been prompted by instrumental considerations to enhance the political sustainability of regional and global market integration, there are sound, normative, human security reasons as well as to why social protection measures are vital in an era of rapid globalization.

The point to emphasize is the worldwide shift in thinking in the last decade towards embracing some form of social support system for individuals and groups caught up in the dislocations, insecurities, and uncertainties associated with contemporary globalization. In a 2001 edition, the arch liberal economic news journal, *The Economist*, acknowledged the importance of social safety nets, public services, and a limited amount of redistribution to ensure the sustainability of globalization (Crook 2001). More recently, Martin Wolf, a renowned proponent of globalization, noted in the *Financial Times* that "more generous government-financed services", which included at least education for the disadvantaged and universal health insurance, were needed if the United States was to remain a vibrant and internationally open society (Wolf 2007). What a growing number of authors are saying simply is that competitiveness and social support should not be seen in zero-sum terms — they have always been, and continue to remain, two sides of the same coin, both in theory and policy practice. It was only the neoliberal ideology (and its associated policies), which reigned supreme for much of the 1990s, that rendered them asunder.

SOUTHEAST ASIA:
AVOIDING THE FATE OF THE "MISSING MIDDLE"

The issues raised by the preceding discussion were first debated in November 2005 at a workshop organized by the S. Rajaratnam School of International Studies (then known as the Institute of Defence and Strategic Studies, IDSS), a research graduate school of the Nanyang Technological University in Singapore. The themes first discussed at the 2005 workshop were subsequently expanded, with the various chapters in this edited volume focusing on a selected set of key competitiveness and social challenges that Southeast Asia needs to confront amidst globalization and the phenomenal rise of the Asian powerhouses, India and China.

While it is common to think of India and China as Southeast Asia's competitors, the two chapters that respectively discuss India and China emphasize the complementarities as well in the relationship of these two economic giants with Southeast Asia, or ASEAN. Both India and China have signed cooperative agreements with ASEAN, with the ASEAN-China Free Trade Agreement already in the implementation stage. Although India and ASEAN signed a Framework Agreement on Comprehensive Economic Cooperation in 2003, negotiations on an ASEAN-India free trade agreement continues well into 2007. The signing of both these agreements reflects the views of Southeast Asian governments that while both countries pose a competitive threat to their own economies, there are also benefits to be gained from closer economic cooperation and integration with India and China.

Thus, Rahul Sen and Sadhana Srivastava in Chapter 2 analyse in some detail the competitive, and especially the complementarities, in the economic structure and growth strategies of the ASEAN countries on the one hand, and India on the other. Examining trade, investment, services, and manpower flows between ASEAN and India, Sen and Srivastava conclude that while there is limited competition between the two entities in information technology (IT) services, ASEAN and India have a largely complementary economic relationship in a wide range of other economic sectors, which offers much scope for both parties to gain. Firms from ASEAN countries are already benefiting from contracts in India in a number of areas, including infrastructure development, while ASEAN already utilizes the expertise of the knowledge workers that India is now famous for. Thus, even in the area of IT services, both authors note the potential for cooperation. They see the future ASEAN-India FTA as a boon to both India and ASEAN, provided the agreement is comprehensive in coverage in order to maximize the gains in joint liberalization as the adverse consequences expected in some areas are balanced by the gains from other sectors. However, in an echo of the Dieter chapter, Sen and Srivastava also emphasize the need to ensure that the rules of the FTA are simple for businesses to utilize. Their conclusion is heartening — there is much to be gained by Southeast Asian countries from closer cooperation with India.

Liu Yunhua similarly identifies the potential for ASEAN to gain from the market and investment opportunities created by a rising China. While the competitive elements of the ASEAN-China relationship are clearly higher than the economic relationship between India and ASEAN, Liu points to the dramatic increase in exports from ASEAN to China in the past ten years as evidence that there is room for the Southeast Asian countries to find their respective niches in the expanding networks of production that are emanating from, and linked to, China. Liu also examines how six ASEAN countries have adjusted their domestic policies to cope with the emergence of Chinese competition and opportunities. He suggests that more needs to be done by regional policymakers in terms of suitable policy responses to exploit the economic opportunities offered by the China market. Like Sen and Srivastava, Liu ends on a positive note — he points out that the evolving pattern of trade and investment between ASEAN and China suggests that the "missing middle" thesis may be overblown. His findings lead him to suggest that the six ASEAN countries he has studied are increasingly drawn into a "continued chain" market in which each country is able to find its own niche in a varied and expanding production network centred on China, provided, of course, that the ASEAN countries continue to upgrade their competitiveness.

Chapters 2 and 3, while drawing optimistic conclusions from the detailed analysis of their respective authors on the relationship between Southeast Asia and India/China, also emphasize the need for governments and firms to be able to enhance their competitiveness if they are to gain from the economic opportunities offered by India and China. The authors of both chapters also highlight the benefits that formal economic cooperation between ASEAN and India and China can yield. Sen and Srivastava note, however, that for such an outcome, the rules governing these agreements must be kept simple.

Drawing from the theoretical discussion in the first part of this chapter and the two chapters on India and China, we identify three key competitiveness challenges for the region. Two of these challenges are well-known, namely (1) the problem of adequate technological and innovative capacity in the region, and (2) the problem of managing labour in a world driven by the competitiveness imperative. A third competitiveness challenge — one that we feel has been little explored — stems from the region's burgeoning bilateral trading arrangements. Although sold to domestic publics as arrangements that will enhance market access, the implication of these arrangements for the competitiveness of firms has been under-researched.

Heribert Dieter leads the charge in Chapter 4 with his masterful and comprehensive analysis of how bilateral economic arrangements affect firms. He focuses on the rules of origin that are central to all preferential trading arrangements, including bilateral agreements, arguing that it is this feature of bilateral agreements that undermines the competitiveness of firms, and eventually of the economy at large. While much of the discussion on bilateral FTAs has focused on their potential to enhance market access, Dieter unravels the complexities associated with rules of origin, how they operate in practice, and their impact on firms and production in Southeast Asia. He argues that as a result of these complex rules, firms operating in countries which negotiate multiple bilateral FTAs are likely to experience higher costs, even if these bilateral agreements are WTO-consistent. Moreover, transnational production that involves utilizing inputs from more than one country in the region, such as the case of automotive production in Southeast Asia, will suffer as the bilateral agreement slices through and fragments these production chains.

Dieter expands his critique of the bilateral instrument by demonstrating how in practice, bilateral agreements, especially if they involve negotiations with a powerful negotiating partner, have onerous effects on the less powerful partner. He shows this through his examination of two bilateral FTAs negotiated by two Southeast Asian countries — Singapore and Thailand — with the powerful United States, and compares these with the Australia-United States agreement. Even the latter agreement, although between two close, industrial countries that are military allies, yielded disproportionate benefits for the United States while denying true market access for Australia's most competitive agricultural sectors. Dieter, in short, argues persuasively against such thinking in the region, especially by the region's politicians, that bilateral FTAs pose little anti-competitive effects while yielding gains from enhanced market access instead.

The next two chapters take a closer look at two firm-level competitiveness issues — technological capabilities and labour productivity. The preceding discussion has shown how these two factors play key roles in determining the overall competitiveness of firms and the economy at large. Rajah Rasiah's approach in Chapter 5 to the subject of firm-level technological and innovative capacities is to compare electronic firms in East and Southeast Asia to show how the surrounding high technology environment within which firms are embedded has a key impact on their technological and innovative capacity. Using quantitative regression analysis, Rasiah shows that electronics firms in two East Asian countries (Korea and Taiwan) displayed higher capabilities in these areas compared with firms in four Southeast Asian countries (Thailand, Indonesia, Malaysia, and the Philippines) because of what Rasiah identifies as the higher network strength of the former. Network strength comprises a set of institutional factors that include education and training, health support, the transport and telecommunication infrastructure, research and technology support from universities, and R&D laboratories, as well as R&D incentives and grants to firms from the government. Based on his findings, Rasiah calls on governments to improve their institutional infrastructure in these areas to enhance the competitiveness of local firms.

Labour productivity is a key issue in this region and elsewhere, with a wide variety of factors determining productivity growth, such as education, training, costs of hiring and firing, and the use of productive technology, among others. In Chapter 6, Chew Soon Beng and Rosalind Chew focus on the role of unions in managing labour for competitiveness, because unions, they argue, can affect how all these factors come together in influencing labour productivity. Theirs is a more theoretical discussion, of two key approaches to managing labour in firms — the labour market approach and the industrial relations approach — with the authors suggesting that sound industrial relations can have a positive effect on competitiveness. The authors also advocate an approach to industrial relations that turns trade unions into strategic partners of governments rather than making them antagonists.

Micro-focused unions, in their opinion, rely on the creation of a wage premium to induce workers to join unions, which ultimately threatens the survival of firms, and paradoxically, the security of employment. Macro-focused unions, such as those found in Singapore, take a longer-term outlook and look on the government as a strategic partner. These forms of unions work to set wages at levels that maximize employment, working with the firm's management and the government to enhance worker training to improve competitiveness. The presence of such unions also contributes to labour market flexibility. The authors also discuss how the emergence and success of macro-focused unions depends a great deal on the political and social environment in a country. Singapore's conditions makes macro-focused unions possible, according to the authors, while the fragile political and social conditions in other Southeast Asian countries such as Malaysia, Thailand, Indonesia, and the Philippines work against the emergence of macro-focused unions and further undermines labour market flexibility.

Their chapter raises many interesting issues and questions that can form the basis of further work on this theme. One key issue is whether macro-focused unions are able to succeed in countries such as Singapore because of the availability of an implicit social contract in the form of high wages, employment opportunities, subsidized housing, and retirement financing. If so, then the question is whether recent wage cuts, the introduction of flexible wages, retrenchments, and cutbacks to the pension scheme, all responses by the Singapore government to growing competitive pressures (Yeung 2006), will undermine the attractiveness of the macro-focused union approach to labour management. To what extent can such an approach be replicated in settings with vastly different forms of political governance?

The discussion on labour market flexibility by Chew and Chew emphasizes labour market freedom as a key contributor to competitiveness. Labour market freedom is viewed as a composite of a variety of factors, including low or no minimum wages, ease of hiring and firing, and low levels of unemployment benefits. To put it differently, competitiveness seems to be inversely related to social protection in this conception of labour market freedom. Carolina Guina in Chapter 7 takes a different position from Chew and Chew in discussing whether labour regulations are a boon or bane for competitiveness. Guina's is the first of three chapters in Part 3 of the volume that focus on social issues — labour and social protection, social security, and corporate social responsibility — and their implications for competitiveness. The authors of these final three chapters address the question of whether responding to the competitive challenges of globalization also means forgoing or ignoring social development and social protection issues.

Guina reviews the empirical evidence on the impact of labour regulations on international competitiveness and finds that contrary to the popular perception that labour standards raise labour costs, well-designed labour regulations can result in long-run gains for the economy that far outweigh the short-run adjustment costs that firms have to bear. From the available empirical evidence, Guina shows that labour regulations, especially those pertaining to child labour, trade union rights, minimum wages, and employment security, either do not hamper economic growth and the inflow of foreign investment, or they have neutral effects. There are, however, short-term costs to firms, and this explains why business actors often lobby against raising labour standards. Yet, because labour regulations offer long-run gains for investors in terms of overall social and political stability, Guina calls on the region's policymakers to take a broader view of labour market policies, going beyond their immediate impact on firms' costs to the overall macro gains such regulations produce for the economy. She argues that there is room in Southeast Asia for designing labour policies that preserve workers' rights without impinging on the overall economic health of the economy.

While Guina's chapter addresses current working conditions, Mukul Asher and Amarendu Nandy in Chapter 8 look to the welfare of workers when they stop working. They focus on social security policy on retirement financing, discussing in some detail the core objectives of any social security system and the trade-offs of these goals against labour market flexibility, economic growth, and fiscal prudence. Asher and Nandy then examine the highly diverse social security systems in Southeast Asia, identifying the key challenges facing these countries' social security arrangements in terms of coverage, adequacy, administrative efficiency and transparency, and governance and regulation. In proposing a number of shifts that are needed in Southeast Asian thinking and practice in this area, the authors emphasize that ultimately, an appropriate social security system can only emerge if policymakers and business actors realize that social security is an essential part of international competitiveness and not something that undermines it.

Bala Ramasamy in the final chapter examines whether firms have social responsibilities that go beyond the task of maximizing profits for their shareholders to include non-economic activities such as taking care of the welfare needs of their employees and the broader community in which the firm operates, including its environmental responsibility. Ramasamy traces how the increasingly attractive notion of corporate social responsibility (CSR) is changing the way business leaders view the roles and responsibilities of their firms, particularly in western societies, and how that impacts on firms' profitability. He makes the case for viewing CSR as an investment rather than a cost. Indeed, because many multinational firms consider the CSR performance of their prospective partners before making a decision on whether to invest, Ramasamy suggests that CSR promotion amongst local firms could enhance the attractiveness of the region to foreign investment. Unfortunately, there is a long way to go before CSR practices in firms across the region improve to levels that make a positive impact on the individual, the community, and the environment. Ramasamy warns that profit maximisation as the sole objective of firms is no more a sustainable option, and competitiveness defined in terms of low production costs, no longer tenable. As western society increasingly demands its firms to be socially responsible, the internationalization of these firms, coupled with rising local awareness, will combine to transform the way firms in this region see themselves and how local communities and workers — stakeholders — regard the firm and its responsibilities.

CONCLUSION

The preoccupation of policymakers with international competitiveness is here to stay in spite of the sound arguments Paul Krugman put forward more than a decade ago for reviewing our obsession with the phenomenon. The increasingly intense competition from India and China suggests that international competitiveness will remain a desideratum of governments as they compete with other countries for access to markets and capital, and a chance to be part of the world's growing production networks. The emphasis on competitiveness will not be wasted if policymakers focus on appropriate policies and strategies to enhance productivity in firms and across the economy more generally. The worry, however, is that policymakers will adopt misguided policies that fail to build up such capabilities in a sustained manner, and instead securing short-term fixes that do not translate into long-run competitive strength.

Protectionist policies, including the use of low exchange rates, are obvious examples of misguided short-term strategies used to enhance the export competitiveness of domestic firms. However, policies that have been framed in terms of securing access to foreign markets and capital — the bilateral FTA being a notable recent example — can also work against firms by raising costs and undermining their participation in regional or transnational production networks. Worse, many bilateral FTAs, in reality, contain anti-competitive components that deny market access to even the most competitive producers. Instead of such policy fixes, a focus on enhancing the technological and innovative capabilities of firms and their labour productivity will be a far more rewarding task. However, this region displays weaknesses in both these areas, which can act to undermine the region's competitiveness and that of its firms.

Although the competitiveness imperative often leads policymakers to view social policies, particularly on a variety of labour standards and social protection, as a bane for competitiveness, there is much theoretical and empirical work that suggests that such thinking is flawed. Instead, embracing such policies will, over the long run, raise the growth potential and competitiveness of the economy, even if there are short-run costs on individual firms. The call is for judiciously crafted social protection policies and labour standards that enhance the stability of the environment for investors while securing the rights and economic security of individuals. As firms themselves increasingly come to see the firm as more than just an entity that engages in profit maximization as its sole objective, but an integral part of society and community, we may find ourselves not only striving for competitiveness, but also equally engaged with securing social protection for individuals and the community at large.

The various authors writing in this volume provide useful discussions on these issues and suggest tentative answers. While theirs will not be the last word on how Southeast Asia is likely to fare in the global economy in the years to come, they have highlighted a set of key issues that need to be addressed if the region is to reap the rewards of participating in the global economy while minimizing the adverse consequences of this.

Notes

1. See press release from the World Bank, "Book Examines Global Implications of India and China's Growth", 21 January 2007. <http://web.worldbank.org/WBSITE/EXTERNAL/NEWS> (accessed 6 February 2007).
2. Ibid.
3. The World Economic Forum is under the supervision of the Swiss Federal Government, and claims to be impartial, "tied to no political, partisan or national interests". <http://www.weforum.org/en/about/index.htm> (accessed 15 February 2007).
4. The Global Competitiveness Report is the flagship report of the Global Competitiveness Network of the WEF. <http://www.weforum.org/en/initiatives/gcp/index.htm> (accessed 15 February 2007).
5. On the limitations of government capacity in Southeast Asia, see Hamilton-Hart (2003).

References

Bhagwati, Jagdish, David Greenaway and Arvind Panagariya. "Trading Preferentially: Theory and Policy". *Economic Journal* 108 (1998): 1128–48.

Bowring, Philip. "Behind Thai Currency Crisis, China's Heavy Hand". *International Herald Tribune*, 19 December 2006.

Castanda, Jorge. "Latin America's Left Turn". *Foreign Affairs* 85, no. 3 (May/June 2006): 28–43.

Cooper, Richard. "A False Alarm: Overcoming Globalisation's Discontents". *Foreign Affairs* 83, no. 1 (January/February 2004): 152–55.

Crook, Clive. "Globalization and its Critics: A Survey of Globalization". *The Economist*, 29 September 2001.

Desker, Barry. "In Defence of FTAs: From Purity to Pragmatism in East Asia". *Pacific Review* 17, no. 1 (2004): 3–26.

Freeman, Nick and Denis Hew. "Overview: Rethinking the East Asian Development Model". *ASEAN Economic Bulletin* 19, no. 1 (2002): 1–5.

Garret, Geoffrey. "Globalization's Missing Middle". *Foreign Affairs* 83, no. 6 (November/December 2004): 84–96.

Hamilton-Hart, Natasha. "Asia's New Regionalism: Government Capacity and Cooperation in the Western Pacific". *Review of International Political Economy*, 10, no. 2 (2003): 222–45.

Kahler, Miles. "Economic Security in an Era of Globalization: Definition and Provision". In *Globalization and Economic Security in East Asia: Governance and Institutions*, edited by Helen E. S. Nesadurai, pp. 23–39. London and New York: Routledge 2006.

Kapstein, Ethan. "Winners and Losers in the Global Economy". *International Organisation* 54, no. 2 (2000): 359–84.

Krugman, Paul. "Competitiveness: A Dangerous Obsession". *Foreign Affairs* 73, no. 2 (1994): 28–44.

Lopez-Claros, Augusto. "Executive Summary". In *The Global Competitiveness Report 2006–2007*, pp. xii–xxviii. Geneva: World Economic Forum, 2006.

Louth, Nick. "What Latin American Nationalism Means For Miners'. *Money Week*, 19 June 2006.

Nesadurai, Helen E.S. *Globalization, Domestic Politics and Regionalism: The ASEAN Free Trade Area*. London and New York: Routledge, 2003.

————. "Conceptualising Economic Security in an Era of Globalization: What Does the East Asian Experience Reveal". In *Globalization and Economic Security in East Asia: Governance and Institutions*, edited by Helen E. S. Nesadurai, pp. 3–22. London and New York: Routledge, 2006.

Scollay, Robert and John P. Gilbert. *New Regional Trading Arrangements in the Asia-Pacific*. Washington D.C.: Institute for International Economics, 2001.

Thakur, Ramesh. "From National to Human Security". In *Asia-Pacific Security: The Economics-Politics Nexus*, edited by Stuart Harris and Andrew Mack, pp. 52–80. St Leonards, New South Wales: Allen & Unwin, 1997.

Thomas, Caroline. "Developing Inequality: A Global Fault-Line". In *The New Agenda for International Relations*, edited by Stephanie Lawson, pp. 71–90. Cambridge: Polity Press, 2002.

Wang, Zhengyi. "China Confronts Globalization: Conceptualizing Economic Security and Governance". In *Globalization and Economic Security in East Asia: Governance and Institutions*, edited by Helen E. S. Nesadurai, pp. 63–84. London and New York: Routledge, 2006.

Winters, L. Alan and Shahid Yusuf. "Introduction: Dancing with Giants". In *Dancing with Giants*, edited by L. Alan Winters and Shahid Yusuf. New York and Singapore: The World Bank and the Institute of Policy Studies, 2007.

Wolf, Martin. "Better Government Services May Be Key to the Survival of an Open Society". *Financial Times*, 15 February 2007.

Yeung, Henry Wai-Chung. "Institutional Capacity and Singapore's Developmental State: Managing Economic (In)security in the Global Economy". In *Globalization and Economic Security in East Asia: Governance and Institutions*, edited by Helen E. S. Nesadurai, pp. 85–106. London and New York: Routledge, 2006.

PART ONE

Southeast Asia/ASEAN
and the Asian
"Giants"

2

ASEAN AND INDIA
Exploring Complementarities

Rahul Sen and Sadhana Srivastava

INTRODUCTION[1]

While the past three decades saw rapid growth of the ten member countries of ASEAN and their deeper integration with the world economy through flows of trade, investments, technology, manpower as well as bilateral and multilateral loans, globalization and its associated technological changes have, in the past decade, ushered in an era of economic uncertainty for ASEAN. In particular, the East Asian economic crisis of 1997–98, whose proximate cause was the devaluation of the Thai baht on 2 July 1997, considerably reduced ASEAN's earlier dynamism and affected its medium term growth prospects adversely. Nevertheless, most ASEAN countries have since rebounded from the crisis and are striving to regain their lost competitiveness in the wake of an increasingly knowledge-based globalized world. As a result, the need for greater economic coordination and cooperation to manage and adjust to the challenges of globalization is now widely recognized in Asia.

It is in this context that ASEAN's increasing engagement with India assumes significance. The scope and density of relations between India and ASEAN have been steadily transforming since the initiation of India's "Look-East" Policy in 1991. This policy aimed to expand India's trade, investment, and security linkages with the rest of Asia, particularly ASEAN, and to learn from the latter's experiences in managing globalization. India's growing economy and outward orientation meant that there was some basis or substantive value to this policy. Thus, starting from being a sectoral dialogue partner in 1992, India is now a summit-level full dialogue partner of ASEAN, and has already engaged the grouping and its members towards enhancing sub-regional and bilateral economic cooperation.

An important milestone in this relationship has been the signing of a Framework Agreement on Comprehensive Economic Cooperation between India and ASEAN at the Bali Summit in 2003. This agreement is expected to encompass a strategic and political partnership, thus going well beyond a traditional FTA agreement (Bhattacharya and Ariff 2002). At the Laos Summit in 2004, the two sides signed a long-term Partnership for Peace, Progress and Shared Prosperity. Concomitantly, India has entered into a Comprehensive Economic Cooperation Agreement (CECA) with Singapore, and is negotiating bilateral FTAs respectively with Thailand and Malaysia. On a subregional basis, India has also engaged the newer ASEAN members such as Vietnam, Thailand, Myanmar, and Laos through economic cooperation initiatives.[2] India views these different subengagements to be consistent with strengthening its ties with ASEAN as a whole.

Against this backdrop, this chapter examines the extent to which both parties can cooperate to manage jointly the challenges arising from globalization, highlighting in particular, the potential complementarities in that relationship from which both sides can gain. Following this introduction, the chapter analyses the economic drivers of ASEAN and India and identifies the complementarities in their economic structures and growth strategies. This is followed by an analysis of the linkages between the two parties in merchandise trade, services, investment, and manpower flows. In the next section, the chapter identifies some key areas of cooperation between ASEAN and India that can create synergies for mutual gains and help both parties adjust to the forces of globalization.

COMPLEMENTARITIES IN ECONOMIC STRUCTURE AND GROWTH STRATEGIES

Tables 2.1 and 2.2 present the major domestic and external macroeconomic indicators for both India and six ASEAN members (henceforth ASEAN-6), namely Indonesia, Malaysia, Philippines, Singapore, Thailand, and Vietnam.[3] From these tables, the following observations may be made.

TABLE 2.1

Domestic Macroeconomic Indicators of ASEAN-6 and India, 2003

Countries	GDP (US$ bn)	GDP Growth (%)	Population (mn)	Per capita GDP (US$)	PPP GDP (US$ bn)	Inflation Rate (%)	Investment Rate (%)	Savings Rate (%)	Manufacturing (% of GDP)	Services (% of GDP)
Indonesia	208.3	4.1	215.0	968.6	758.8	6.6	16.0	21.5	43.6	39.9
Malaysia	103.2	5.2	25.0	4,118.5	207.8	1.1	21.8	42.9	42.1	45.5
Philippines	79.2	4.5	81.1	977.2	390.7	3.1	18.9	18.9	34.8	53.5
Singapore	91.3	1.1	4.2	21,748.1	109.4	0.5	13.4	46.7	31.4	66.4
Thailand	143.2	6.7	64.0	2,238.4	477.5	1.8	25.2	32.8	44.2	46.3
Vietnam	36.7	7.2	80.9	453.3	203.7	3.1	35.1	28.2	36.6	38.2
ASEAN-6	661.9	5.4	470.2	1,407.5	2,147.9	2.7	21.7	31.8	38.8	48.3
India	575.3	8.1	1,073.0	536.2	3,033.0	4.0	23.3	24.2	15.7	51.1
World	36,252.7	3.8	6,379	5,683.0	51,480.0	—	—	—	—	—
TOTAL	2,646.2		2,915.3	5,627.3	11,629.9					

Source: Compiled from ADB (2004); WTO (2004).

TABLE 2.2
External Macroeconomic Indicators of ASEAN-6 and India, 2003

Countries	Merchandise Exports (US$ bn)	Service Exports (US$ bn)	Total Merchandise Trade (US$ bn)	Services Trade (US$ bn)	Trade/GDP (%)	FDI Inflow (US$ bn)	FDI Outflow (US$ bn)	FDI/GDP (%)	FDI/GDCF (%)
Indonesia	70.3	n.a.	112.4	n.a.	54.0	-0.6	0.01	-0.3	-1.4
Malaysia	117.9	13.5	217.0	30.8	210.4	2.5	1.4	2.4	11.3
Philippines	41.9	3.0	86.8	7.4	109.6	0.3	0.2	0.4	2.3
Singapore	144.1	30.4	272.1	57.6	297.9	9.3	3.7	12.5	83.2
Thailand	80.5	15.7	156.3	34.0	109.2	1.9	0.5	1.3	5.0
Vietnam	20.7	n.a.	45.7	n.a.	124.6	1.4	n.a.	3.8	10.2
ASEAN-6	475.4	62.5	890.3	129.8	134.5	13.4	5.8	2.5	18.4
India	60.0	25.0	137.4	46.6	23.9	4.3	0.9	0.7	3.1
World	7,502.9	1,796.5	15,281.0	3,578.9	42.2	632.6	617.0	1.5	

Source: Computed from ADB (2004); WTO (2004).

First, ASEAN's total population is about half that of India's which is over one billion people. The most populous and largest country in ASEAN, Indonesia, has about a fifth of India's population. However, in per capita terms, ASEAN's income in current prices at US$1,407 is nearly two and a half times that of India. This implies that although ASEAN's market size may be half that of India, it is collectively richer than India, and hence presents significant investment opportunities to be tapped by Indian businesses. Although this gap is expected to narrow, there is unlikely to be any reversal in the income pattern in the medium to longer term (Sen, Asher, and Rajan 2004).

Second, Table 2.1 shows that the gap between the GDP of ASEAN and India in current dollars has narrowed significantly, especially since ASEAN suffered an economic crisis during the 1996–2001 period. During this time, ASEAN grew at an average annual rate of 3.7 per cent, while the corresponding growth rate for India was 5.7 per cent. Apart from Vietnam, most of the other ASEAN members experienced a severe decline in their growth prospects in the crisis year of 1998, but have since recovered, although on average, their growth rate has remained lower than that of India.

Third, there are significant complementarities in the economies of ASEAN and India with respect to their economic drivers. While ASEAN's GDP has been significantly driven by both manufacturing and services, the services sector contributes to more than half of India's GDP. Since 1993, the share of the manufacturing sector in India's GDP has remained almost static at about 15–16 per cent, whereas that of the services sector has been increasing, albeit at the cost of a rapidly declining share of the agricultural sector (World Bank 2004). Thus, while the ASEAN-6 economies continue to be highly dependent on the manufacturing sector for their growth, in the case of India, the services sector has emerged as the main engine of growth.

As for the external sector, the stark contrast between the ASEAN-6 and India is evident from Table 2.2. ASEAN continues to be far more integrated with the world economy than India, as indicated by its merchandise trade to GDP ratio which is more than five times that of India (Table 2.2). This is largely attributed to the differences in growth strategy adopted by ASEAN and India over the past two to three decades. While the ASEAN-6 have always been outward looking and open to trade from that time, India's economic policy was largely inward looking, with an emphasis on import substitution and industrial licensing until the 1990s. India embarked on an economic reform process and was exposed to globalization forces only after 1991.

As a result of its particular growth strategy, the ASEAN economies have generally been highly dependent on foreign direct investment (FDI) to drive their export and growth dynamics, indicated by their high FDI to GDP, and FDI to GDCF ratios, compared with India. The economy of city state Singapore alone constituted nearly two-thirds of the ten-member grouping's total FDI inflows and outflows in 2003 (Table 2.2). Neither India's exports nor its growth dynamics have been highly dependent on FDI, as evinced by its significantly smaller magnitudes of FDI inflows and outflows compared with the ASEAN-6 as a whole over the past decade. However, India has recently attracted larger amounts of FDI compared with most of the ASEAN-6 countries, while it also experienced higher volumes of FDI outflows in comparison.[4]

Unlike ASEAN, India's growth strategy is built around its relatively robust corporate sector that strongly encourages entrepreneurial talent (Khanna and Huang 2003). An important consequence of its liberalization and rapid growth has been the growing involvement of Indian companies abroad (Merchant 2004; Ramakrishnan 2004). The total FDI stock of Indian companies was US$6 billion in 2004 and is rising rapidly. The Indian government is actively encouraging companies to expand linkages abroad, and prefers this route to accumulating higher reserves passively. Simultaneously, India is welcoming and wooing FDI in many areas recently, particularly in infrastructure.[5]

India's current growth strategy is increasingly focusing on export-oriented growth and greater integration with the world economy. The growth of India's exports of goods and services nearly doubled in the post-reform period, with its share in India's GDP increasing substantially. Its merchandise trade showed a growth rate of more than 180 per cent in the decade till 2003 as against a growth of 83 per cent for the ASEAN-6 countries. The growth of India's services trade has been even more rapid, growing at a decadal average rate of 389 per cent over the 1993–2003 period, compared to 60 per cent for the ASEAN-6 economies.[6]

Finally, on average, India's tariff regime remains much more protected than that of the ASEAN-6 (Table 2.3), although the difference has narrowed considerably. India's average tariff rate for non-agricultural goods was below 15 per cent in 2005, and the country is committed to reducing tariffs to East Asian levels by 2007. In spite of this, existing tariff and non-tariff barriers faced by India's exporters to ASEAN countries could emerge as a possible constraint towards expanding bilateral merchandise trade linkages. A recent study by the Associated Chambers of Commerce and Industry of India (ASSOCHAM) observes:

TABLE 2.3
Tariff Barriers in India and ASEAN-6

	Year	Binding Coverage	All Products (%) Simple Mean Bound Rate	Simple Mean Tariff	Weighted Mean Tariff	Primary Products (%) Simple Mean Tariff	Weighted Mean Tariff	Manufactured Products (%) Simple Mean Tariff	Weighted Mean Tariff
India	1990	n.a.	n.a.	79.0	56.1	69.8	34.1	79.9	70.8
	2004[b]	73.8	46.1	28.3	28.0	30	36.9	27.9	25.3
Indonesia	1989	n.a.	n.a.	19.2	13.0	18.2	5.9	19.2	15.1
	2003[b]	96.6	37.5	6.4	5.2	8.0	3.1	6.1	5.8
Malaysia	1988[b]	n.a.	n.a.	14.5	9.7	10.9	4.6	14.9	10.8
	2003[b]	83.7	14.0	7.3	4.2	4.5	2.1	7.8	4.6
Philippines	1988	n.a.	n.a.	28.3	22.4	29.9	18.5	27.9	23.4
	2003[b]	66.8	25.3	4.5	2.6	5.7	5.0	4.2	2.0
Singapore	1989	n.a.	n.a.	0.4	1.1	0.2	2.5	0.4	0.6
	2003[b]	69.8	6.9	0	0	0	0	0	0
Thailand	1989	n.a.	n.a.	38.5	33.0	30.0	24.3	39.0	35.0
	2003	75	19.2	14.0	8.3	16.4	4.4	13.5	9.3
Vietnam	1994	n.a.	n.a.	14.8	20.6	20.9	46.7	13.9	13.1
	2004[b]	n.a.	n.a.	13.7	13.7	18.1	16.7	12.9	12.5

Source: World Bank (2005).

While Singapore will emerge as a major trade partner for India in ASEAN in services, banking and the legal profession, its trade prospects in other ASEAN countries such as Thailand, Malaysia, Indonesia, Philippines and Vietnam will suffer because of protective measures, both tariff and non-tariff, which these nations are unlikely to lift until the Free Trade Agreement (FTA) between India and ASEAN is executed by 2012 (ASSSOCHAM 2005).

This indicates that while India is continuing to reduce its tariff barriers to ASEAN, similar steps should be reciprocated from the ASEAN side if the ASEAN countries are to reap the gains from expanding bilateral trade with India, which currently stands at about US$14 billion.

India recently announced its first ever National Foreign Trade Policy for 2004–09, which integrates foreign trade with broader economic growth and employment generation strategies, just as the ASEAN countries have done, and successfully, for several decades. This policy aims to double India's share of global merchandise trade from 0.8 per cent to between 1.5–2 per cent by 2009, and to increase substantially its current 1.4 per cent share in global trade in commercial services (Asher and Sen 2005).

India is increasingly becoming a major player in global trade in commercial services. As observed by Sen, Asher, and Rajan (2004), India ranked twenty-first in terms of its global export share of commercial services in 2003, higher than Singapore (eighteenth), Thailand (twenty-eighth), Malaysia (twenty-ninth), and Indonesia (fortieth). In the same year, India ranked twenty-first compared with Singapore (seventeenth), Thailand (twenty-fifth), Indonesia (twenty-sixth), and Malaysia (twenty-eighth) in terms of its share of global imports of commercial services. India's total value of commercial services trade was worth US$47 billion in 2003, which was higher than that of all the ASEAN-6 economies, except for Singapore (Table 2.2). While it is not likely to be as integrated with the world economy in conventional terms as the ASEAN-6, India is becoming the hub for outsourcing of software and business processes (Farrell 2004). More than 100 of the Fortune 500 companies and European multinational corporations (MNCs) are setting up Research and Development (R&D) centres in India. While detailed data on such service transactions remain unavailable, it is becoming clear that the impact of work done in India on global technological and other developments is not insignificant and is expected to rise over time (Asher and Sen 2005).

The discussion thus far indicates that there are significant complementarities with respect to the economic structures and growth strategies of the ASEAN-6 and India, and that the economic drivers of the two entities are significantly different. While ASEAN-6 is well integrated with the world economy and is heavily dependent on trade and FDI for growth, India has only just embarked on this strategy, and its growth dynamics are not yet that significantly dependant on the external sector.

COMPETITION AND COMPLEMENTARITIES IN TRADE, INVESTMENT, AND MANPOWER FLOWS

Merchandise Trade

In order to ascertain whether the trade patterns of the ASEAN-6 and India are competitive or complementary, Table 2.4 identifies the top twenty products exported by the ASEAN-6 countries and India to the rest of the world in 2003. These products made up close to, or more than half, of total exports in both India and the ASEAN-6 countries. Apart from gems and jewellery, which form the bulk of India's manufacturing exports (and about 18 per cent of the total), textiles are the other mainstay of India' exports. With the expiry of the Multifibre Arrangement (MFA) quotas on textile exports of developing countries into the markets of the developed countries in 2005, India's textile exports are expected to increase further.

In contrast, the top twenty export products of the ASEAN-6 are mainly electronic product parts and components as well as petroleum products. It is important to note that there are only two products in India's top ten exports, namely SITC 0361 and 0423 (frozen crustaceans and milled and semi-milled rice), both agricultural products, accounting for 3.2 per cent of its total exports, that overlap with Thailand's (3.5 per cent), Vietnam's (8.7 per cent) and Indonesia's (1.4 per cent) top ten exports. Among the top twenty products of the Philippines and Thailand, there are only two manufacturing products, namely SITC 7812 and 7843 (motor vehicles and auto parts) that overlap with those of India. Overall, we find that Thailand and Vietnam's export structures have more products overlapping with that of India, compared with the other ASEAN-6 economies. The composition of trade highlighted above indicates that significant complementarities exist in the merchandise exports of India and ASEAN-6 as they do not export similar products to the rest of the world.

On the import side, Table 2.5 shows that India relies heavily on imported crude petroleum that accounted for almost a quarter of its total imports in

TABLE 2.4
Top 20 Products Exported by India and ASEAN-6, 2003

	India			Indonesia	
Commodity Code	Commodity Description	Share in Total (%)	Commodity Code	Commodity Description	Share in Total (%)
6672	Diamonds. excl. industrial	14.4	3431	Natural gas, liquefied	10.1
8973	Gold, silver jewellry, ware	3.5	3330	Crude petroleum	9.2
6513	Cotton yarn, excl. thread	2.2	4222	Palm oil, fractions	4.0
5429	Medicaments, nes	1.9	3212	Oth.coal,not agglomeratd	3.2
2815	Iron ores and concentrates, not agglomerated	1.7	2831	Copper ores and concentrates	3.0
5169	Organic chemicals, nes	1.7	6343	Plywood,solely of wood	2.5
8454	T-shirts, singlets and other vests	1.6	2312	Natural rubber exc. latex	2.4
0361	Crustaceans, frozen	1.6	7649	Parts, telecommun. equipt	1.6
0423	Rice, milled, semi-milled	1.6	3344	Fuel oils, n.e.s.	1.6
6585	Curtains, oth. furnishings	1.5	7638	Sound, video recordng etc	1.6
8427	Blouses, shirts and textile material	1.4	7599	Parts, data proc. etc. mch	1.6
0813	Oil-cake, oilseed residue	1.3	8512	Sports footwear	1.5
8415	Shirts	1.2	0361	Crustaceans, frozen	1.4
9310	Special transactions and commodities n.e.s	1.2	8215	Furniture, nes, of wood	1.3
6531	Fabric, synth. filmnt. yarn	1.1	2515	Chem. wood pulp, soda, blch	1.3
7812	Motor vehicles, n.e.s.	1.0	8211	Convertible seats, parts	1.0
6752	Flat-rolled. hi-speed stl	0.9	6424	Paper, paperboard, cut, nes	0.9
5311	Synth. organic dyestuffs	0.9	6531	Fabric, synth. filmnt. yarn	0.9
6974	Tbl, ktchn, h. hold art. nes	0.8	6353	Buildrs. joinery, wood etc	0.8
7843	Other parts, motor vehicl	0.8	6518	Yarn, staple fibres, etc.	0.8
	Total	43.2		Total	51.6

Malaysia			Philippines		
Commodity Code	Commodity Description	Share in Total (%)	Commodity Code	Commodity Description	Share in Total (%)
7764	Electronic microcircuits	16.5	7764	Electronic microcircuits	36.1
7599	Parts, data proc. etc. mch	7.9	7599	Parts, data proc. etc. mch	7.3
4222	Palm oil, fractions	4.4	7527	Storage units	6.1
7522	Digital automatic D/P machines	4.0	7763	Diodes, transistors etc.	4.3
3330	Crude petroleum	4.0	7522	Digital automatic D/P machines	3.9
3431	Natural gas, liquefied	3.3	7768	Elctrn comp pts, crystals	2.5
7763	Diodes, transistors etc.	2.5	7843	Other parts, motor vehicl	2.5
7526	Input or output units for automatic D/P machines	2.1	7731	Insultd wire, etc. condctr	1.5
7643	TV, radio transmittrs etc	1.9	4223	Coconut oil, fractions	1.4
7638	Sound,video recordng etc	1.8	7526	Input or output units for automatic D/P machines	1.1
7611	Television receivers, colour (including video monitors/projectors)	1.7	8811	Cameras, flash equipt, etc	1.0
7768	Elctrn comp pts,crystals	1.6	0573	Bananas (including plantains), fresh or dried	0.9
7649	Parts, telecommun. equipt	1.4	7725	Switch. apparatus, <1000 v	0.8
7722	Printed circuits	1.4	7649	Parts, telecommun. equipt	0.8
7529	Data processing equipment, n.e.s.	1.2	8426	Trousers, bib and brace overalls, breeches and shorts,	0.8
9310	Special transactions and commodities nes	1.1	7643	TV, radio transmittrs etc	0.8
6343	Plywood, solely of wood	1.0	6821	Copper; anodes; alloys	0.8
7641	Line telephone etc. equip	1.0	7722	Printed circuits	0.5
8482	Plastc, rubbr, apparel, etc	0.9	8414	Trousers, bib and brace overalls,	0.5
8215	Furniture, nes, of wood	0.9	7812	Motor vehicles for the transport of persons, n.e.s.	0.4
	Total	61.4		Total	74.5

TABLE 2.4 (continued)

	Singapore			Thailand	
Commodity Code	Commodity Description	Share in Total (%)	Commodity Code	Commodity Description	Share in Total (%)
7764	Electronic microcircuits	20.3	7764	Electronic microcircuits	5.3
7527	Storage units, whether or not presented with the rest of a data processing	7.9	7599	Parts, data proc. etc. mch	4.5
7599	Parts, data proc. etc. mch	6.6	7527	Storage units, whether or not presented with the rest of a data processin	3.2
9310	Special transactions and commodities not classified according to kind	3.5	2312	Natural rubber exc. latex	2.8
7763	Diodes, transistors etc.	2.1	7821	Goods vehicles	2.3
7649	Parts, telecommun. equipt	1.9	9310	Special transactions and commodities nes	2.2
7768	Elctrn comp pts, crystals	1.8	0423	Rice, milled, semi-milled	2.2
7643	TV, radio transmittrs etc	1.8	7526	Input or output units for automatic data processing machines, whether or	2.2
5157	Oth. heterocycl. comp. nucl	1.8	7649	Parts, telecommun. equipt	1.9
7526	Input or output units for automatic data processing machines, whether or	1.2	7415	Air conditioning mch, pts	1.8
8987	Other recorded media	1.2	7763	Diodes,transistors etc.	1.6
7529	Data processing equipment, n.e.s.	1.0	7611	Television receivers, colour (including video monitors and video projector	1.4
7725	Switch. apparatus, <1000 v	0.9	8973	Gold, silver jewellery, ware	1.4
5156	Lactams; heterocycl comp.	0.9	0371	Fish, prepard, presrvd, nes	1.4
7239	Pts nes, cvl. enging. mach	0.9	0372	Crustacea, mollc. prpd nes	1.3
5154	Organo-sulphur compounds	0.8	7641	Line telephone etc. equip	1.3
7786	Electrical capacitors	0.7	7843	Other parts, motor vehicl	1.2
5146	Oxygen-funct. amino-comp.	0.7	7929	Parts, nes, aircraft, equip	1.1

7638	Sound, video recordng etc	0.6
7722	Printed circuits	0.6
	Total	57.8

0361	Crustaceans, frozen	1.1
7812	Motor vehicles for the transport of persons, n.e.s.	1.0
	Total	42.2

Vietnam

Commodity Code	Commodity Description	Share in Total (%)
3330	Crude petroleum	18.9
8512	Sports footwear	5.6
0361	Crustaceans, frozen	5.1
0423	Rice, milled, semi-milled	3.6
8514	Oth. footwear, lthr. uppers	2.6
0711	Coffee, not roasted	2.5
8215	Furniture, nes, of wood	2.1
2312	Natural rubber exc. latex	1.8
0362	Crustaceans, other than frozen, including flours	1.7
8414	Trousers, bib and brace overalls	1.7
7599	Parts,data proc. etc.mch	1.6
8453	Jerseys, pullovers, cardigans, waistcoats	1.5
7731	Insultd wire, etc. condctr	1.4
8513	Footwear, nes, rubber, plst	1.4
0577	Edible nuts fresh, dried	1.4
8442	Suits, dresses skirts etc	1.4
0363	Molluscs	1.4
8413	Jackets and blazers	1.3
8415	Shirts	1.2
8454	T-shirts, singlets and other vests	1.0
	Total	60.2

Source: Computed from UN-Comtrade Database.

TABLE 2.5
Top 20 Products Imported by ASEAN and India from the World, 2003

ASEAN-6			India		
Commodity Code	Commodity Description	Share in Total (%)	Commodity Code	Commodity Description	Share in Total (%)
7764	Electronic microcircuits	11.2	3330	Crude petroleum	24.7
7768	Elctrn comp pts,crystals	7.7	6672	Diamonds. excl. industrial	9.2
3330	Crude petroleum	6.9	9710	Gold, nonmontry excl ores	8.6
7599	Parts, data proc. etc.mch	6.0	7643	TV, radio transmittrs etc	2.5
7643	TV, radio transmittrs etc	1.8	4222	Palm oil, fractions	2.4
7763	Diodes, transistors etc.	1.5	3212	Oth. coal, not agglomeratd	1.4
7649	Parts, telecommun. equipt	1.5	7599	Parts, data proc. etc.mch	1.1
7843	Other parts, motor vehicl	1.4	7935	Spec. purpose vessels etc	1.0
9310	Special transactions and commodities not classified according to kind	1.2	7921	Helicopters	0.9
7284	Mach. appl. spcl indus nes	1.1	2475	Wood, non-conif, rough,unt	0.9
7722	Printed circuits	1.0	5223	Inorganic acid, oxide etc	0.9

Source: UN Comtrade Database.

2003. Electronic products and transport equipment made up the other major component of India's imports, with SITC 7843 (motor vehicle parts) being the only manufacturing product in that category to be both exported and imported by India in the top twenty category. In contrast, ASEAN countries imported a number of electronic parts, components, and accessories that India also exports, indicating a high level of intra-industry trade in electronic products. This is largely due to the trade in electronic parts, components, and accessories (Athukorala 2003).

The preceding discussion shows that merchandise trade patterns of ASEAN and India are largely complementary, and that expansion of bilateral merchandise trade from the current level of US$13 billion would be mutually beneficial to both parties. However, the analysis above is based on trade shares only, which is an absolute measure. There is a need to estimate a relative measure of trade patterns for a better understanding of the complementarities in ASEAN and India's merchandise trade. Therefore, the export similarity pattern for the individual ASEAN-6 countries vis-à-vis India for all products was estimated using the export similarity indices for 2003 (Table 2.6). This index measures the degree of similarity of the exports of any two entities to a third market, with possible values ranging from 0 (no similarity) to 100 (complete similarity), as described in Appendix 2.I.

The results show that the economies of India and ASEAN have a greater degree of complementarity in manufactured exports. ASEAN's major manufactured exports have been electronics while India's competitiveness lies in ready-made garments. As shown in Table 2.7, the overall export

TABLE 2.6
Estimates of Export Similarity of India
and ASEAN-6 Countries, 2003

Country	Value
Indonesia	26.8
Malaysia	18.2
Philippines	17.1
Singapore	20.0
Thailand	33.3
Vietnam	27.1
ASEAN-6	27.5

Source: Authors' calculations.

TABLE 2.7
Export Similarity Indices for ASEAN-6 and India's Merchandise
Exports to World and the United States, 1993–2003

	1993	1998	2003
Total Exports to the World	26.4	24.7	27.5
Exports to the U.S.	20.0	19.3	21.0

Source: Authors' calculations.

similarity index for ASEAN and Indian merchandise exports to the world market has increased only marginally over the 1993–2003 period from 26.4 to 27.5, indicating that about three-quarters of the products exported by both parties are completely dissimilar in pattern. Thus, it appears that the overall similarity between the exports of the ASEAN-6 and India is very low, due particularly to the divergence in the composition of their respective export baskets.

The index is also found to be lower than the global value when India's and ASEAN'S exports to the United States are compared. The United States is the major trading partner for both parties. The level of similarity is as low as 20 per cent, which further confirms our earlier findings of complementarity between ASEAN and India's merchandise exports. This suggests that a removal of tariff barriers and trade promotion measures by both the ASEAN-6 and India in a potential FTA will bring about significant mutual gains for both parties.

Services Trade

With services trade gaining importance in world trade, it is also essential to analyse complementarity and competition in the services sector between the ASEAN-6 and India. It is, however, important to note at the outset that the services trade sector is generally more complex than that of merchandise trade as services trade involves not only international movements of capital and labour, but it also involves the transfer of knowledge and technology across international borders.

Table 2.8 presents the composition of commercial services exports of the ASEAN-5 (comprising the ASEAN-6 minus Vietnam) and India in 2002. In 2002, computer, communication, and other services (including information and communication technology or ICT-enabled services and

TABLE 2.8
Composition of Commercial Services Exports of ASEAN-5 and India, 2002
(% of service exports, BoP)

	Communications, computer, etc.	Insurance and financial services	Transport services	Travel services
India	76.2	1.5	10.3	12.3
Indonesia	4.8	0.0	16.2	81.1
Malaysia	31.6	1.4	19.3	48.2
Philippines	20.2	2.2	20.8	57.4
Singapore	44.2	2.5	38.6	14.8
Thailand	26.5	0.6	21.4	51.9

Source: World Bank (2004).

professional business services, including business processes outsourcing or BPO) constituted more than three-quarters of India's commercial service exports. In contrast, travel services (including tourism) constituted the bulk of the ASEAN-5's commercial service exports (especially for Indonesia, the Philippines, Thailand, and Malaysia). Likewise, transport and logistics services constituted about 40 per cent of the ASEAN-5's imports of commercial services (due to the presence of Singapore in ASEAN as a logistics and manufacturing hub), while it accounted for about 14 per cent of Indian imports (World Bank 2004). These figures indicate that even in services trade, the ASEAN-5 and India are more complementary than not in the global market.

Table 2.9 presents a summary estimate of the export similarity index for the ASEAN-6 and India in their global services exports in order to assess the extent of trade complementarity. The overall index in 2002 was higher than that for merchandise trade, particularly for ICT and professional services (which also include offshoring and BPO activities). In the other categories, there was hardly any degree of export similarity, indicating yet again the presence of complementarities. Except for some limited competition in this category of services exports, significant complementarities are found in general, between the ASEAN-6 and India in both merchandise as well as service exports. Thus, both are likely to gain not just from tariff reduction, but also from deeper liberalization of bilateral services trade under an ASEAN-India FTA, provided proper regulatory mechanisms are in place. Since bilateral services trade data of either ASEAN or India are unavailable, the export

TABLE 2.9
Export Similarity Indices for ASEAN-6 and India's Commercial Services Exports to the World Market, 2002

Sector	Index Value
Computer, communications, and other services	32.3
Insurance and financial services	1.5
Transport services	10.3
Travel services	12.3
Overall	56.4

Source: Authors' calculations.

similarity indices for ASEAN and India's service exports to the United States cannot be computed. However, given the overall complementarities, we expect these results to be similar to those for service exports to the world market.

There is no published source on bilateral services transactions between ASEAN and India. Thus, any detailed analysis on this aspect of their economic relationship is not possible. However, anecdotal evidence from several studies, for instance, Sen, Asher, and Rajan (2004) and Asher and Sen (2005) have suggested that potential gains from cooperation in this sector are likely to be significant for both parties. These gains are likely to come from cooperation ranging from ICT and professional business services to financial services,[7] logistics, travel and tourism, education, and healthcare services.

Travel and Tourism

In particular, travel and tourism holds significant potential for expansion between ASEAN and India. In this context, Sen, Asher, and Rajan (2004) note:

> Indonesia, Malaysia, Philippines, and Singapore have already developed considerable expertise and competitive advantage in tourism, with Vietnam also developing into an important tourist destination in recent years. However, India has realized the potential in this area rather belatedly, and is taking steps to implement an integrated tourism industry.[8] India aims to not only attract substantially larger number of international visitors than the 3.5 million visitors in 2004, but also provide a conducive atmosphere and money-for-value services to increase their stay and expenditure per day.[9]

A comparison of world tourist arrivals and foreign exchange earnings from tourism (tourism receipts) indicates that India attracts fewer visitors per year than ASEAN countries and earns far less foreign exchange from this activity. Nonetheless, the average stay of a tourist in India is about thirty days, which is far greater than in most ASEAN countries. Furthermore, India also has a strong domestic tourism sector that generates about 100 million visitors per year. This indicates that there are considerable opportunities for the ASEAN countries to provide tourism services in India.

Trends in visitor arrivals from India to the ASEAN-5 indicate that the total number of visitors has increased from 421,000 in 1992 to 744,300 (4.7 per cent of total visitors) in 2003. In general, Singapore attracted nearly half of all Indian visitors to the ASEAN-5 during the 1995–2003 period, followed by Thailand, Malaysia, and Indonesia (ASEAN Statistical Yearbook 2004). In contrast, the flow of ASEAN visitors to India was quite small. In 2003, visitors from the ASEAN countries to India numbered only about 140,000, less than one-fifth of the number of Indian tourists visiting ASEAN. Of the ASEAN countries, visitors from Malaysia constituted the largest proportion of ASEAN visitors to India (41 per cent), followed by Singapore (31 per cent) and Thailand (13 per cent). The share of business travellers from key ASEAN countries, such as Singapore, has also been growing. In 2003, about 35 per cent of visitors from Singapore to India travelled on business visas (Aggarwal 2004). This indicates that the balance of trade in tourism services is likely to favour the ASEAN countries significantly. India needs to be more proactive in attracting visitors from ASEAN.

In operational terms, several important developments in the tourism sector in both ASEAN and India have taken place in the past few years. During the Bali Summit in 2003, India offered unilateral liberalization of air travel for ASEAN carriers. ASEAN air carriers are now permitted to fly directly to twenty-one tourist destinations in India. In addition, ASEAN air carriers can now fly to four metropolitan areas in India without any limit during the busy tourist months. This is expected to be of significant benefit to national carriers from Malaysia, Thailand, and Singapore. Indian private domestic carriers have already started to fly to destinations in ASEAN. This has improved the connectivity between India and ASEAN. Increased competition in the skies is expected to reduce airfares between India and ASEAN, currently among the highest in the world on a per-mile basis.

These developments are expected to boost tourism flows and help enhance business interactions between ASEAN and India. The granting of visa-on-arrival facilities for Indian visitors to Thailand, and more recently by Malaysia and Indonesia, are measures that could enhance such interactions. For the less developed ASEAN countries, Indian visitors could constitute a new source of tourists, and they should also consider visas on arrival to enhance their gains from this activity, although unlike Thailand and Malaysia, their pricing of visas will need to reflect their lower competitiveness.

ASEAN and India in the Global Offshoring Market

Notably, although ICT services trade may have some limited areas of mutual competition between ASEAN and India (particularly in the global offshoring market), it is also a potential area of cooperation that would simultaneously require an expansion of bilateral investments and more secure and easier movement of natural persons between India and ASEAN. In this context it is important to understand the competitive advantages of India and the individual ASEAN countries in the offshoring and BPO services sector, to analyse their competitive positions in the global offshoring market, and the extent to which their core competencies in this sector differ or overlap with that of India. The phenomenon of offshoring involves breaking up service functions across countries to take advantage of lower costs of service provision overseas. It takes place either through contractual arrangements or intrafirm sourcing via FDI (which is also known as captive offshoring).

Global offshoring in services is a relatively new phenomenon that has opened up opportunities for export-oriented services in many developing countries. Spurred by the forces of globalization and rapid advancement in international communication technology, this phenomenon is gaining momentum and has generated new growth opportunities in services, not only in low-to-mid skill-intensive activities such as IT-enabled-BPO services (examples include call centre support and other back-end business process operations such as data entry and handling, coding, medical and legal transcriptions, etc.) but also in more sophisticated and high-skill areas such as software development, research and development (R&D), patent writing, product design and development, which is also dubbed knowledge-process outsourcing (KPOs).

According to a recently released report by A.T. Kearney, which ranked global offshoring destinations, a number of top ranked destinations are located in Asia, with India being ranked overall as the number one destination for global offshoring, compared with Malaysia (in third place), Singapore (fifth) and the Philippines (sixth) among the ASEAN economies (A.T. Kearney. 2004) (Table 2.10). These rankings are drawn on a weighted average of

TABLE 2.10

Core Competencies and Global Rankings of ASEAN Economies and India in the Global Offshoring Market, 2004

	Core Competencies	Overall Ranking as Global Offshore Destination	Ranking According to Skill Availability	Ranking According to Business Environment	Ranking According to Financial Structure	Process Maturity/Competitiveness
India	Application maintenance and support, application development, contact centres, and financial processing services.	1	1	15	1	Well developed IT/BPO industry with suppliers capable of handling high volume as well as varied technology business. However, there exists a large number of small BPO companies that do not have the required competencies to address the outsourcing market.
Philippines	Call centres, transcriptions, animation, business process outsourcing (shared services, finance & accounting, logistics, telesales).	3	11	22	3	Voice based BPO operation is one of the key competency of the Philippines — contributes more than 50% of export revenues. There are about 100 call centres and BPO companies in the Philippines. Since the population as such is small, the quick scaling up of operations is a major issue with these BPO companies.

TABLE 2.10 *(continued)*

	Core Competencies	Overall Ranking as Global Offshore Destination	Ranking According to Skill Availability	Ranking According to Business Environment	Ranking According to Financial Structure	Process Maturity/Competitiveness
Malaysia	Application development, application maintenance, e-business, multimedia & animation, data processing.	5	20	9	10	Emerging as a key BPO destination.
Singapore	Application development, application maintenance, systems integration; regional service functions and high-end offshoring.	6	8	1	21	Attractive for regional service functions and high-end offshoring activities.

Source: A.T. Kearney (2004) and neoIT (2004).

rankings based on three main factors that determine the attractiveness of a country as an offshoring destination, namely availability of skilled manpower, business environment, and financial structure. Table 2.10 indicates that India ranked as the top offshoring site with respect to skills availability and financial structure, but ranked poorly in terms of business environment, while Singapore was ranked top in terms of business environment for offshoring due to its excellent infrastructure, which is a critical factor in determining offshore locations.

India has gained a global edge as an offshoring hub for a number of reasons, including the widespread use of English, internationally competitive wages, its large pool of science and engineering graduates, and the presence of strong indigenous service sector enterprises. This has helped it in developing its core competencies in this market not only in low-to-mid skill areas such as call centres and routine data-crunching tasks, but also increasingly towards more sophisticated and skills-based services, including software development, research and development (R&D), financial portfolio analysis, patent writing, and product design and development — activities defined as knowledge-process outsourcing (KPOs). The market size of the Indian IT and BPO market was estimated to be worth US$9.6 billion in 2003. According to a study by Swami and Shekhar (2005 p. 47), the share of India in the global KPO market in 2003–2004 was 56 per cent compared with 36 per cent in the BPO market. By 2010–2011, India's share in the global KPO market has been projected to expand to 71 per cent, increasing in value from US$0.72 billion to US$12 billion, growing at a compounded annual average rate of 49.5 per cent. In spite of these successes, sustaining this competitive edge would require Indian policymakers to address the weaknesses in infrastructure facilities, which international firms have cited as a major bottleneck to the expansion of their offshoring activities in India.

Among the ASEAN countries, Malaysia is rapidly emerging as a favourite destination for offshoring of services, primarily due to its low-cost infrastructure and strong government support in the development of the ICT sector, particularly along the Multimedia Super Corridor (MSC) in Cyberjaya and Putrajaya. Malaysia has developed core competencies in the area of application development, application maintenance, e-business, multimedia & animation, and data processing. Although it is emerging as a serious competitor for India in the offshoring of certain services (such as multimedia and animation), its market of twenty-two million is unlikely to offer firms the scale advantages that India offers. Furthermore, Malaysia also needs to improve its intellectual property (IP) regime and tackle the piracy problem if it is to sustain its competitiveness in this market.

The city state of Singapore, on the other hand, enjoys a competitive advantage in the area of high-end outsourcing and has developed core competencies in areas such as application development, application maintenance, systems integration, and regional service functions. It is targeting knowledge-based offshoring functions in technology-intensive areas such as remote and robotics management, healthcare, and genetic diagnostics. In spite of its high labour costs, Singapore is preferred as an offshoring destination because of its high-quality infrastructure and a business environment that gives high importance to data security and IP protection, which is a paramount concern for companies that undertake offshore operations. According to A.T. Kearney (2004), many Indian IT companies have utilized this opportunity and set up their regional hub for IT services in Singapore.

The Philippines has already established itself as a leading offshoring destination for voice-based BPO services and call centres. It has developed core competencies in the area of call centers, transcriptions, animation, business process outsourcing (shared services, finance & accounting, logistics, telesales), which also overlaps with that of India. As in the case of India, it also possesses a competitive advantage of low costs and an English-speaking population. However, the quality of the business environment needs to improve if the Philippines is to sustain its competitiveness and move up the value chain towards higher-end offshoring activities. The government has already designated five special economic zones for the setting up of IT, BPO, and call centres, which will also enjoy special incentives for investors.

Figure 2.1 shows the relative positions of India and ASEAN in the global offshoring market. It appears that most ASEAN countries would need to improve their workforce skills, and some of them would also need to improve their respective business environments in order to sustain their global competitiveness in the offshoring market.

While limited competition does exist between India and some ASEAN countries in this market, this should not preclude them from cooperating simultaneously with each other, as has become the norm in many industries globally. Thus, ASEAN corporations can cooperate with Indian firms to utilize India's strengths in outsourcing, design, and research and development, to enhance their global competitiveness as aggressively as their Western counterparts, and this is a source of synergy still waiting to be tapped.

FIGURE 2.1

**Comparison of ASEAN Countries and India as an
Offshoring Destination in Asia**

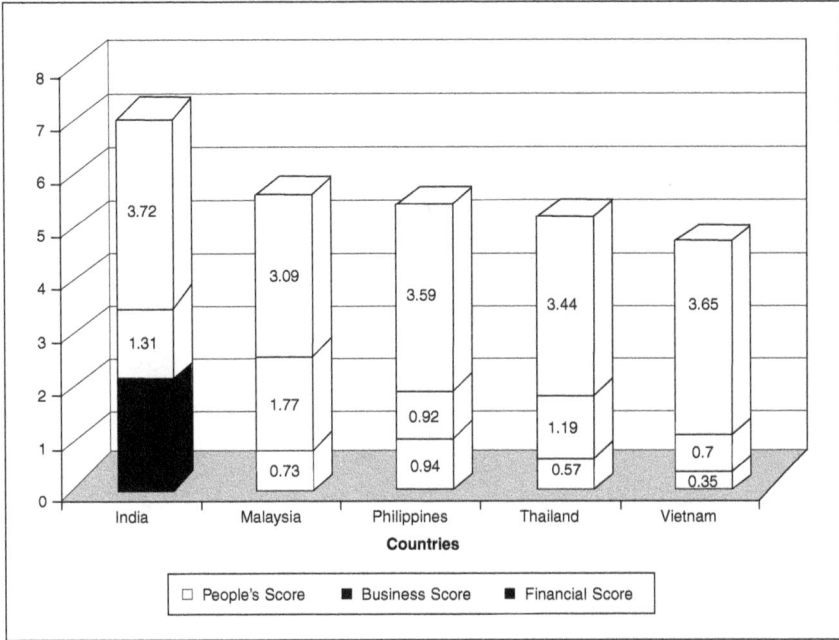

Note: The above represents a weight distribution of three categories in the ratio 4:3:3.
Thus, financial structure is rated on a scale from 1 to 4, while business environment and
people's skill and availability scores are rated on a scale from 1 to 3.
Source: A.T. Kearney (2004).

Investment Flows

As already observed, unlike ASEAN, India has not been traditionally open to
foreign investment flows. However, with the economic reforms in 1991, both
inward and outward investment policies were gradually liberalized, making
the Indian economy more receptive to foreign investment flows. The actual
levels of FDI in the 1990s averaged about US$2.5 to US$3 billion annually,[10]
reaching US$5.5 billion by 2004–05, while that of portfolio investment
inflows surpassed FDI inflows and significantly expanded to reach about
US$9 billion by the 2004–05 period (Figure 2.2). In contrast, the ASEAN-5
as a region has always been a major recipient of FDI inflows, particularly
Japanese FDI directed towards developing ASEAN as a production base for

FIGURE 2.2
Foreign Investment Inflows in India, 1990–91 to 2004–05

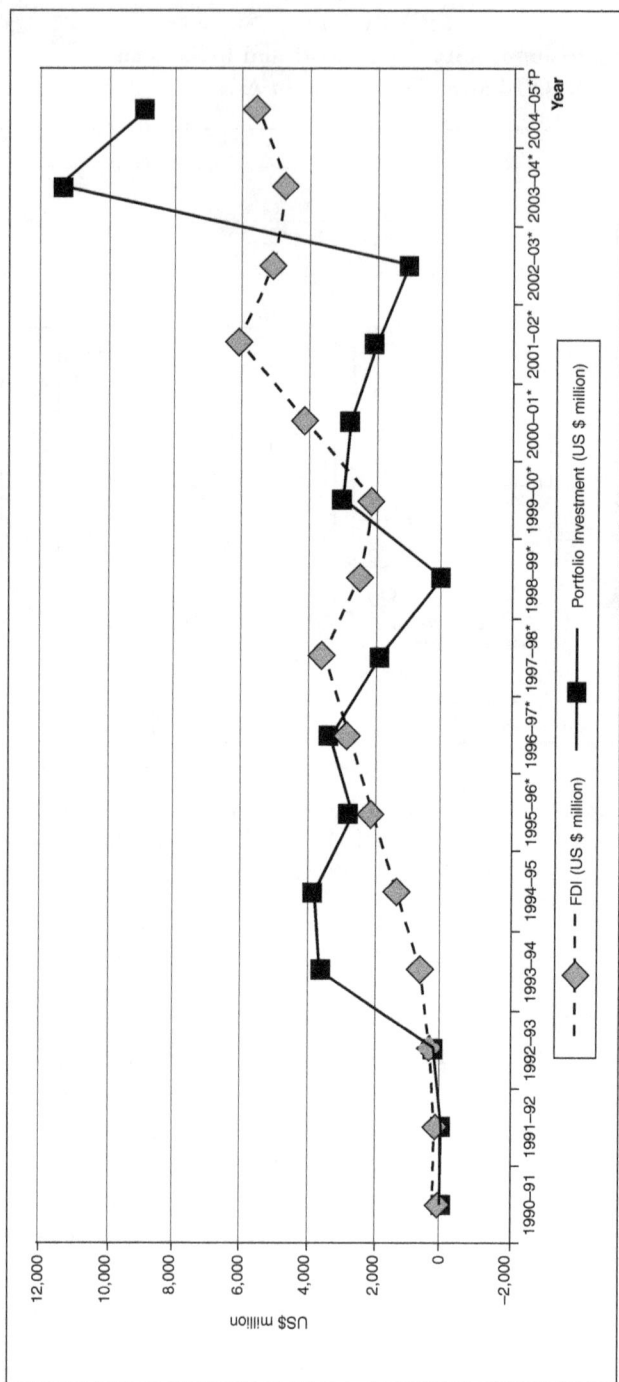

Notes: 1. Data on FDI have been revised since 2000–01 with expanded coverage to approach international best practices. Data from 2000–01 onwards are not comparable with FDI data for earlier years.

2. Negative (–) sign indicates outflow.

P : Provisional.

* Includes acquisition of shares of Indian companies by non-residents under Section 6 of FEMA, 1999. Data on such acquisitions are included as part of FDI since January 1996.

Source: RBI (2005).

Japanese labour-intensive manufacturing exports. Although FDI inflows into ASEAN declined significantly during the Asian economic crisis — from a peak of US$29.7 billion to US$19.2 billion — they have remained steady thereafter.

The sectoral breakdown of FDI inflows for both ASEAN and India is shown in Table 2.11. In the case of India, FDI is mainly concentrated in services, comprising ICT, power, and the hotel and tourism sectors. According to a survey by Munjal and Pohit (2001), these sectors have received the largest amount of FDI in the past five years. Since many of these services have been enhancing their export potential (namely call centres, insurance, and medical transcription and financial services), the potential for enhancing export-oriented FDI through the services sector in the Indian economy is clearly evident. In contrast, for the ASEAN countries, financial intermediation and the services sector continue to draw a large portion of investments flowing into the region. Also, FDI into ASEAN is heavily concentrated in the labour-intensive manufacturing sector. Since India does not compete with ASEAN for global FDI in the manufacturing sector, therefore, it can be argued that it is not a direct competitor of ASEAN, and, therefore, there exist complementarities between ASEAN and India in the area of investment flows as well.

However, these complementarities have not yet been reaped. As noted by Sen, Asher, and Rajan (2004):

> The existing investment relations between ASEAN and India have started growing only since 2001. Malaysia and Singapore in particular have been investing fairly aggressively in India. While Malaysia has been primarily investing in infrastructural projects in India, there has been steady investment by Singapore-based companies in India, primarily in the telecommunications, IT, ports, logistics and health care sectors. In this aspect, Malaysia's and Singapore's experience and competencies in infrastructural development complements [sic] India's need for physical infrastructure. At the same time, India is in a position to cooperate with ASEAN-6 in substantially lowering costs of essential drugs, including those for HIV-AIDS, as well as cooperating in food and energy security.

Investment by the ASEAN countries in India during 2000–03 amounted to only US$350 million, accounting for about 3 per cent of total FDI inflows to India. From the Indian point of view, the first phase of internationalization of Indian firms started in the ASEAN region, the major recipient countries being Indonesia, Malaysia, and Thailand. However, these investments have been modest thus far, with India accounting for only 0.5 per cent of FDI

TABLE 2.11
Sectoral Composition of FDI Inflows in ASEAN-6 and India

| | ASEAN | | | | | India | | | |
| | 1999 | | 2003 | | | 1999 | | 2001 | |
Economic Sectors	US$ million	% share	US$ million	% share	Economic Sectors	US$ million	% share	US$ million	% share
Agriculture, Fishery, and Forestry	−16.7	−0.1	178.0	0.88	Food and Dairy Products	121.0	7.7	49	1.7
Mining and Quarrying	2,086	7.5	4,081.3	20.1	Engineering	326.0	20.6	231	7.9
Manufacturing	6,578	−23.6	4,630.8	22.8	Electronic & Electrical	172.0	10.9	659	22.4
Construction	−70.9	−0.3	109.8	0.54	Chemicals and Products	120.0	7.6	67	2.3
Trade/Commerce	4,332	15.6	2,237.7	11.0	Pharmaceuticals	54.0	3.4	69	2.3
Financial Intermediation and Services	6,530	23.4	5,395.4	26.6	Domestic Appliances	—	0.0	—	0.0
Real Estates	624.3	2.2	697.2	3.4	Computers	99.0	6.3	368	12.5
Services	2,126	7.6	−275.2	0.0	Finance	20.0	7.3	22	0.7
Others	5,063	18.2	2,291.3	11.3	Services	116.0	35.0	1,126	38.3
					Other Industries	553.0		396	38.3
Total	**27,853**		**20,304.4**		**Total**	**1,581.0**		**2,938.0**	**13.5**

Source: ASEAN Statistical Yearbook, 2004, CEIC Database.

flows to the region in 2003. There is thus substantial scope for the promotion and facilitation of bilateral investment flows, as there is underutilization of India as a source for FDI flows to ASEAN, compared with FDI inflows to ASEAN from the rest of the world.

Manpower Flows and Demographic Complementarities

As indicated above, A.T. Kearney (2004) has identified that one of India's greatest competitive strengths is the presence of large pools of internationally competitive and scientific manpower accustomed to operating in a multicultural environment. Although there is insufficient data detailing the extent of actual manpower flows between India and ASEAN, this is an area where India's excess supply matches the demand shortfall of similar skills in some ASEAN members (Singapore, Malaysia, and Thailand), particularly for middle and high skill levels. In this sense, there are complementarities to be reaped.

As noted by Sen, Asher, and Rajan (2004):

> The presence of MNCs in both ASEAN and India has already increased the need for movement of skilled manpower across their borders to optimize resource utilization. Indian professional and technical manpower are making positive contributions to sustaining [the] competitiveness of many ASEAN countries. Professionals from some ASEAN countries like Singapore and Malaysia are also playing a similar role in the Indian economy. Bilateral agreements between individual ASEAN countries and India involving areas such as mutual recognition of professional and technical qualifications, and flexibility in the temporary movement of natural persons could help in further enlarging the scope of mutually beneficial cooperation.

The demographic dynamics of the two parties also involve complementarities. Table 2.12 presents the trends in population ageing across several countries, including those in ASEAN and India. Almost all the ASEAN-5 countries have already begun, or are likely, to experience rapid ageing of their population within three decades, with an increasing proportion of the elderly in the population (Figure 2.3). In contrast, India is entering the phase of the "demographic gift", when the share of the working-age population is likely to increase over the next three to four decades.

Complementarities such as these provide a strong reason for ASEAN countries such as Singapore, Malaysia, and Thailand to utilize India's

FIGURE 2.3

Proportion of Elderly in Total Population of Selected Countries Including ASEAN and India

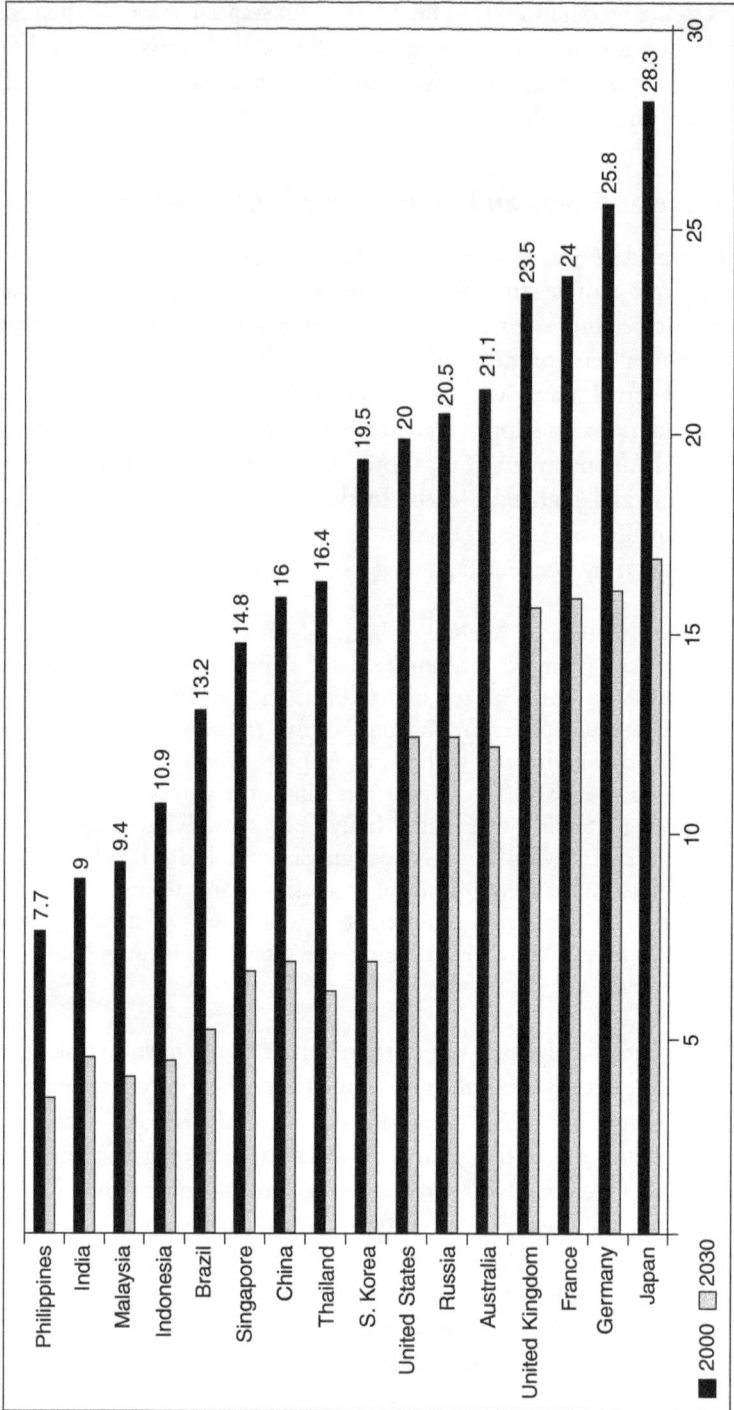

Source: Asher and Vasudevan (2005).

TABLE 2.12
Population Ageing in Selected Countries Including ASEAN and India

	Population (In Millions)		% of Population Over 65		Population Over 65 (Numbers in Million)	
	2000	2030	2000	2030	2000	2030
China	1,262	1,483	7.0	16.0	88	237
India	1,014	1,437	4.6	9.0	47	129
USA	276	351	12.6	20.0	35	70
Indonesia	225	313	4.5	10.9	10	34
Brazil	173	203	5.3	13.2	9	27
Russia	146	133	12.6	20.5	18	27
Japan	127	117	17.0	28.3	22	33
France	59	62	16.0	24.0	9	15
U.K.	60	61	15.7	23.5	9	14
S. Korea	47	54	7.0	19.5	3	11
Malaysia	22	35	4.1	9.4	1	3
Australia	19	23	12.4	21.1	2	5
Singapore	4	9	6.8	14.8	0	1

Source: Asher and Vasudevan (2005).

knowledge-based human resources without having to consider long-term immigration issues. In this way, these countries can extend their economic space by partnering India. It is noteworthy that businesses from the OECD countries, which have already experienced rapid ageing (Figure 2.3) are already substantially enhancing their competitiveness by partnering India in variety of knowledge-intensive service activities (Farrell 2004).

AREAS OF MUTUAL ECONOMIC COOPERATION BETWEEN ASEAN AND INDIA[11]

As the Indian economy continues to grow, the opportunities for ASEAN for mutually beneficial economic cooperation are likely to multiply. These opportunities are likely to exist in a range of areas such as food and energy security, oil and mineral exploration, health care, infrastructure development, ICT cooperation in IT related services, and sourcing of manpower, agriculture and natural resource monitoring, establishing institutional linkages in the financial sector, gems and jewellery, education services and human resource development, and technical assistance. Table 2.13, adapted from Sen, Asher,

TABLE 2.13
ASEAN and India: Areas of Mutual Economic Cooperation in a Globalized Era

Countries	Important Areas of Mutual Economic Cooperation with India
Indonesia	Food and energy security, oil exploration, health care, Infrastructural development, ICT cooperation in IT related services, and sourcing of manpower
Malaysia	Infrastructural development, ICT cooperation in IT related services and sourcing of manpower, health care, oil exploration, education services
Philippines	Health care, ICT cooperation in IT related services and sourcing of manpower, education services
Thailand	ICT cooperation in IT related services and sourcing of manpower, gems and jewellery, food processing, heritage tourism
Singapore	ICT cooperation in IT related services and sourcing of manpower, financial services, logistics and infrastructure development, tourism, education services
Myanmar	Food security, technical assistance, development of infrastructural links, agriculture and natural resource monitoring, establish institutional linkages in financial sector
Vietnam	Food security, technical assistance, development of infrastructural links, ICT cooperation in IT related services and sourcing of manpower, health care, oil and mineral exploration, education services
Cambodia and Laos	Food security, technical assistance, development of infrastructural links, ICT cooperation in IT related services and sourcing of manpower, health care, oil exploration, education services
Brunei	Energy security, oil exploration

Source: Compiled from Sen, Asher, and Rajan (2004).

and Rajan (2004), lists some possible areas of mutual cooperation that each ASEAN country may consider exploring with India.

Initial efforts have already been launched to enhance mutually beneficial economic cooperation in some of these areas. As an example, India's national oil company is already involved in a joint venture to explore oil and natural gas in Vietnam. Furthermore, in the mid-1990s, the President of Laos invited an Indian company, Kirloskar Brothers Ltd. (KBL), to partner Laos in addressing challenges from floods and drought in rice production. High quality, well-tested, but reasonably priced pumps from KBL used for irrigation and for mitigating floods enabled Laos to increase its rice production twenty times, making it at least self-sufficient in this key consumption commodity. Similar possibilities exist for Cambodia and Myanmar.

Another area of economic cooperation between India and ASEAN is in infrastructure development, with Malaysian businesses being particularly successful in securing contracts for roads and highway projects in India. India is hopeful of security contracts in Malaysia and in the railways sector, a sector in which it has a good record in Malaysia. The Port of Singapore Authority (PSA) has been involved with the development and management of the Tuticorin Port in Tamil Nadu and the Pipavav Port in Gujarat. Temasek Holdings, a Singapore government holding company, and Keppel, a government owned real estate company in Singapore, have opened offices in India. The Government Investment Corporation (GIC) of Singapore and government venture capital companies ought to follow suit. There is considerable scope for Singapore to provide venture capital for Indian firms not only in IT, but also in biotechnology and life sciences, thereby extending Singapore's entrepreneurship reach.

In the area of educational services, two Indian Schools (Bhavan's Global Indian International School [GIIS] and the Delhi Public School [DPS]) are already operating in Singapore.[12] The former has plans to operate these schools in Malaysia and the latter already has a presence in Indonesia. Apart from these areas, other potential areas of cooperation are in the entertainment and multimedia sector. Firms from ASEAN and India could consider joint production of films, television programmes, and Internet content for both domestic and international audiences, particularly those whose main language is Malay or Bahasa Indonesia. Restrictive practices in this area among ASEAN countries need to be reviewed if gains from cooperation in this area are to be realized. India could also cooperate with ASEAN in the pharmaceutical and health care service sectors. Given the rapidly rising health care costs in many ASEAN countries due to population and individual ageing, as well as the rise in sexually transmitted diseases, opportunities exist for mutually beneficial cooperation in health care activities, and in the production of generic and other drugs, including HIV/AIDS drugs.

Another possible area of cooperation between ASEAN and India is in space technology and its application for development purposes. Despite a budget of only US$450 million a year, which is about one-thirtieth of NASA's annual budget, India has sent thirteen satellites into orbit, produced some of the world's best remote imaging satellites, and launched its first unmanned mission to the moon in 2008 (Rhode 2004). India is using satellite technology to reclaim farmland, bring medical care to remote villages, as well as to predict natural disasters. ASEAN countries could cooperate with India in gaining expertise in applying satellite technology for their own development needs.

Of the ASEAN countries, Myanmar is the only country that shares a 1,600 km long border with India. Strategically it is, therefore, a very important country for India in the context of the overall ASEAN-India relationship. Myanmar could, therefore, develop as a gateway to ASEAN from India's Northeast, an area India wants to develop for both economic and security reasons.[13] It is important to note that success of economic cooperation has often been matched by political and security cooperation, which plays a very significant role in enhancing economic relations. As Myanmar is part of ASEAN, India and ASEAN consequently also share a land boundary. India also shares maritime frontiers with three ASEAN members, namely, Indonesia, Thailand, and Myanmar. The Andaman and Nicobar Islands, which are strategically located near the Straits of Malacca, are geographically closer to the ASEAN members than to India. Apart from this, India shares its exclusive economic zone (EEZ) with Malaysia. The presence of Indian diaspora in the ASEAN region, especially in Malaysia and Singapore, is another enduring bond between ASEAN and India. Consequently, India's security and prosperity are invariably linked to the well-being of the ASEAN region.

CONCLUDING REMARKS

It is evident from the above analysis that ASEAN and India share a largely complementary relationship with regards to their economic structures, demographics, and trade patterns, and that in a post-Cold War globalized era, both parties stand to gain significantly from mutually beneficial economic cooperation, primarily led by their businesses. Therefore, the potential FTA between the two is likely to be mutually beneficial.

However, in order to reap gains from the FTA, both parties must ensure that the final agreement is comprehensive in scope and covers liberalization and facilitation of trade in goods, services, investments, movement of professionals, as well as broader economic cooperation in strategic areas outlined above and to address competitiveness challenges in the globalized world jointly. The two sides must also ensure that the rules used in the FTA for preferential treatment are simple and attractive for businesses. The presence of substantial complementarities suggest that if the FTA is implemented properly, an ASEAN-India economic partnership would yield a win-win outcome for both parties in the medium to longer term, providing opportunities for global risk diversification.

APPENDIX 2.I
Export Similarity Index

Many countries have an unusual pattern of export specialization in relation to the rest of the world. Often, some product exports, typically manufacturing, have grown more rapidly than the average of world exports. It is not clear, however, to what extent these results reflect a common tendency among countries, and to what extent the results are driven by the performance of individual countries. The export similarity (XS) index based on Finger and Kreinin (1979) provides useful information on distinctive export patterns from country to country. It is defined as:

$$XS_{j,k} = \text{sum } [\min (X_{ij}, X_{ik}) * 100]$$

where X_{ij} and X_{ik} are industry i's export shares in country j's and country k's exports, and usually covers a group of countries or competitors. The index varies between zero and 100, with zero indicating complete dissimilarity and 100 representing identical export composition. This measure is subject to aggregation bias (as the data are more finely disaggregated, the index will tend to decline) and hence embodies a certain arbitrariness due to product choice.

Notes

1. The authors would like to thank Mukul Asher and Amarendu Nandy for useful comments and suggestions on this chapter. The chapter has benefited from discussions with Mukul Asher on some of his earlier works in this area. This chapter also draws from earlier works of one of the authors on this subject, namely, Sen, Asher, and Rajan (2004) and Asher and Sen (2005). The usual disclaimer applies.

2. These include the Mekong-Ganga Cooperation (MGC) and the BIMST-EC (Bay of Bengal Initiative for Multi-Sectoral and Technical Economic Cooperation). The first summit of the heads of state of BIMST-EC took place in 2004. Bhutan and Nepal joined this grouping at this summit. During the Ministerial meeting from 6–12 February 2004, the BIMST-EC members evolved a framework

for establishing a regional trade and investment agreement among themselves (*Business Line*, 13 February 2004).

3. Brunei, Cambodia, Laos, and Myanmar are excluded because of the lack of comparable data.

4. By 2004, Singapore was the only ASEAN country to have received FDI inflows greater in magnitude than India. It was also the only country to have experienced larger FDI outflows than India in the same year.

5. See Virmani (2004) for a discussion on FDI policies and strategies in India.

6. Author's calculations from Government of India (2004) and ASEAN Secretariat (2004).

7. See Nageswaran and Krithivasan (2006).

8. Its "Incredible India" tourism advertisements have had a degree of success. This is indicated by the fact that the Readers' Travel Awards 2003 conducted by Condé Nast Traveller placed India among the top ten must-see countries <http://www.india-tourism.com>.

9. Average length of stay of international tourists is twenty-nine days. Thus, in 2003, India received eighty million nights of visitors per year, a fraction of its potential.

10. The FDI figures in India need to be interpreted carefully, since the official FDI figures do not report reinvested earnings, intracompany loans, and some part of portfolio flows before the year 2000 (Srivastava 2003). These are subcomponents of FDI flows, which constitute quite a significant proportion of the volume of inward FDI, and thus remain underestimated in the case of India a few years ago when compared with IMF standard measurement guidelines. This is particularly important to note while making international comparisons of India's FDI flows with other countries.

11. This section draws on Sen, Asher, and Rajan (2004).

12. Since these currently cater mainly, but not exclusively, to the children of expatriate Indians from the region, their presence suggests that they expect substantial presence of these groups of Indians to continue. If Singapore liberalizes its current restrictive rules concerning its citizens not being eligible to join international schools, then substantial benefits may accrue, especially to its citizens of Indian origin.

13. In 2002–03, the two-way trade between India and Myanmar was US$412 million, with Myanmar's exports being US$337 million. Indeed, India is now Myanmar's largest export market. See Devare (2006) for further analysis on the India-Myanmar relationship.

References

Aggarwal, N. "Corporate Travel to India Takes Off". *Straits Times* (Singapore), 2 February 2004.

ASEAN Secretariat. *ASEAN Statistical Yearbook 2004*. Available electronically at <http://www.aseansec.org>.

Asher, M.G. and R. Sen. "India-East Asia Integration: A Win-Win for Asia". *Economic and Political Weekly* XL, no. 36 (3 September 2005): 3932–41.

Asher, M.G. and D. Vasudevan. "Emerging Economies: Growth, Demographic Dynamics and Pension Reform". Paper presented at the Swiss Finance Conference, Zurich, 3–4 February 2005.

Asian Development Bank (ADB). *Key Indicators of the Asian-Pacific Economies.* Manila: ADB (2004).

Associated Chambers of Commerce and Industry of India (ASSOCHAM)."India-ASEAN FTA: Business Complementarities, Trade Advantages & Rules of Origin". Report submitted to Ministries of Commerce and Industry and Finance, Government of India, New Delhi, 2005.

A.T. Kearney. *Making Offshore Decisions.* A.T. Kearney's 2004, Offshore Location Attractiveness Index, A.T. Kearney Inc., Chicago, 2004.

Athukorala, P. "Product Fragmentation and Trade Patterns in East Asia". *Trade and Development Discussion Paper 2003/21*, Division of Economics, Research School of Pacific and Asian Studies, The Australian National University, Canberra, 2003.

Bhattacharya, B. and M. Ariff. "Study on AFTA-India Linkages for the Enhancement of Trade and Investment". A report submitted to the Government of India and the ASEAN Secretariat, May, 2002.

Devare, S. *India and Southeast Asia: Towards Security Convergence.* Singapore: ISEAS, 2006.

Farrell, D."How Germany Can Win From Offshoring". *The McKinsey Quarterly_No. 4,* downloaded from <www.mckinseyquarterly.com>.

Finger, J.M. and M.E. Kreinin. "A Measure of 'Export Similarity' and Its Possible Uses". *Economic Journal* 89 (1979): 905–12.

Government of India. *Economic Survey 2004–05.* Ministry of Finance, New Delhi, 2004.

Khanna, T. and Y. Huang. "Can India Overtake China?". *Foreign Policy,* 8 December 2003.

Merchant, K."Indian Firms Spread Around the Globe". *Gulf News,* 1 February 2004, p. 37.

Munjal, P. and S. Pohit. "Perceptions of Impact of FDI on Economy". A report prepared for CUTS Centre for International Trade Economics and Environment, 2001 mimeo.

Nageswaran, A. and S. Krithivasan. "Capital Market Reforms in India and ASEAN: Avenues for Cooperation". In *India-ASEAN Economic Relations: Meeting the Challenges of Globalization,* edited by Nagesh Kumar, Rahul and Mukul Asher. Singapore: ISEAS, and New Delhi: RIS, 2006.

neoIT. "Mapping Offshore Markets 2004 Update". *Offshore Insights White Paper* 2 no. 6 (2004). Available electronically at <www.neoIT.com>.

Ramakrishnan, N. "The Age of Indian MNC Has Finally Dawned". *Business Line,* 31 March 2004.

Reserve Bank of India (RBI). "Handbook of Statistics on the Indian Economy". Mumbai: Reserve Bank of India, 2005.

Sen, R., M.G. Asher and R. Rajan. "ASEAN-India Economic Relations: Current Trends and Future Prospects". *Economic and Political Weekly* XXXIX no. 29 (2004): 3297–3309.

Srivastava, S. "What Is the True Level of FDI Flows to India?". *Economic and Political Weekly*, no. 38 (15 February 2003): 608–11.

Swami, P. and S. Sekhar. "India: From BPO to KPO". *Business India*, 29 August– 11 September 2005.

World Bank. *World Development Indicators CD-Rom*, 2004.

———. *World Development Indicators*. Washington D.C.: The World Bank, 2005.

Virmani, A. "Economic Reforms: Policy and Institutions Some Lessons From Indian Reforms". *Working Paper No. 121, ICRIER*, New Delhi (January 2004).

UNCTAD. *UN Comtrade Database*, UNCTAD: Geneva, 2004.

World Trade Organization (WTO). *International Trade Statistics 2004*. Geneva: WTO, 2004.

3

ASEAN AND CHINA
Managing Competition and Exploring Complementarities

Liu Yunhua

INTRODUCTION

The emergence of China as an economic powerhouse raises both challenges and opportunities for its neighbouring, developing countries. The economies of ASEAN (Association of Southeast Asian Nations), in particular, find themselves uncomfortably close to rising Chinese influence given their geographical location close to China. One of the concerns of these economies is that their traditional export markets in the world may be taken away by China if China turns into the world's low-cost manufacturing workshop. Another challenge facing ASEAN is the outflow of foreign direct investment (FDI) to China. Meanwhile, trade has expanded dramatically between ASEAN and China during the past decade, growing at an annual average of 19 per cent. China's exports to the five original members of ASEAN (referred to as the ASEAN-5 and comprising Indonesia, Malaysia, the Philippines, Singapore, and Thailand) grew from US$10 billion in 1995 to US$44 billion in 2004 while ASEAN's exports to China grew from US$8.2 billion in 1995 to US$42.2 billion in 2004. China's accession to the World Trade Organization (WTO) and the anticipated completion of a free trade area (FTA) between ASEAN and China will further change trade relations between the two areas.

Faced with the rapid increase of China's impact on Southeast Asia, how should the ASEAN economies respond to the variety of challenges and opportunities posed by a rising China? This chapter examines this crucial issue in the following three dimensions. First, it looks at previous trade patterns and the movement of FDI between China and ASEAN with a view to uncovering the areas of possible competition between these two areas. This discussion will also analyse the possible impact of such competition on the ASEAN economies, particularly their implications for specific industries. The analysis will cover the ASEAN-5 economies in some detail, while the case of Vietnam is discussed briefly. Second, the chapter examines the implications of the expanding Chinese economy on the emerging market opportunities of the ASEAN countries. Third, the chapter explores how these countries have responded through policy to a rising China, and highlights the consequences of these policies.

THE ASEAN ECONOMIES AND RECENT CHALLENGES

The Asian financial crisis that struck the region in 1997 posed critical challenges for the ASEAN economies, with the future at that point in time looking uncertain and dismal (Table 3.1). Before the crisis, however, the ASEAN economies documented high growth rates during the 1980s and early 1990s. Given their low levels of technology, limited market size, and inadequate financial resources, outward looking policies that emphasized trade and foreign investment were the most feasible choices for ASEAN. Exports of labour-intensive products and inflow of FDI eventually transformed ASEAN into one of the fastest growing regions in the last two decades of the twentieth century.

The performances of the individual ASEAN economies were, however, quite different. Among them, Singapore may be singled out as coming closest to achieving developed economy status; Malaysia and Thailand display relatively high levels of industrialization, while the Philippines and Indonesia are at the less developed end of the spectrum. Major economic indicators of the ASEAN-5 in the last decade are listed in Table 3.2.

One common experience of all the ASEAN-5 is that per capita GDP did not change very much during the past decade, with only Singapore and Malaysia registering a small increase. Trade volume for these countries, however, all increased moderately. This may be attributed to the depreciation in the value of their respective currencies, which itself

TABLE 3.1
Real GDP Growth Rate of ASEAN-5 and China, 1987–2004
(In percentages)

	Indonesia	Malaysia	Philippines	Singapore	Thailand	China
1987	4.9	5.4	4.8	9.4	9.5	11.1
1988	5.8	8.9	6.3	11.1	13.3	11.3
1989	7.5	9.2	6.1	9.2	12.3	4.3
1990	7.1	9.7	2.7	8.3	11.6	3.9
1991	6.6	8.7	−0.7	6.7	7.9	8.0
1992	5.8	8.5	0.0	5.8	7.5	13.2
1993	5.9	8.4	1.0	9.9	7.7	13.5
1994	7.5	9.2	4.4	11.4	9.0	12.7
1995	8.2	9.8	4.7	8.0	9.3	10.5
1996	7.8	10.0	5.8	7.6	5.9	9.6
1997	4.7	7.3	5.2	8.5	−1.4	8.8
1998	−13.1	−7.4	−0.6	0.1	−10.8	7.8
1999	0.8	6.1	3.4	5.9	4.4	7.1
2000	4.8	8.9	4.4	9.6	4.8	8.0
2001	3.8	0.3	1.8	−2.0	2.2	7.5
2002	4.4	4.1	4.3	3.2	5.3	8.3
2003	4.9	5.3	4.7	1.4	6.9	9.5
2004	5.1	7.1	6.1	8.4	6.1	9.5

Source: Asian Development Bank (2005).

could be the result of overall decreasing competitiveness of their respective economies.

The 1997 financial crisis led to unstable currencies and the significant withdrawal of FDI from the region. The world economic recession in 2000 further increased uncertainty for these countries. Among the ASEAN-5, Indonesia and the Philippines suffered high unemployment rates and fluctuating currency values, while Malaysia and Singapore suffered more from the decline in economic growth as well as relatively high unemployment. The economy of Thailand, however, revealed a relatively smoother pattern of unemployment. Compounding these domestic problems was the growing competition from a newly rising China, high oil prices, and rapid globalization of the world economy. These are three very important international factors that have impacted on the ASEAN economies in recent times.

TABLE 3.2
Key Economic Indicators of ASEAN-5 and China, 1995–2004

Country/Item	1995	1996	1997	1998	1999	2000	2001	2002	2003	2004
Indonesia										
Per Capita GDP, US$	1,038	1,154	1,083	467	675	802	788	948	1,116	1,191
Unemployment rate, %	7.2	4.9	4.7	5.5	6.4	6.1	8.1	9.1	9.9	...
Exports, US$ billion	45.4	49.8	53.4	48.8	48.6	62.1	56.3	57.1	60.9	77.8
Imports, US$ billion	40.6	42.9	41.6	27.3	24.0	33.5	30.9	31.2	32.5	51.7
Exchange rate, rupiah/US$	2,249	2,342	2,909	10,014	7,855	8,422	10,261	9,311	8,577	8,939
Malaysia										
Per Capita GDP, US$	4,294	4,764	4,623	3,254	3,485	3,844	3,665	3,880	4,142	4,604
Unemployment rate, %	3.1	2.5	2.4	3.2	3.4	3.0	3.5	3.5	3.6	3.5
Exports, US$ billion	73.7	78.2	78.9	73.4	84.5	98.1	88.1	93.3	104.9	126.5
Imports, US$ billion	77.6	78.4	79.0	58.3	65.4	82.1	73.3	79.5	82.7	104.2
Exchange Rate, ringgit/US$	2.50	2.52	2.81	3.92	3.80	3.80	3.80	3.80	3.80	3.80
Philippines										
Per Capita GDP, US$	1,083	1,183	1,149	889	1,015	987	907	957	970	1,035
Unemployment rate, %	8.4	7.4	7.9	9.6	9.6	10.1	9.8	10.2	10.1	10.9
Exports, US$ billion	17.3	20.5	25.2	29.4	35.4	38.2	32.1	35.1	36.2	46.7
Imports, US$ billion	28.2	31.7	39.1	29.5	30.7	34.4	33.0	35.4	37.5	47.8
Exchange Rate, peso/US$	25.7	26.2	29.4	40.8	39.0	44.1	50.9	51.6	54.2	56.0

Singapore

Per Capita GDP, US$	23,807	25,106	25,143	20,922	20,891	23,042	20,774	21,206	22,071	25,192
Unemployment rate, %	2.0	2.0	1.8	3.2	3.5	3.1	3.3	4.4	4.7	4.0
Exports, US$ billion	118	125	125	109	114	137	121	125	144	179
Imports, US$ billion	124	131	132	101	111	134	116	116	127	162
Exchange Rate S$/US$	1.41	1.41	1.48	1.67	1.69	1.72	1.79	1.79	1.74	1.69

Thailand

Per Capita GDP, US$	2,829	3,032	2,490	1,828	1,984	1,972	1,844	2,008	2,246	2,547
Unemployment rate, %	1.1	1.1	0.9	3.4	3.0	2.4	2.6	1.8	1.5	1.5
Exports, US$ billion	57.2	55.7	57.5	54.4	58.4	68.9	65.1	68.8	80.3	97.4
Imports, US$ billion	73.6	73.3	62.8	43.1	50.3	61.9	62.0	64.7	75.8	95.3
Exchange Rate, baht/US$	24.9	25.3	31.3	41.3	37.8	40.1	44.4	42.9	41.4	40.2

China

Per Capita GDP, US$	581	671	730	762	791	856	924	992	1100	1273
Unemployment rate, %	2.9	3.0	3.1	3.1	3.1	3.1	3.6	4.0	4.3	4.2
Exports, US$ billion	148	151	182	183	194	249	266	325	438	614
Imports, US$ billion	132	138	142	140	165	224	243	295	412	569
Exchange Rate, yuan/US$	8.35	8.31	8.28	8.27	8.27	8.27	8.27	8.27	8.27	8.27

Source: Asian Development Bank (2005).

CHALLENGES AND OPPORTUNITIES FOR
ASEAN IN FACING A RISING CHINA

Although China's pledge to avoid depreciating its currency during the financial crisis helped the ASEAN region emerge fairly rapidly from the downturn, some critics believe that the devaluation of the Chinese yuan in 1994, which led to a rapid expansion of China's exports in labour-intensive products, was an important contributing factor to the crisis. The Chinese economy, consequently, led to the unprecedented shock that was the financial crisis, which impacted not only the Southeast Asian region but also the rest of the world.

Competition in World Export Markets

The success of China's economic reforms led to a tremendous rise in its economic power as a huge trading nation and acted as a magnet for international investment capital. Its abundant labour and land have turned China into the world's production factory for labour-intensive products. China's WTO entry in 2001 further ensured that the country would have market access to world markets for its exports. Within ten years, China's exports increased from US$120 billion in 1994 to US$762 billion in 2005, and led to the country being ranked as the second largest exporting country in the world after Germany.

Given the slow but steady growth in world demand for labour-intensive goods over the past ten years, the rapid expansion of China's exports will inevitably take away market share from countries traditionally producing labour-intensive products. The ASEAN economies are likely to be among those immediately affected by this trend, with Singapore likely to be the most adversely affected. This is revealed by the large proportion of China's export production that is relocated from Taiwan and Hong Kong, two countries that produce goods similar to those manufactured in Singapore. Table 3.2 shows that since the 1997 financial crisis, ASEAN's exports experienced drastic fluctuations while China's exports generally grew at a high rate of more than 20 per cent.

More specifically, we may check the degree of export competition between the ASEAN-5 and China in the U.S. market. Table 3.3 shows the quantity of exports of ASEAN and China to the U.S. market. Table 3.4 indicates that ASEAN's exports to the United States from the mid-1990s did not reveal the sort of high growth rates of the late eighties to mid-nineties, while China's exports to the United States registered mainly double digit growth

TABLE 3.3
U.S. Imports from ASEAN-5 and China
(US$ billion)

	World Total of U.S.	Indonesia	Malaysia	Philippines	Singapore	Thailand	ASEAN-5	China
1987	424.4	4.0	3.1	2.5	7.3	2.3	19.2	3.1
1988	459.5	3.6	3.7	2.6	9.5	3.3	22.7	3.5
1989	492.9	4.3	4.9	3.3	10.7	4.5	27.7	4.7
1990	517.0	4.2	5.2	3.3	11.7	5.5	29.7	5.8
1991	508.4	4.2	6.0	3.3	11.9	6.3	31.7	6.8
1992	553.9	5.3	7.9	4.0	13.6	7.6	38.5	9.6
1993	603.4	6.1	10.2	4.6	15.1	8.3	44.3	18.4
1994	689.2	6.7	12.7	5.3	17.6	9.6	51.8	22.5
1995	770.9	7.5	15.7	6.4	21.2	10.3	61.0	26.0
1996	822.0	8.1	14.9	7.4	23.2	10.4	63.9	28.9
1997	899.0	8.5	15.2	9.2	23.1	11.8	67.8	35.4
1998	944.4	8.5	16.4	10.3	22.0	14.0	71.2	41.2
1999	1,059.4	8.6	19.2	11.1	22.6	13.5	75.0	47.4
2000	1,259.3	9.4	22.8	12.5	23.6	15.5	83.8	62.3
2001	1,180.1	7.7	17.8	8.9	18.7	13.2	47.8	54.3
2002	1,202.3	7.5	18.8	8.6	19.1	13.5	48.6	70.0
2003	1,305.1	7.3	20.5	7.2	20.5	13.6	48.8	92.6
2004	1,525.3	10.5	23.7	8.1	23.5	15.5	57.9	139.7

Source: 1. Asian Development Bank (2005) for ASEAN and China.
2. <http://www.oecd.org/statisticsdata/> for United States' imports total.

TABLE 3.4
Growth Rate of Imports of the U.S. from ASEAN-5 and China
(In percentages)

	World Total of U.S.	Indonesia	Malaysia	Philippines	Singapore	Thailand	ASEAN-5	China
1988	8.3	−9.8	17.6	5.7	29.9	42.5	18.0	12.5
1989	7.3	18.3	32.4	26.3	12.8	39.7	22.3	33.8
1990	4.9	−2.6	6.2	−1.5	8.8	20.0	7.2	22.5
1991	−1.7	1.0	16.5	0.6	2.1	15.2	6.7	17.5
1992	9.0	27.0	32.1	22.9	13.8	21.5	21.5	41.5
1993	8.9	15.4	28.2	13.7	11.2	8.4	15.0	91.7
1994	14.2	8.5	24.7	14.6	16.8	15.8	17.1	22.1
1995	11.8	12.2	23.4	21.1	20.0	7.5	17.6	16.0
1996	6.6	8.2	−4.8	15.7	9.6	0.9	4.9	10.9
1997	9.4	5.3	2.0	24.5	−0.4	13.3	6.0	22.4
1998	5.0	−0.4	7.7	12.3	−4.6	18.7	5.0	16.6
1999	12.2	1.4	17.0	8.3	2.4	−3.4	5.3	14.9
2000	18.9	9.3	18.8	12.6	4.4	14.8	11.7	31.4
2001	−5.6	−18	−21.9	−28.8	−20.8	−14.8	−43	−12.8
2002	1.9	−2.6	5.6	−3.4	2.1	1.5	1.7	28.9
2003	8.9	−2.7	9.0	−7.0	7.3	0.7	0	32.2
2004	16.9	43.8	15.6	12.5	14.6	14.0	18.6	50.9

Source:

1. Asian Development Bank (2005) for ASEAN and China.
2. <http://www.oecd.org/statisticsdata/> for United States imports total.

rates. Although there could be other reasons for the fluctuation in ASEAN's exports to the U.S. market, the export growth data, nevertheless, suggest that competition from China has been an important factor.

The econometric analysis undertaken by Liu and Luo (2004) further confirms the impact of competition from China on ASEAN and shows the period during which such competition affected different types of industry. Liu and Luo drew up a competition matrix based on estimates as shown in Table 3.5. The market share regression model is specified in the equation:

$$MS_i = a + bMS_c + u \tag{1}$$

where MS_i is the individual ASEAN member's total market share in the United States for a particular type of product, MS_c is China's market share in the United States for the same type of product. The assumption is that the sign of parameter b should be negative if competition took place between ASEAN members and China for that particular type of product. If a positive sign appears for parameter b, the assumption that there is competition between China and ASEAN will not hold for the particular product group examined. In statistical terms, this method should overcome the possible problems of heteroscedasticity, when different products are pooled into one group. Another assumption is that the sum of the market shares of the two regions maintains a stable trend. The data cover one-digit and two-digit SITC goods and two time periods, 1987–92 (Chew and Liu 1998) and 1987–2000 (Liu and Luo 2004). The results are presented in Table 3.5.

In general, the results show that competition took place for primary goods between the four ASEAN members (Indonesia, Malaysia, the Philippines, Thailand) and China, while competition between Singapore and China was mostly in the manufacturing sector. During the period 1987–92 (Chew and Liu 1998), there was also no competition between Singapore and China except for miscellaneous manufactured goods (SITC 81-89). However, after extending the analysis to the period 1987–2000, the major category of basic manufactures (SITC 61-69) turned out to be significantly negative, and regression on a bigger group comprising products of SITC 5-9 also turned out to be significantly negative. Overall, we can conclude that export competition in the U.S. market between Singapore and China became severe beginning from the early to mid-1990s. These results are not surprising and are consistent with our common understanding that although Singapore has a relatively advanced production level, China caught up very quickly over time, in terms of basic and

TABLE 3.5

Competition Matrix for ASEAN-5 and China for Different Types of Products in the U.S. Market, 1987–2000

Products	N	ASEAN-5	Indonesia	Malaysia	Philippines	Singapore	Thailand
Primary goods (SITC 0,1,2,3,4)	70	−5.82 (−2.25)	0.10 (0.31)	−3.39 (−4.08)	−4.73 (−4.03)	0.15 (3.45)	2.05 (9.33)
Manufactures (SITC 5,6,7,8,9)	70	0.02 (0.12)	0.13 (4.81)	0.05 (2.12)	−0.21 (−1.78)	−0.08 (−2.06)	0.13 (8.41)
Food & beverages (SITC 00-12)	168	3.44 (15.01)	0.43 (4.37)	0.08 (3.11)	0.39 (3.75)	0.17 (4.35)	2.36 (12.73)
Crude materials (SITC 21-43)	224	−0.87 (−2.58)	−0.18 (−1.13)	−0.38 (−2.46)	−0.18 (−1.75)	−0.06 (−2.17)	−0.07 (−1.25)
Chemical & related (SITC 51-59)	126	−0.05 (−0.56)	−0.01 (−0.31)	0.02 (0.77)	0.001 (0.07)	−0.09 (−1.30)	0.01 (1.28)
Basic manufactures (SITC 61-69)	126	0.10 (0.63)	−0.04 (−0.33)	0.03 (1.16)	0.02 (1.35)	−0.02 (−3.42)	0.12 (3.05)
Machines, transport (SITC 71-79)	126	1.70 (5.81)	0.12 (11.13)	0.74 (8.23)	0.21 (6.85)	0.37 (1.86)	0.26 (7.97)
Miscellaneous manufactured (SITC 81-89)	112	0.10 (2.91)	0.08 (5.27)	−0.01 (−1.10)	0.02 (1.71)	−0.03 (−4.16)	0.05 (4.28)

Note: N is the number of observations; numbers in the parentheses below the estimators are *t*-values.
Source: Liu and Luo (2005).

mid-range industrial products. It means that in the coming years, Singapore will face further pressure from China, given China's ability to learn fast and move up the value chain. After 2000, we should expect the competition to intensify for all five ASEAN members.

Competition in Attracting FDI

It appears that the diversion of FDI from Southeast Asia to China is an obvious fact. The pattern of FDI inflows to Asia has changed in recent years, with more than 70 per cent of incoming FDI now flowing into China instead of Southeast Asia as in the past. Table 3.6 shows FDI flows into Singapore and China over the past two decades, and suggests that FDI diversion may be a reality.

Historically, Singapore has relied heavily on FDI for economic expansion and upgrading its industry level. Despite the small size of the economy, FDI inflows to Singapore only fell behind China significantly after 1991. Less capital inflow and own capital outflow could mean lower economic

TABLE 3.6
FDI Inflows of China and Singapore
(US$ million)

Year	China	Singapore	Year	China	Singapore
1980	57	1,236	1992	11,156	2,204
1981	265	1,660	1993	27,515	4,686
1982	430	1,602	1994	33,787	8,550
1983	636	1,134	1995	35,849	11,503
1984	1,258	1,302	1996	40,180	9,303
1985	1,659	1,047	1997	44,237	13,533
1986	1,875	1,710	1998	43,751	7,594
1987	2,314	2,836	1999	40,319	13,245
1988	3,194	3,655	2000	40,772	12,464
1989	3,393	2,887	2001	46,846	10,949
1990	3,487	5,575	2002	52,700	7,655
1991	4,366	4,887	2003	53,500	5,528

Source:

1. *World Trade Analyzer (WTA)* CDROM, 2001 and International Monetary Fund (2001).
2. Data after 2000 are from <http://www.singstat.gov.sg/keystats/economy.html> and <http://www.uschina.org/statistics/fdi_cumulative.html>.

TABLE 3.7
FDI Inflow of China and ASEAN-5 in the Past Eleven Years
(US$ billion)

	1993	1994	1995	1996	1997	1998	1999	2000	2001	2002	2003
China	27.5	33.7	35.8	40.1	44.2	43.7	38.7	38.3	44.2	49.3	53.5
Indonesia	2.0	2.1	4.3	6.1	4.6	–0.3	–2.7	–4.5	–3.2	–1.5	–0.5
Malaysia	5.0	4.3	4.1	5.0	5.1	2.1	3.8	3.7	0.5	3.2	2.4
Philippines	1.2	1.5	1.4	1.5	1.2	2.2	1.7	1.3	0.9	1.7	0.3
Singapore	4.6	8.5	11.5	9.3	13.5	7.5	13.2	12.4	10.9	7.6	5.5
Thailand	1.8	1.3	2.0	2.3	3.8	7.3	6.1	3.3	3.8	0.9	1.9
ASEAN-5	14.7	17.9	23.5	24.4	28.4	19.0	22.2	16.4	13.1	12.0	9.6
China and ASEAN-5 Total	42.2	51.7	59.4	64.6	72.7	62.7	60.9	54.8	57.3	61.3	63.1
ASEAN-5/Total	35	35	40	38	39	30	36	30	23	20	15
China/Total	65	65	60	62	61	70	64	70	77	80	85

Source: Asian Development Bank (2005).

growth and fewer jobs. Some scholars have argued that FDI competition could appear at any time and jobs might be in jeopardy if a country's economic environment is not sufficiently competitive. These views suggest that care is needed when attributing a slowdown in FDI inflows simply to its diversion to other sites; other perspectives need to be considered to gain a comprehensive understanding of the situation (Chen and Ku 2003). Nevertheless, the diversion hypothesis is a plausible one. Table 3.7 also shows that during the past decade, competition between China and ASEAN in attracting FDI became more severe, with the relative share of ASEAN in FDI inflows down to 15 per cent compared with an 85 per cent share for China.

The Increasing Importance of China's Market to ASEAN

While ASEAN faces considerable challenges posed by a rising Chinese economy, there are also opportunities for ASEAN countries in China's large market. For the past decade, all of the ASEAN-5 experienced rapid increases in their trade with China, with an annual average growth rate of more than 14 per cent (Table 3.8).

Interestingly, in 2003 and 2004, Singapore's exports rebounded. registering sharp increases of 15 and 28 per cent respectively compared with the 3 per cent increase in 2002 (Table 3.2). From examination of the destinations for Singapore's exports over the past ten years in Table 3.9, it is clear that the China market expanded the fastest for Singapore. In 2004, Singapore's exports to China increased by 51.5 per cent. In 2004, the trade volume between the two countries reached US$31.5 billion, increasing by 48.6 per cent and accounting for 9.2 per cent of Singapore's total trade. Back in 1995, China's share was only 2.8 per cent. In 2004, China replaced Hong Kong as Singapore's fourth largest trading partner after Malaysia, the United States, the European Union, and Japan. The year 2004 also was when the sum total of Singapore's trade with China and Hong Kong combined overtook that with Malaysia, and the two together became Singapore's largest market. These major shifts have been taking place only since 1995. Imports of Singapore from China show another facet of its trade relationship with China, namely the increasing complementarity of trade between the two. In fact, Singapore has been recording trade deficits with China more often in the past ten years as China has become an important supplier of diverse resources, manufactured products, and technology to Singapore, especially in consumption goods and production parts (Chew and Liu 1998).

TABLE 3.8
ASEAN's Trade with China, 1995–2004
(US$ million)

Country/Item	1995	1996	1997	1998	1999	2000	2001	2002	2003	2004	1995–2004, Average %
Indonesia											
Exports	1,741	2,057	2,229	1,832	2,008	2,767	2,200	2,903	3,802	5,870	14.5
Imports	1,495	1,597	1,518	906	1,242	2,022	1,842	2,427	2,957	5,693	16.0
Malaysia											
Exports	1,889	1,882	1,852	1,994	2,318	3,028	3,821	5,253	6810	8,460	18.1
Imports	1,709	1,876	2,232	1,849	2,139	3,237	3,804	6,157	7,300	10,339	22.1
Philippines											
Exports	209	328	244	344	575	663	793	1,356	2,145	5,342	43.3
Imports	660	653	972	1,199	1,040	786	975	1,252	1,798	3,539	20.5
Singapore											
Exports	2,759	3,395	4,053	4,065	3,920	5,377	5,329	6,863	10,134	15,392	21.0
Imports	4,042	4,439	5,668	4,851	5,697	7,116	7,195	8,869	11,073	16,211	16.7
Thailand											
Exports	1,642	1868	1,744	1,769	1,861	2,806	2,863	3,553	5,707	7,103	17.6
Imports	2,096	1,953	2,260	1,822	2,495	3,377	3,711	4,928	6,067	8,185	16.3
Vietnam											
Exports	361	340	474	440	746	1,536	1,417	1,518	1,883	2,321	23.0
Imports	329	329	404	515	673	1,401	1,606	2,158	3,138	4,557	34.0

Source: Asian Development Bank (2005).

TABLE 3.9
Direction of Singapore's Exports and Imports
(US$ billion)

Country	1995	1996	1997	1998	1999	2000	2001	2002	2003	2004
Exports, total	118.2	125.1	125.3	109.8	114.7	137.9	121.7	125.0	144.1	179.4
1. Malaysia	22.7	22.5	21.8	16.7	18.9	25.0	21.1	21.8	22.7	27.2
2. U.S.	21.6	23.1	23.1	21.8	22.0	23.8	18.7	19.1	20.5	23.2
3. Hong Kong	10.1	10.2	12.0	9.2	8.8	10.8	10.8	11.4	14.4	17.6
4. Japan	9.2	10.2	8.8	7.2	8.5	10.4	9.3	8.9	9.6	11.5
5. China, P. R.	2.8	3.3	4.0	4.0	3.9	5.3	5.3	6.8	10.1	15.3
6. Thailand	6.8	7.0	5.7	4.2	5.0	5.8	5.3	5.7	6.1	7.7
7. Korea	3.2	4.7	3.6	2.5	3.5	4.9	4.6	5.2	6.0	7.3
8. Germany	4.0	3.8	3.6	3.3	3.2	4.2	4.2	4.0	4.4	6.2
9. Netherlands	3.1	2.8	3.0	3.7	3.8	4.0	4.0	4.3	4.6	5.4
10. Australia	2.6	2.8	2.9	3.1	3.1	3.2	3.1	3.3	4.6	6.6
Imports, total	124.4	131.3	132.5	101.6	111.0	134.6	116.0	116.4	127.9	162.9
1. Malaysia	19.3	19.7	19.9	15.6	17.2	22.8	20.0	21.2	21.5	24.9
2. U.S.	18.7	21.5	22.3	18.7	19.0	20.2	19.1	16.6	18.0	20.7
3. Japan	26.3	23.8	23.2	17.0	18.5	23.1	16.0	14.5	15.3	19.0
4. China, P. R.	4.0	4.4	5.6	4.8	5.6	7.1	7.1	8.8	11.0	16.2
5. Thailand	6.4	7.1	6.8	4.8	5.2	5.8	5.1	5.4	5.5	6.7
6. Korea	5.4	4.8	4.1	3.0	4.1	4.8	3.8	4.3	4.9	6.9
7. Germany	4.3	4.7	45	3.4	3.6	4.2	3.8	3.9	4.8	5.6
8. Saudi Arabia	3.8	4.9	5.3	3.2	3.2	4.3	4.2	3.8	3.9	5.0
9. Hong Kong	4.1	4.2	3.9	2.8	3.1	3.5	2.7	2.8	3.0	3.6
10. Philippines	1.1	1.3	1.9	2.3	2.9	3.3	2.5	2.5	2.8	4.2

Source: Asian Development Bank (ADB) — Key Indicators 2005 <www.adb.org/statistics> May 2006.

Impact of China's WTO entry and FTA with ASEAN on ASEAN's Exports

One major concern that Asian countries had with respect to China was that a rising China could pose an economic and political threat to them. Recent developments in the relationship between China and Asian countries, however, reveal that the strong demand for investment and consumption in the fast growing Chinese economy has become a leading force turning around the economies of China's neighbours from stagnation or downturn to growth. The rapid increase in exports from Japan, Malaysia, and Singapore to China in recent years showed these trends. The "world largest market" is clearly functioning well.

With China's WTO entry and with the FTA between China and ASEAN progressing well, the impact of China's tariff reductions and removal of other trade restrictions on trade and investment flows could be substantial. To examine the effect of these policy and institutional changes in China on specific industries in ASEAN, we use the results of Liu and Luo (2005). A model of ASEAN's exports related to the exchange rate, China's tariff reduction, and time trend is estimated using SITC data for the period 1987 to 2000:

$$EX = a_0 + a_1 ER + a_2 TR + a_3 YEAR + u \qquad (2)$$

where EX = ASEAN's exports to China (US$ thousand),

ER = exchange rate between the Chinese yuan and that of individual ASEAN member countries (current Chinese yuan/ASEAN member country currency),

TR = China's import tariff in terms of average tariff rate in a specific industry (%).

Tariff and exchange rates are two of the many factors that influence trade. This model allows us to analyse the effect of changes in the two variables on trade. According to economic theory, both tariff and exchange rates share an inverse relationship with trade value. Therefore, the sign of the parameter of both tariff and exchange rates should be negative. Another variable added to our model is the year variable. This variable helps to account for changes in trade value attributed to economic factors other than tariffs and exchange rates.

Within the primary sector, there are five individual industries. Hence, four dummy variables were introduced into the model. Dummy variables help to capture effects that are due to changes in any industries within the primary sector. Three dummy variables were also introduced into the manufacturing sector model for the same reason. The results are presented in Table 3.10.

TABLE 3.10

Tariff Export Matrix For Different Types of Products in China Market from ASEAN-5, 1987–2000

Products	N	Indonesia	Malaysia	Philippines	Singapore	Thailand
Primary goods (SITC 0,1,2,3,4)	168	-888.16 (-2.62)	-195.30 (-0.90)	-36.35 (-1.33)	-732.63 (-1.88)	-203.95 (-1.29)
Food & beverages (SITC 00-12)	72	20.88 (0.75)	-21.38 (-1.32)	2.94 (0.09)	392.32 (2.26)	-218.49 (-1.27)
Crude materials (SITC 21-43)	96	-2,510.72 (-2.52)	812.96 (1.30)	-93.40 (-1.40)	-2,537.54 (-2.49)	-333.82 (-0.84)
Manufactures (SITC 5,6,7,8,9)	210	-231.13 (-1.23)	-412.98 (-2.09)	-119.37 (-1.48)	-602.82 (-1.56)	-205.96 (-1.02)
Chemical & related (SITC 51-59)	54	-163.64 (-0.79)	-47.85 (-0.26)	-105.16 (-2.33)	60.31 (0.15)	72.48 (0.19)
Basic manufactures (SITC 61-69)	54	-682.93 (-0.96)	-581.39 (-1.57)	-173.71 (-1.78)	-153.08 (-2.30)	232.54 (1.94)
Machines,transport (SITC 71-79)	54	-69.64 (-0.32)	-529.31 (-1.97)	-33.72 (-0.08)	-636.27 (-2.33)	-418.88 (-2.42)
Miscellaneous manufactures (SITC 81-89)	48	79.98 (3.04)	-73.52 (-2.28)	-4.36 (-0.89)	-168.58 (-2.54)	-53.70 (-1.43)

Note: N is the number of observations; due to the conversion from Harmonized System to SITC code, and the difference in general tariff rates, the number of observations does not follow the pattern that within each year there are five observations (for SITC 0, 1, 2, 3, 4). Estimators are tariff's coefficients; numbers in the parentheses below the estimators are t-values.

The results show that Singapore and Malaysia benefit more from China's tariff reduction in manufacturing goods, while Indonesia benefits more in primary goods. Singapore benefits substantially in all manufactures, with gains ranging from US$153,080 to US$636,270 for each SITC two-digit item for a 1 per cent tariff reduction in China. The potential for gains for ASEAN are, therefore, large, given that the current average tariff of China is 11.3 per cent. By the end of the fifth year of China's WTO entry, the average tariff rate of China should fall to 9 per cent, while completion of the China-ASEAN FTA in 2010 will see tariffs removed completely. The largest gains are in crude materials, which includes Singapore's refined oil exports. If tariffs are removed completely, Singapore's exports will certainly get a big boost.

POLICY RESPONSES AND ADJUSTMENT OF ASEAN COUNTRIES

Faced with rapid economic globalization as well the challenges and opportunities associated with the rising Chinese economy, the ASEAN countries have, in fact, actively managed their policies to cope with the changing world and regional economic environment. Although policy changes adopted in these countries are not necessarily all due to the pressure of the rising Chinese economy, competition from China, nevertheless, has been one of the more important reasons for domestic reforms.

Policies to Cope with Competition

During the past decade, the ASEAN countries have collectively initiated a number of policies to cope with increasing world economic competition. At the regional level, they adopted regional cooperation by forming the ASEAN Free Trade Area (AFTA), while also expanding the free trade zone to include China (an ASEAN plus one arrangement). At the national level, each of the countries separately signed free trade agreements with third parties, particularly to secure market access. To avert direct competition with China, these countries have made considerable efforts to move up the technological ladder to ensure that they are always ahead of China. They are also focusing on developing niche areas of economic specialization to avoid head-on competition with China. Relatively large economies such as Indonesia, Malaysia, Thailand, and Vietnam have adopted a two-track approach. On the one hand, they have continued with export-oriented development, albeit with some differences in view of the emergence of China. On the other hand, these countries have also turned inwards to develop their domestic market as a new source of economic growth.

The ASEAN countries initiated the ASEAN Free Trade Area (AFTA) as far back as 1992. AFTA may not have been initiated as a direct response to the rise of China, but was rather aimed at integrating a regional market economy comprising 500 million people in Southeast Asia. On this free trade platform, intra-ASEAN industrial linkages can be forged with the ultimate aim of developing the ASEAN region as a viable international production centre. Such a move is economically beneficial to all the countries. Firstly, industries in the region can enjoy massive economies of scale. Secondly, the comparative advantage of each country can be exploited and intraregional trade expanded. Finally, through industrial linkages, an integrated production and trade system could be developed such that the region as a whole can withstand the onslaught of severe competition in the international market.

Apart from AFTA, the ASEAN countries also extended their regional cooperation into the area of investment. These include the formation of the ASEAN Investment Area (AIA), the ASEAN Industrial Cooperation (AICO) scheme, the ASEAN Framework Agreement on Services, e-ASEAN, and the ASEAN Integration of Preferences. These regional cooperation efforts were initiated, like AFTA, not so much to avert the so-called threat from the rise of China (Zainal Aznam 2003), but rather because the rise of China made these agreements an urgent necessity as a self-help approach to sustaining regional economic growth.

At the national level, it is natural that each ASEAN member country responded differently to competition according to its own special circumstances.

Singapore

Restructuring the economy, expanding potential export markets, and cutting down business cost were the three major strategies used in Singapore to cope with increasing global competition. To address the problems arising from the 1997 crisis, Singapore initiated a series of policy changes that were not only a response to the challenge from China, but were also strategies to cope with the increasing competition from rapid globalization. For Singapore, the disappearance of the country's traditional competitive advantage was the essential challenge. That is, while labour and land costs were reaching the levels found in the developed economies, production technologies were not the same as in the developed economies.

Once the multinational companies began relocating their headquarters and production factories to China, the weaknesses of indigenous enterprises emerged. Upgrading the level of industries and finding and creating new advantages become unavoidable, with Goh Chok Tong, then Prime Minister of Singapore, urging Singaporeans to remake their economy. The Singapore economy had long been characterized by strong state control and foreign investment and state and foreign entrepreneurship has been the driving force in the economy, while the local private sector in comparison has been relatively weak, particularly in industry (relative to commerce and services). Large scale government linked companies (GLCs) and many statutory boards monopolized major social resources in infrastructure, financial services, telecommunications, health services, education, port shipping services, and housing, allowing the private sector little space to develop its capabilities. With the declining returns on GLC investment, bold reforms have been carried out in privatizing many state-controlled business.

Singapore's long-term strategy is to invest in research and development in new industries such as the biochemical industry and life sciences to create new comparative advantages, and to reform the education system to encourage innovative thinking and talent to fit the demands of a knowledge-based economy. To meet its long-term goal towards becoming a knowledge-based economy, Singapore has been actively cultivating intellectual capital and advanced infrastructure to ensure the country builds industries with competitive levels of innovation and technology.

To facilitate the new knowledge-based economy, the government is making further improvements in infrastructure. Some of these improvements include the building of a third terminal at Singapore's Changi Airport, which will increase the capacity of the airport to sixty million passengers a year. Singapore will also be the first country in the world to be connected by a single broadband network. Singapore ONE's collaboration with U.S.-based @Home Network will also expand its services beyond the domestic market. In addition, the National Science and Technology Plan 2000 was aimed at spending more than S$4 billion over five years to strengthen indigenous technological capabilities to support private R&D work. The Singapore government is also spending S$2 billion on information technology for education. Accompanying the industrial upgrading strategy were measures to improve the quality of the labour force. The policy to attract international talent to Singapore has been made more flexible while reforms in the education system have been adopted to support the creation of a knowledge-based economy.

For the short term, business policies were changed to improve the investment environment by cutting corporation taxes and wages to keep Singapore attractive as a regional base for company headquarters and factories. In cutting business costs, the Singapore government has reduced land rent, office rent, as well as water and electricity prices. It has also reduced labour wages and changed the wage structure to a more flexible wage scheme. Finally, corporation tax was reduced to 20 per cent from 22 per cent.

Another strategy was that of expanding international markets for Singapore's exports by forging new trade pacts and enhancing regional cooperation in investment and production to overcome Singapore's size constraint. Since 2001, Singapore has successfully concluded FTA agreements with the United States (2004), Japan (2002), Australia (2003), New Zealand (2001) and with the European Free Trade Association (2003). Agreements being negotiated include those with Canada, Jordan, India, Korea, Mexico, the Pacific Three (Singapore with Chile and New Zealand), and Sri Lanka, while the ASEAN-China and ASEAN-India agreements involve Singapore as a member in a larger negotiating group made up of the ASEAN states.

Malaysia

An inward-focused strategy aimed at reducing Malaysia's heavy reliance on foreign capital to sustain economic growth, promoting a knowledge-based economy, and upgrading the manufacturing sector were the major measures Malaysia has adopted to face the competition from China. Incentives for domestic investment were provided, while a corporation tax cut benefited both local and foreign firms. Incentives were also granted to companies to reduce the cost of doing business and to encourage exports.

Another strategy was to promote new sources of growth, particularly in the services sector. In view of the fact that the service sector accounts for 55 per cent of Malaysia's GDP, service industry promotion packages were offered to attract companies to establish their operational headquarters, regional distribution centres, and representative offices in Malaysia. Efforts were also made to exploit opportunities for "exporting" certain services, particularly tourism, education, and health (Zainal Aznam 2004). With a very much similar export structure but higher labour costs than China, Malaysia has very limited choices in the manufacturing sector except to upgrade the manufacturing sector by moving up the value-added chain. Developing a highly educated work force and increasing the expenditure on research and development (R&D) are the two most important measures for this purpose.

Thailand

Like Malaysia, Thailand has also emphasized a balance between external reliance and domestic strength in order to mitigate the problem of over-dependence on a possibly volatile external sector. A dual track policy of maintaining the export-oriented economy whilst fostering domestic sources of consumption and investment was adopted. The former emphasizes export-oriented manufacturing spearheaded by multinational corporations (MNCs) while the latter strategy involves providing strong support to local enterprises leveraging indigenous skills and resources. In the short run, the government strategy is to stimulate domestic demand through its expenditure on the rural and agricultural sectors. In the meantime, the second domestic track aims to develop new local industries as part of the diversification away from the traditional economic model, including adopting measures to assist businesses move up the value chain, to keep ahead of direct Chinese competition.

The dual track policy has allowed Thailand to achieve a reasonable rate of economic growth following the Asian financial crisis. Growth of the Thai economy accelerated from 2.2 per cent in 2001 to 6.1 per cent in 2004, although real GDP growth recorded a slowdown of 3.5 per cent in 2005 due to the tsunami disaster of December 2004. Inflation was recorded at less than 3 per cent during 2001–04 although it accelerated to 4.2 per cent in 2005 due to higher oil prices in the latter part of 2005.

Philippines and Indonesia

As the Philippines and Indonesia have different resource endowments compared with China, much of the trade between either of them and China is of the interindustry variety while export competition with China in the world market is not significant, as indicated in Table 3.5. Both Philippine and Indonesian economic policies have been more focused on addressing their respective domestic economic problems. The rise of China, however, has prompted these two countries to seek out economic opportunities in China's growing market.

Policies to Build on Complementarities

Aside from the competition that China poses to the ASEAN countries, the complementarities between the two areas have considerable potential for expanding trade and investment ties between them in a mutually beneficial manner. The market opportunities provided by the growing Chinese economy to ASEAN countries have already been outlined in Tables 3.8 and 3.10. The growing Chinese economy has become another engine of growth for ASEAN.

The most important policy mechanism that will allow ASEAN to exploit these complementarities is the ASEAN-China Free Trade Area, which is expected to be completed by 2010. Adopted in 2001, the ASEAN-China FTA covers commodity and services trade as well as investment. Under the agreement, the free trade zone will be established among the developed ASEAN countries and China by 2010 and extended to the less developed ASEAN countries (Vietnam, Laos, Myanmar, and Cambodia) by 2015. Such a regional approach can provide synergy among countries in this region to boost and sustain economic development further, based on complementarities and economies of scale. ASEAN, being a region richly endowed with natural resources, will be able to meet the increasing demand for raw materials, especially oil and gas, by China for its industrial production. At the same time, China will serve as an assembly and export platform for ASEAN manufactured exports, especially in the electronics and telecommunication sector. Chantasasawat et al. (2004) find that China's FDI receipts and other Asian countries' FDI receipts are positively correlated. This evidence, together with increasing intraregional trade, confirms the existence of an integrated production system in Asia, including in ASEAN, one that is based on a regional (international) division of labour.

Besides the regional approach, each ASEAN country has also formulated strategies and policy responses to exploit the complementarities with China and integrate its economy with the Chinese economy. Since China is richly endowed with cheap labour, Singapore and Malaysia are attempting to move up their technological ladders such that their production systems become well integrated with that of China. In this case, the two countries are concentrating on manufacturing intermediate electronic components for export to China for assembly as final consumer products for onward export to third countries. At the same time, ASEAN countries that are richly endowed with natural resources, such as Indonesia, Malaysia, Myanmar, and Thailand, are exporting raw materials including oils and gas to China. Such complementarities have resulted in a rapid rise in intraregional trade. In fact, while China has a trade surplus with the United States, it has trade deficits with almost all the ASEAN countries.

China also offers substantial investment opportunities for the ASEAN countries, each of which has significant ethnic Chinese citizens. Through their cultural affinity, ethnic Chinese businesses have been investing in China, with the pace gathering momentum following China's open door policy in 1978. Ethnic Chinese businesses were able to exploit these cultural resources for investment in China (Gao 2001; Dhales 2005) and together with Chinese from Hong Kong and Taiwan, they accounted for about 60 per cent of FDI to China.

Singapore, in particular, accelerated its investment in China since its regionalization drive adopted in 1992. Its main investment drive in China began with the establishment of the Suzhou Industrial Park, which followed the model of the Jurong Industrial Park in Singapore. The project was a joint venture between the Suzhou provincial government and the Singapore Government and was strongly supported by the Central Government in China. In the initial years, Singapore held a majority share in this venture, which led to some conflict between the two investing parties. The dispute was eventually settled amicably when the Suzhou provincial government became the major shareholder. In the case of Malaysia, ethnic Chinese businesses invest in China as part of their strategy to overcome the discriminatory effects of the New Economic Policy (NEP) on ethnic Chinese domestic investment. The NEP is an affirmative action policy aimed at according the country's ethnic Malay majority population with economic privileges (Ng 1998). Ethnic Chinese businesses in Indonesia were also forced to invest in China as part of their strategy of diversifying investment during the period of political uncertainty in the country following the 1998 downfall of President Soeharto.

With its huge external reserves and also as a strategy to neutralize capital inflows, China began to invest abroad since early 1979. However, investment abroad gained significant momentum from 2001 when huge amounts of capital flowed into China in anticipation of its currency appreciation. Cumulatively, China invested the second largest amount of its funds in the ASEAN region (13.2 per cent) after the European Union (15.3 per cent) (Wong and Chan 2003). Among the ASEAN countries, the largest recipient was Thailand, followed by Cambodia, Indonesia, Vietnam, and Myanmar. At the same time, about a hundred Chinese companies have been listed on the Singapore Stock Exchange.

Vietnam and China

Among the ASEAN members, Vietnam has emerged as a regional economic star, displaying steadily high growth rates during the past decade and outperforming all the ASEAN member countries (Table 3.11). Although it began its reform process rather late in the 1980s, Vietnam has undertaken some important reforms to integrate its economy with the world economy. These policy reforms include shifting from a centrally planned economy to a multisector market economy, creating favorable conditions for business activities to ensure domestic and foreign investment, and creating a legal framework for the market economy. These policies of *Doi Moi* (or renovation) have led to significant improvements in Vietnam's economic performance.

Table 3.12 shows that Vietnam experienced an average growth rate of 23.8 per cent in exports to China during the last decade and an even higher average growth rate of 38.6 per cent in imports. Geographically adjacent to China, Vietnam stands in a much better position to link its economy with China, compared with the other ASEAN members, as the diversified economic resources and products of China provide Vietnam with various sources of complementarity between the two countries to aid its economic development. No doubt, in the coming years, Vietnam will benefit more from the rising Chinese economy and its pursuit of a WTO entry will eventually lead to steady trade relations with China and the rest of world.

CONCLUDING REMARKS

China may be seen as a threat to the ASEAN economy, as shown by some empirical indicators discussed in this chapter. However, there is also evidence to show that this "threat" can be turned into a range of potential opportunities, provided sound policy responses are adopted that aid such a transition. While the regional or collective approach towards the rise of China may be a rational and positive step forward, ultimately, the effectiveness and success of ASEAN's economic engagement with China will depend largely on strong political commitment and cooperation from each individual ASEAN member.

It is surprising that the trade expansion between ASEAN and China developed so rapidly given the moderate similarities in their levels of economic development, suggesting that simply classifying comparative advantage based on low-tech versus high-tech cannot adequately explain trade relations between ASEAN and China. The pattern of economic links between the two areas undermines the notion that the ASEAN countries, due to their position as middle-income economies, are invariably squeezed by globalization. The unfolding pattern of trade between ASEAN and China indicates that we

TABLE 3.11
Main Economic Indicators of Vietnam, 1996–2005

	1996	1997	1998	1999	2000	2001	2002	2003	2004	2005
GDP, %	9.3	8.2	5.8	4.8	6.8	6.9	7.1	7.3	7.8	8.4
Exports, US$ billion	7.4	9.4	9.3	11.5	14.4	15.0	16.7	20.1	25.8	30.8
Imports, US$ billion	11.2	11.8	11.3	11.7	15.6	16.2	19.7	25.2	33.2	39.9
Unemployment, %	—	—	4.5	4.4	2.3	2.8	2.2	2.2	2.1	2.1

Source: ADB Statistics online, 2006.

TABLE 3.12
Vietnam's Trade with China, 1996–2005
(US$ million)

	1996	1997	1998	1999	2000	2001	2002	2003	2004	2005	1995–2004, Average %
Exports	340	474	440	746	1,536	1,417	1,518	1,883	2,321	2,317	23.8
Imports	329	404	515	673	1,401	1,606	2,158	3,138	4,557	6,203	38.6

Source: ADB Statistics online, 2006.

should not view these countries as producing one or another category of goods. Instead, we should view the export market as a "continued chain" market, in which every country at a different level of production will have its own place or niche in the expanding production network. It is interesting to note the growth of intra-industry trade in the basic manufacturing sector between the Philippines and China (Palanca 2004). Other countries are also showing a similar trend. With new patterns of economic integration between the ASEAN and China unfolding, we should be confident that economic cooperation between the two areas has much potential and that we are only at the starting stage of a bright future.

References

Asian Development Bank. *Key Indicators of Developing Asian and Pacific Countries*. 2005.

Chantasasawat, Busakorn, K.C. Fung, Hitomi Iizaka, and Alan Siu. "Foreign Direct Investment in China and East Asia". *Stanford Center for International Development (SCID) Working Paper No. 233*, November 2004.

Chen, Tain-Jy and Ying-Hua Ku. "The Effect of Overseas Investment on Domestic Employment". *NBER Working Paper* 11266 (2003).

Chew Soon Beng and Liu Yunhua. "Competition in Trade between China and ASEAN". *Advances in Pacific Basin Business, Economics and Finance* 3 (1998): 141–59.

Dahles, Heidi. "Culture, Capitalism and Political Entrepreneurship: Transnational Ventures of the Singapore-Chinese in China". *Culture and Organization* 11 (2005): 45–58.

Fung, K.C., Hitomi Iizaka, and Alan Siu. "The Giant Sucking Sound: Is China Diverting Foreign Investment from East Asia and Latin America?" <tdctrade. com>. Accessed January–February 2005.

International Monetary Fund. *International Financial Statistics*. Washington, D.C.: International Monetary Fund, 2001.

Lian, Daniel. "Singapore Economy Dominated by State and Foreign Entrepreneurship". *Morgan Stanley Dean Witter Economists*, 5 June 2000.

Liu, Yunhua. "Facing the Challenge of Rising China: Singapore's Responses". *Journal of Policy Modeling* (forthcoming).

Liu Yunhua and Luo Hang. "Impact of Globalization on International Trade between ASEAN-5 and China: Opportunities and Challenges". *Global Economy Journal* 4, Berkeley Electronic Press (2004); <http://www.bepress.com>.

Looney, Robert. "Thaksinomics: A New Asian Paradigm?". Center for Contemporary Conflict, Strategic Insight, <http://www.ccc.nps.navy.mil/rsepResources/si/dec03/eastAsia.asp>.

Ninn Naing Oo. "The Singapore Approach to FTAs in a Multilateral Trading World". A presentation at National University of Singapore on 29 January 2004.

Palanca, Ellen H. "China's WTO Entry: Effects on its Economy and Implications of the Philippines". Philippine Institute for Development Studies, 2004.

Panitchpakdi, Supachai. *Financial Times*, 23 November 2000.

Straits Times, 21 September 2002.

Wong, John and Sarah Chan. "China's Outward Direct Investment: Expanding Worldwide". *China: An International Journal* 1 (September 2003): 273–301.

Yang, Yongzheng. "China's Integration into the World Economy: Implications for Developing Countries". IMF *Working Paper, WP/03/245*, 2003.

Zainal Aznam Yusof. "Malaysia's Response to the China Challenge". *Asian Economic Papers* 2 (2003): 46–73, and 2004 updated version presented at the conference "Rising China and the East Asian Economy", Seoul, Korea, 2004.

PART TWO

Securing International Competitiveness

4

BILATERAL ECONOMIC ARRANGEMENTS IN THE ASIA-PACIFIC
Implications for Competitiveness

Heribert Dieter

INTRODUCTION

The character of regionalism in the Asia-Pacific is changing significantly. Whereas up to the turn of the century most countries in the region concentrated on participating in the multilateral trade regime, there is now a marked shift, with almost all countries in the Asia-Pacific embarking on a new course for their trade policy. Bilateral trade agreements are mushrooming all over the world, but the Asia-Pacific is the region with the most prolific supporters of bilateralism. The superficial explanation for this trend is that in bilateral agreements, countries agree on measures that liberalize trade much faster than would be possible in the multilateral regime, that is, within the regulations of the World Trade Organization (WTO). On closer inspection, this explanation does not hold water. Bilateralism has to be evaluated not only in comparison with the multilateral regime, but also in comparison with unilateral liberalization.

In this chapter, I will analyse the utility of bilateral trade agreements and their effects on the competitiveness of companies. This requires understanding both the benefits as well as the costs of such agreements. Since both dimensions cannot be fully appreciated at an abstract theoretical level, I will examine the fine print of a few trade agreements in the Asia-Pacific. The key question is whether there is a gap between the free trade rhetoric associated with bilateral arrangements and the reality of such agreements.

Of course, the rapid growth of the number of bilateral agreements requires a selection of cases that can be analysed within the limits of this chapter. Therefore, three cases will be analysed in some detail. First, the agreement between Australia and the United States will be analysed. Although the United States has been negotiating a number of free trade agreements (FTAs) in recent years, the economies concerned are mostly relatively small, e.g. with Jordan, Bahrain, Chile, or Singapore. In contrast, Australia is a relatively large, developed economy with twenty million inhabitants and a GDP of over US$600 billion (in 2004). This agreement, an example of a North-North agreement, will have repercussions not only for trade in goods, but also for trade in services.

The chapter next discusses Singapore's trade policy. Singapore has probably been the most active proponent of bilateral trade agreements in the Asia-Pacific. It has not only concluded agreements with Australia, New Zealand, and the United States, but also succeeded in concluding an FTA with Japan, which continued to put priority on the multilateral regime longer than most other countries in the region. Singapore is a particularly interesting case: The country has one of the most liberal trade regimes of all 150 WTO member countries. Since Singapore functions as a trading hub for the entire Southeast Asian region, tariffs and other restrictions on imports have traditionally been low. Consequently, very few economic benefits from the liberalization of its import regime could have been expected. Whilst Singapore clearly has a motive to secure market access to, say, the American market, what rationale drove the United States? In the absence of significant tariffs, there could hardly have been any benefit from the liberalization of bilateral trade in goods. Other factors, in particular, trade in services, apparently played a more important role.

In the third part of the chapter, Thailand's bilateral initiatives are analysed. Thailand is — in a different way — as much a pioneer of bilateral trade agreements as Singapore. It was the first country to conclude a free trade agreement with China, and this agreement has been implemented with astonishing swiftness. Thailand has concluded an agreement with Japan and is currently negotiating an agreement with the United States. These two agreements show that free trade agreements paradoxically can have a very protectionist dimension. They are — more often than not — preferential rather than free trade agreements.

Before examining those three country cases, I will briefly lay out the logic of bilateral trade agreements and some issues that have to be taken into consideration. In the next section, I will discuss the advantages and disadvantages of bilateral trade agreements. Are these agreements positional goods, that is, do they lose their utility if more and more countries implement them? All free trade agreements require rules and certificates of origin. Without a certificate of origin, no product qualifies for duty-free access in a bilateral free trade agreement. But what exactly are the consequences of rules and certificates of origin? What consequences do they have for competitiveness? These general reflections on bilateral free trade agreements will be followed by the three case studies of Australia, Singapore, and Thailand. In conclusion, I will sum up the findings and make recommendations for an improvement of the rules on bilateral agreements under the ambit of the WTO.

THE DEBATABLE LOGIC OF BILATERAL
TRADE AGREEMENTS

In the Asia-Pacific, the financial crisis of 1997 and 1998 continues to be a watershed. Since that crisis, the strategies for shaping external economic relations have changed, both in trade and in finance. Before 1997, the emphasis was on multilateral organizations, that is, on the International Monetary Fund (IMF) and the WTO. Today, two trends are emerging — monetary regionalism in finance and bilateralism in trade (Dieter and Higgott 2003). This chapter analyses the latter trend. In trade, the change is more visible than in finance, where progress to date is somewhat limited (Dieter 2005, pp. 302–17). By contrast, bilateral trade agreements are truly mushrooming in East Asia. For instance, China has already sealed, or is currently negotiating, free trade agreements with twenty-five countries — up from zero two years ago (*Wall Street Journal*, 3 October 2005, p. 1).

Conventional regional integration, that is, free trade areas and customs unions with more than two participating countries, is in decline in the region. Asia-Pacific Economic Cooperation (APEC) in particular is no longer exhibiting the dynamics of the early 1990s. APEC is too large to be effective, and suffers from American dominance. After the crisis of 1997, Asian countries were wary of the excessive influence of the United States in regional institutions such as APEC. Therefore, both bilateral trade agreements and the emerging monetary cooperation scheme in the Asia-Pacific are implemented without U.S. participation. Prominent exceptions are the Australian-American and the Singapore-U.S. free trade agreements, both of which will be discussed later.

The current wave of bilateral and other preferential trade agreements is having severe repercussions for the WTO. In 2005, for the first time ever, more trade will be governed in preferential agreements than under the most-favoured-nation (MFN) clause, the famous Article I of the General Agreement on Tariffs and Trade (GATT).[1] The most-favoured-nation clause has degenerated into the least-favoured-nation clause. Although other countries have been pushing bilateral agreements lately, the European Union was the original culprit. Due to a number of initiatives, some of them overlapping, the European Union has contributed to the undermining of the multilateral trade regime. As a result of the generalized system of preferences, the everything but arms initiative, and free trade agreements, the European Union trades with fewer than a dozen — out of 150 WTO member countries — under the most-favoured-nation clause (World Trade Organization 2004, p. 21).

Today, there are more than 300 free trade agreements and a few customs unions either already implemented or being negotiated. Until a few years ago, the entire Asia-Pacific region was not participating in this trend. For example, Japan and South Korea were committed supporters of the multilateral regime. This, however, has changed dramatically in the last five years. Partly because there is a momentum for bilateral agreements, partly because some countries in the region are using these agreements to fast-forward their economic and political position in the region, almost no country in the region is willing to abstain from being part of the current trend.

The analysis of the systemic consequences of this trend, that is, the consequences for the WTO, is not the main goal of this chapter. However, they must be considered briefly. The previous debate on this issue has been characterized by the stepping-stone or stumbling block argument. Bilateral or minilateral agreements could be either: Whether they contribute to improving the multilateral regime or undermining it, the end result is that bilateral arrangements are in competition with the established regime. Hitherto, there has not been any direct stimulation of the WTO. Bilateral agreements exist parallel to the WTO, and there are features of bilateral agreements that suggest they undermine the multilateral order. For instance, many bilateral deals contain dispute settlement mechanisms outside the WTO. This feature of bilateral agreements should not be necessary, because dispute settlements could continue to be conducted in Geneva. The fact that this is not the case, especially in agreements in which the United States participates, indicates that bilaterals are competing with, rather than complementing, the multilateral regime.

Bilateral Trade Agreements as Positional Goods

One aspect of bilateral trade agreements that has been somewhat overlooked is the possibility that bilaterals are positional goods. Fred Hirsch has suggested that positional goods will lose their utility if others are using the same good. For instance, using a car has a higher utility when very few others are doing the same thing. If everybody drives a car, the utility of having a car declines sharply.

Bilateral trade agreements could also be positional goods. If all other countries rely on market access via the multilateral regime, then a bilateral free trade agreement could be beneficial, provided that market access is unrestricted in the bilateral agreement and is more restricted under WTO regulations. For example, if Australia were the only country that had a free trade agreement with the United States, Australia would have an economic advantage. If all other WTO member countries also negotiate similar free trade agreements with the United States, there would not be any additional benefit for Australia from a bilateral trade agreement, compared with other countries, whilst the disadvantages of bilateral free trade agreements would continue to exist. In other words, the more countries use bilateral agreements, the more limited is their utility. There continue to be advantages for early starters, but as other countries catch up, the usefulness of bilateral agreements declines.[2]

Another factor to consider is the importance of dispute settlement. Prior to the creation of the WTO in 1995, the accused party could veto dispute settlement. Today, the WTO is one of the few multilateral organizations where small countries can take the European Union or the United States to court, and have a fair chance of receiving justice, even if it is only after some time. No party can veto the dispute settlement mechanism of the WTO. The implementation of the dispute settlement mechanism in the WTO has been a milestone for the creation of a rules-based system of international trade.

Transferring dispute settlement to the bilateral level is a step backwards. In many bilateral schemes, there is an option to use either the bilateral dispute settlement or multilateral dispute settlement. The bilateral route clearly offers many opportunities for the more powerful partner to promote its case. Hierarchy and power — always present in international trade — have a more prominent role in bilateral trade agreements than in the multilateral regime. The existence of an alternative to the WTO dispute settlement mechanism provides the more powerful countries with an additional choice, but for weaker countries, this is a complication. Furthermore, it may also be a drawback for producers that are more competitive. With bilateral trade agreements, less efficient producers could be inclined to increase their lobbying efforts since protection can be tailor-made for a specific product. For example, there is ample evidence that the American sugar industry successfully lobbied against the inclusion of sugar in the Australian-American FTA. Lobbyism is not limited to the bilateral arenas, but there are more options to tackle protectionist tendencies in the multilateral regime.

Another weakness of bilateral free trade agreements is the administrative burden that rules of origin cause. Even if there is no significant utility of bilateral free trade agreements, these disadvantages will remain. There are two reasons for the assumption that rules of origin have negative effects on competitiveness. First, their administration costs significant amounts of money. Second, they can have welfare-reducing effects because they can divert trade.

Arduous Rules of Origin

All free trade areas require rules of origin to establish the "nationality" of a product. This is because participating countries in FTAs continue to have diverging external tariffs. One country might have a high tariff on a specific product in order to protect domestic producers, whilst the other might have a low or no tariff on that product. Since only goods produced within the free trade area qualify for duty free trade, there have to be procedures that differentiate between goods produced with the FTA, and goods from the rest of the world. The preferential system becomes complicated. And expensive: on average, the cost of issuing and administering certificates of origin is estimated to be 5 per cent of the value of a product (Dieter 2004).

Since the 1950s, the use of rules of origin has changed significantly. After decolonization, many developing countries used rules of origin as instruments to enhance their economic development. Rules of origin were used to increase the local content of manufactured products and to protect infant industries in those economies against foreign protection. This function of rules of origin is of minor importance in the twenty-first century. Today, developed countries use stringent rules of origin to protect their ageing domestic industries. There is, however, a caveat. Companies can avoid the complexity of rules of origin. By paying the appropriate tariff, they can be easily circumvented. Nevertheless, the protectionist effect of rules of origin should not be underestimated since peak tariffs continue to be implemented by Organization for Economic Cooperation and Development (OECD) countries in a range of sectors.

Establishing Origin

At the outset, it is important to understand that there are two categories of certificates of origin — non-preferential and preferential ones. The former are used to differentiate between foreign and domestic products, for instance, for statistical purposes. The latter can distort trade because it provides preferential access to a market.

There are four methods to establish the "nationality" of a product, to establish origin — natural origin and origin due to substantial transformation, with the latter category being subdivided into three other forms, namely a change in tariff heading, a minimum percentage of value added, and specific production processes (Estevadeordal and Suominen 2003). Natural origin (wholly produced or obtained) is the least complicated approach. This applies to raw materials and agricultural products, that is, to a relatively small part of international trade.

A change in tariff heading is far more complicated. The Harmonized System (HS) is a set of regulations that has been agreed upon in the World Customs Organization (WCO). It consists of 1,241 categories at the four-digit level, and more than 5,000 categories at the six-digit level. If a product receives a different tariff heading after the production process, this can be used to qualify for origin. This method has considerable advantages. It is both transparent and easily established. Using the Harmonized System is simple, easy to implement, and costs relatively little. The necessary documentation is undemanding. The trouble is that a change in tariff heading does not necessarily constitute a significant step in the production process. Minor changes to a product can lead to a change in tariff heading. Therefore, purely requiring a change in tariff heading to establish origin is the exception in FTAs. Furthermore, if a final product consists of a large number of components, documenting origin becomes complicated, and, therefore, costly (Woolcock 1996, p. 200).

The minimum value-added rule is probably the most complex method to establish origin. Incidentally, it is also the most widely used scheme. A certain percentage of the value of the product has to be generated within the FTA to qualify for duty-free trade. For example, in the ASEAN Free Trade Area (AFTA), there is a minimum requirement that 40 per cent of the value (free on board) of a product must have been produced in an ASEAN country. Conversely, it is also possible to set an upper limit for maximum inputs sourced from outside the FTA. In AFTA, complicated rules of origin have resulted in less trade facilitation than expected. Furthermore, there have been bitter disputes between ASEAN countries over the implementation and interpretation of rules of origin, plus problems in day-to-day customs routine.

> In the absence of clear and unambiguous rules, even the best intentions and the skills of an experienced customs officer get frustrated by rules that are inadequate to regulate the intra-industry trade flows of the fastest growing trade region of the world (Inama 2005, p. 571f).[3]

Transnational production processes are another factor to consider. What is the procedure if some inputs for a specific product are sourced from outside the FTA?

The Cumulation of Origin

One of the most important issues for competitiveness is the question of whether the cumulation of origin from different FTAs is possible. In overlapping FTAs, can inputs sourced from various member countries be cumulated to achieve origin? The European Union has been actively promoting free trade areas both with other European as well as non-European countries. This has resulted in complicated rules of origin that potentially harm transnational production processes and could reduce the competitiveness of European manufacturers. In Europe, this awareness has led to the Pan-European Cumulation of Origin. In 1997, PANEURO was established, which permits the cumulation of origin between the free trade areas of the European Union and the European Free Trade Area (EFTA). PANEURO today covers as many as fifty FTAs (Estevadeordal and Suominen 2003, p. 16).

What is the cumulation of origin? Bilateral cumulation is the conventional version. It permits the use of intermediate products coming from the other country in an FTA. Diagonal cumulation permits the use of intermediate products from all countries that are participating without risking origin. Diagonal cumulation can also be called the cumulation of origin between free trade areas. Full cumulation of origin is even more comprehensive, because it allows the use of intermediate products from all countries, but this type of cumulation is rare in customs administration (Estevadeordal and Suominen 2003, p. 5; Priess and Pethke 1997, p. 782). Full cumulation would dilute any preferential arrangement, because whatever the geographical source of an input, it would count as an input from within the free trade area. Outside Europe, hitherto there are only limited efforts to permit diagonal cumulation of origin. To date, there are some early attempts in Southeast Asia. However, the rapid increase of bilateral and plurilateral free trade agreements in the region calls for a Pacific-wide diagonal cumulation of origin in order to facilitate trade.

For companies in Asia, complex rules of origin pose a growing challenge. Transnational production requires the sourcing of inputs from the cheapest producer worldwide. If bilateral FTAs result in the limitation of inputs from the two countries involved, the consequence is potentially a welfare-reducing diversion of trade. Take the FTA between Singapore and the United States. If a manufacturer in Singapore will have to use intermediate products from either Singapore or the United States to achieve origin, but the cheapest provider of inputs comes from, say, Thailand, this would be trade diversion. Rather than using the cheapest supplier worldwide, the cheapest supplier from within the free trade area is used. In other words, trade is diverted, which results in — following conventional trade economics — a welfare reduction. When this argument applies to each and every individual bilateral free trade area, it is obvious that they undermine the competitiveness of producers in a region where free trade agreements are mushrooming. Rather than working towards increasing efficiency, companies get preoccupied with achieving origin — a waste of time and resources.

Finally, specific production processes can be identified and agreed on to establish origin. The trouble is that this method both requires complex negotiations on agreed production processes and continuous updating. Due to the changing patterns of production, new forms of production emerge that would constitute substantial transformation, but unless they are listed in the catalogue of approved production processes, they would not qualify for duty free trade.

Rules of origin and their application have to be taken into consideration when evaluating the usefulness of free trade areas. They make transnational production processes more complicated, if not impossible. The inherent need for documentation of the production process leads to additional bureaucratic procedures. Rules of origin — indispensable parts of free trade agreements — do not contribute to trade facilitation. Rather, they can be used as protectionist devices.[4] In particular, badly designed rules of origin can create barriers to intra-industry trade (Inama 2005, p. 577). Of course, there is considerable variation between free trade agreements with regard to the stringency of their rules of origin. However, even when generous limits for establishing origin are chosen, the complex administration remains. Clearly, companies that are unwilling to meet the requirements of rules of origin can always opt out and simply pay the appropriate tariff, which in turn would reduce the utility of the free trade agreement to zero.

Consequences of Bilateral Agreements:
The Case of Transnational Automotive Production

The consequence of more and more bilateral agreements — resulting in the so-called noodle bowl syndrome — is an increasing fragility of production in East and Southeast Asia. The variation of rules between the various bilateral agreements is causing significant problems for the private sector (Montes and Wagle 2006, p. 46). What has been termed "Factory Asia" might be at risk. Richard Baldwin has identified three factors that contribute to this fragility. First, each nation's industrial development and the competitive position of companies in these countries depend on the smooth functioning of intra-industry trade flows. Second, the tariff cutting that created Factory Asia was done unilaterally by most Asian countries. These tariff cuts were not "bound" in the WTO, and consequently, they are not subject to WTO discipline. This so-called bindings-overhang means that tariffs in Asia could go up overnight without violating WTO rules. Third and most important, there is no political regulation in the region that could substitute WTO discipline. By contrast, European regulation involves two types of top-level management, that is, the European Commission, and WTO discipline, because European countries have bound their tariffs at very low levels (Baldwin 2006, p. 1f).

In Asia, car production continues to be dominated by Japanese producers although South Korean companies are quickly catching up. Outside these two countries, major production facilities are found in China, Malaysia, Taiwan, and Thailand (Dicken 2005, p. 15). Foreign direct investment has played a crucial role in the development of car manufacturing in Asia, particularly in Southeast Asia. Many of these production sites are controlled by Japanese companies (Yoshimatsu 1999, p. 495). Through a network of assembly plants and joint ventures with domestic firms, Japanese cars are assembled in Thailand, Malaysia, the Philippines, Indonesia, Taiwan, and China. The market share of Japanese producers reaches surprising dimensions: In Thailand, their share is over 90 per cent of the market (Dicken 2005, p. 15).

Thailand has become the third largest exporter of automotive products in Asia, after Japan and South Korea. Due to the export orientation of foreign investment inflows, Thailand has become the Southeast Asian export hub for Japanese, American, and European manufacturers. There is an emphasis on production of pick-up trucks, small, basic cars, and components. At the end of the 1990s, Thailand already had more than 700 component producers (Dicken 2005, p. 17). The Asian crisis was a major turning point. After the crisis, the lowered exchange rate of the Thai baht was an incentive to expand exports from Thailand. In contrast to the situation before 1997, when Thailand virtually exported no cars, the country by 2000 exported more than 150,000 cars — more than a third of the total production of 420,000 cars (Shimokawa 2004, p. 149).

The development of transnational production networks in Asia by Japanese manufacturers has not been a purely market-led development. Governments, with their capacity to shape markets, have had a decisive influence. High levels of import protection have encouraged Japanese car manufacturers to produce locally. The markets for automobiles in Asia continue to be individual national markets, some of which are heavily protected against imports (Dicken 2005, p. 15). The relocation of production out of Japan to other Asian countries since the 1980s was a response to changes in international and external conditions, for example, exchange rate fluctuations, as well as trade conflicts, in the 1980s, in particular. Japanese transnational corporations have systematically created production networks through accelerated FDI. These changes have not only improved the competitiveness of Japanese firms, but have also contributed to the *de facto* integration processes in Asia and the regionalization of production (Yun 2005, p. 1).

However, without the changes in trade policy that occurred in the 1990s, in particular the liberalization of intra-ASEAN trade, the integration of production in the region would not have been attractive. For automobile manufacturers, unrestricted access to the entire Southeast Asian regional market is essential for achieving economies of scale and for the development of full production, rather than the assembly of completely knock-down kits (Dicken 2005, p. 17). The development of production networks in the region thus reflects the economic policies of the individual countries. The example of the investments of the Japanese electronic components manufacturer Denso illustrates this. Denso's first operations in Southeast Asia were established in Thailand in 1972, followed by investments in Indonesia in 1975, Malaysia in 1980, the Philippines in 1995, and Vietnam in 2001. Today, Malaysia is Denso's most important production site, followed by Indonesia and Thailand (Dicken 2005, p. 17).

Within Southeast Asia, trade and industry policies towards the automotive industry differ sharply. On the one extreme is Malaysia, which has been trying to build up its own car industry, with the Proton. On the other end of the spectrum is Thailand's approach, which has liberalized the automotive industry and has not tried to develop a "national car". However, even Thailand does not employ a liberal trade policy regarding the automotive industry, but continues to employ rather high tariffs for cars.[5] Furthermore, in the early days of industrialization in Southeast Asia, the Thai government provided significant tariff incentives for local assembly of vehicles (Yoshimatsu 1999, p. 497). The creation of regional production networks in automobiles would not have been possible, therefore, without trade policy measures facilitating this regional division of labour. One example of an early, and successful trade policy measure, was the Brand-to-Brand Complementation (BBC) scheme that was adopted by ASEAN countries in 1988 (Yoshimatsu 1999, p. 506). The scheme allows intraregional tariff preferences and local content accreditation. The aim was to enable production of components utilizing economies of scale.

The BBC has been considered a success. Between 1991 and 1996, production of vehicles in the region more than doubled, although this cannot be attributed to BBC alone (Freyssenet and Lung 2004, p. 48). The scheme, which had been promoted by Mitsubishi, has been utilized by Mitsubishi, Toyota, and Nissan (Shimokawa 2004, p. 143). Japanese automakers have also developed a parts complementation scheme based on the BBC. One example is Toyota, which established a regional complementation scheme soon after the approval of its BBC scheme in November 1989 (Yoshimatsu 1999, p. 506). Despite providing benefits, the BBC scheme suffered from Indonesia's exclusion. The government in Jakarta regarded the scheme not only as providing too few benefits to its own auto industry, but also impeding the development of its own parts industry (Yoshimatsu 1999, p. 507). In effect, the BBC scheme is a sector-specific trade policy instrument that is not very comprehensive. It is limited to intracompany trade, and that in itself limits the further division of labour.

The car industry in Southeast Asia has prospered, but this process is increasingly fragile. On the one hand, the Southeast Asian car industry shows a remarkable degree of transnational division of labour. This process has been facilitated by trade liberalization. Even quite restrictive regimes such as the BBC scheme in ASEAN have contributed to the creation of transnational production networks. Yet the process of regionalization is quite fragile. First, the preferences granted are not always WTO bound, that is, countries can terminate them without violating WTO rules. Second, the supranational structures to safeguard unrestricted trade in the region are weak, and even within ASEAN there appears to be little peer pressure in this regard. Third, the recent push towards bilateral preferential trade agreements is hindering further division of labour in the region. As already noted, these preferential agreements require complicated certificates of origin, and in effect, contribute to parallel regulatory spheres. These, in turn, are an obstacle for further division of labour within a region.

Thus, there is ample scope for institutionalizing the existing transnational division of labour. Two proposals should be considered. First, Southeast and East Asia can develop a regime of Pan Asian cumulation of origin. Like the PANEURO regime, which has existed in Europe since the late 1990s, diagonal cumulation of origin should be permitted between participating free trade agreements. For example, consider a semi-finished product made in Indonesia (ASEAN FTA) that is used in a product manufactured in Singapore. This product is then exported to Japan under the FTA between Singapore and Japan. The input from Indonesia would then be "counted" as having Singaporean origin under the diagonal cumulation of origin. Clearly, Pan Asian cumulation of origin is only a second-best solution, but it would represent an improvement over the current complex and increasingly non-transparent trade regime.

The analysis of bilateral trade agreements reveals that they have a number of structural deficiencies. In practice, they display even more negative elements, such as asymmetry in some of these agreements. The FTA between Australia and the United States is a fine example for such an imbalance.

THE AUSTRALIA-UNITED STATES FREE TRADE AGREEMENT

The Australia-United States Free Trade Agreement (AUSFTA) was signed in February 2004. Rather than benefiting from the good political relationship between the two conservative governments, Australia was at the receiving end of a lopsided deal. The richer country, the United States, obtained preferential access to the Australian market. Several questions have, therefore, to be asked. First, is the agreement as bad as its critics suggest? Second, what might have been the motives of the Australian government in agreeing to this deal? Third, is this new strategy providing Australia with the appropriate trade regime for the twenty-first century? In particular, are bilateral deals enabling Australian companies to intensify their integration into the Asian markets?

The disadvantages for Australia are most visible in agriculture (Table 4.1). Sugar, which can be produced competitively in Australia's tropical regions, is excluded from exports to the United States, apart from a relatively small quota that existed before the FTA. For beef and dairy products, there are surprisingly long transitional periods of up to eighteen years before competitive Australian producers will have unrestricted access to the American market.

Australian trade negotiators were apparently unable to open up the U.S. market for sugar. The Australian Government, which had campaigned for the free trade agreement citing agriculture as a potential benefit for

TABLE 4.1
Some Asymmetries in the Australian-American Free Trade Agreement

Consequences for Australian Producers	Consequences for American Producers
Agriculture: Tariffs, quotas, and seasonal restrictions remain, tariffs continue to exist for wool (ten years), wine (eleven years), dairy products, beef, cotton and cut flowers (eighteen years, conditions for application required) Sugar continues to be excluded from free trade indefinitely	Agriculture: No restrictions for imports from the United States from the day the treaty becomes effective, no seasonal restrictions, sugar imports unrestricted
Manufacturing: In general, no restrictions on exports to the United States, but the same rules of origin apply, which are more difficult to comply with for Australian manufacturers Restrictions on the use of Australian-made ferries in the United States continue: Jones Act of 1920 requires the use of American-made ferries for national shipping (passengers and freight) Cancellation of all "Buy Australian" campaigns Exceptions for small companies (fewer than 200 employees)	Rules of origin more easily complied with due to larger supplier base Public procurement may contain minimum U.S.-content requirement Exceptions for small companies (fewer than 1,500 employees)
Consular Affairs: Australian citizens have no right to be granted a U.S. visa if that is necessary for foreign direct investment	Consular Affairs: American citizens have the automatic right to be granted an Australian visa if that is necessary for foreign direct investment

Source: Weiss, Thurnbon, and Mathews (2004), pp. 7–13.

Australia, subsequently had to provide compensation to domestic sugar producers. They will receive AU$444 million, a rather hefty sum of AU$70,000 for each of the 6,500 sugar producers in Australia (Capling 2004, p. 67; Weiss, Thurnbon, and Mathews 2004, p. 147). Equally problematic is the deal on beef. The United States can stop Australian imports if American farmers are threatened by this competition. For more than thirty years, Australia fought a similar approach adopted by the European Union, only to accept it now in the case of the United States (Capling 2004, p. 82). Both the exclusion of sugar and the arbitrary regulations on beef imports are violations of the principles that successive Australian governments have been publicly supporting for decades.

It has been pointed out that the bilateral free trade agreement is a combination of two different treaties: The first is a trade agreement, characterized by many exceptions. The second is an agreement on investment and intellectual property, in which the Australian side had more or less acceded to American regulations on intellectual property (Weiss, Thurnbon, and Mathews, 2004, p. 116). As mentioned in the introduction to this chapter, one of the most disturbing aspects of bilateral trade agreements is that they contribute to a weakening of the dispute settlement mechanism of the WTO. This applies to the AUSFTA as well. Article 21.4 of the Agreement stipulates the following:

(1) Where a dispute regarding any matter arises under this Agreement and under another trade agreement to which both Parties are party, including the WTO Agreement, the complaining Party may select the forum in which to settle the dispute.

(2) Once the complaining Party has requested a panel under an agreement referred to in paragraph 1, the forum selected shall be used to the exclusion of the others (Australia-United States Free Trade Agreement, Article 21.4).

The consequences are far-reaching. There is the opportunity to use bilateral dispute settlement even for cases that affect the participation of the two countries in the multilateral regime. Although the weaker country has a choice of forum, in practice there will be considerable pressure by the more powerful country to use the bilateral mechanism. If this were not the case, it would be hard to understand why the choice of dispute settlement had been suggested in the first place. Weaker countries do not have an incentive to provide a choice between bilateral and multilateral mechanising because they are the ones that benefit most from a rules-based multilateral dispute settlement mechanism.

With the FTA with the United States, Australia does not enjoy the best of both worlds. The bilateral agreement shows very few benefits for Australian companies, but has damaged the reputation of the country in international groupings. The Cairns Group of agricultural producers, known for pushing for multilateral agricultural trade liberalization, is now very weak, and major players within that organization — Brazil in particular — are today using other fora to promote their cause, for instance, at the G-21, founded during the failed WTO ministerial round in Cancún. Bilateral trade agreements in general, and the deal with the United States, in particular, are not in Australia's national interest.

SINGAPORE'S TRADE POLICY REVISITED

Singapore has been the most active proponent of bilateral free trade agreements in the entire Asia-Pacific region (Table 4.2). The country, a founding member of ASEAN, has been implementing a three-tier trade policy in recent years: bilateral, regional, and multilateral. Singapore's bilateral free trade agreements have been presented as new generation, WTO-plus agreements. The scope of these agreements is more comprehensive than the approach of ASEAN. However, traditional attempts to liberalize trade and investment in Southeast Asia have only shown modest improvements (Inama 2005, p. 561). Therefore, the question is why an approach that has not generated much progress at the plurilateral level, namely at the ASEAN level, is expected to perform so much better bilaterally.

In Singapore, the agreement with the United States probably enjoyed the most prominence in the debate on free trade agreements. The real document, however, was probably not seen by many citizens. It is a 1,200-page document, listing every detail of existing and potential bilateral economic relations (*Wall Street Journal*, 3 October 2005, p. 1). The United States-Singapore Free Trade Agreement (USSFTA) has been in force since January 2004 and is reviewed annually. As in the FTA with Australia, the United States has insisted on some asymmetries. Whilst Singapore has eliminated all import tariffs on American goods once the agreement came into force, the United States has maintained some tariffs which will be eliminated over a period of three to ten years (Thangavelu and Toh 2005, p. 1224). With regard to intellectual property rights, Singapore has had to change its regulations. In particular, copyright has been extended to life of the author plus seventy years. Singapore also had to adopt measures against the circumvention of technologies that protect copyright works and change regulations on pharmaceutical products (Thangavelu and Toh 2005, p. 1226).

One of the more humorous aspect of the FTA with the United States is the regulation on chewing gum. Singapore had banned the sale of chewing gum, trying to keep the city state as clean as possible. However, the United States government insisted on liberalizing trade in chewing gum, and — after intense debate — the two parties agreed on a regulation that satisfies both sides. Article 2.11 of the free trade agreement between Singapore and the United States reads as follows:

TABLE 4.2
Singapore's Bilateral Free Trade Agreements

In force/ratified (date implemented)	*Negotiations (year started)*
New Zealand (January 2001)	Mexico (2000)
Japan (30 November 2002)	Canada (2001)
EFTA (1 January 2003)	Pakistan (2004)
Australia (28 July 2003)	Feasibility studies and/or negotiations with Bahrain, Egypt, Panama, Sri Lanka, Peru, Taiwan, United Arab Emirates, Qatar, Kuwait
United States (January 2004)	
Jordan (16 June 2004 — conclusion of negotiations)	
India (29 June 2005 — deal signed)	
Trans-Pacific (Brunei/New Zealand/Chile) (3 June 2005 — deal signed)	
South Korea (4 August 2005 — deal signed)	

Source: Government of Singapore website on FTAs, <http://app.fta.gov.sg/asp/index.asp>.

> Singapore shall allow the importation of chewing gum with therapeutic value for sale and supply, and may subject such products to laws and regulations relating to health products.[6]

The consequence of this path-breaking regulation is that Singaporeans now have the option to see their dentist and get a prescription for buying chewing gum. However, there are other sovereignty-reducing aspects of the agreement. Perhaps the most disturbing is the regulation on capital controls, something that has nothing to do with a free trade agreement.[7] The text of the agreement contains regulations on capital flows. In principle, there should be no restrictions on capital inflows or outflows.[8]

To understand why that commitment by Singapore may be construed as a sovereignty-reducing measure, one has to consider the arrangements that Singapore imposed before the FTA with the United States. Singapore imposed restrictions on borrowing by foreigners in Singapore dollars. The rationale for that measure was that if a player intends to speculate against the Singapore dollar, he has to create an open position, that is, borrow in Singapore dollars and then transfer that money into U.S. dollars, yen, or euro. Without an open position, speculating against a currency will not generate a profit. The measure that Singapore applied — a ceiling on borrowing by foreign individuals and financial institutions — provided the country with an efficient safety net. The United States insisted on dismantling this policy tool, just like in its FTA with Chile.

Singapore's agreement with Japan is probably as important as the deal with the United States. The Japan-Singapore Economic Partnership Agreement (JSEPA) is hailed as a "new age" partnership agreement. It does not only cover trade in goods and services, but also the promotion of foreign direct investment as well as regulatory reform, facilitation of customs procedures, cooperation in science and technology, media and broadcasting, electronic commerce, movement of natural persons, and human resource developments (Thangavelu and Toh 2005, p. 1211). Nevertheless, once carefully scrutinized, these are distinct agreements that have received a joint label. The core continues to be the agreement on free trade in goods and services. The other agreements are side issues that could also be dealt with in different arenas. For instance, the agreement on the movement of people is a traditional consular affair between two countries, which agree on the reduction of restrictions for the movement of people. This assessment does not imply that JSEPA is not useful, but that it is important to differentiate between the various layers of the agreement.

Singapore's strategy is to seek as many bilateral arrangements as possible in order to become a hub for the region. Singapore does not only want to liberalize its own trading relations, but the expectation is that it can transform its previous status as an entrepot trader. This concept is not too well received by Singapore's ASEAN partners, because there is an inherent hierarchy in Singapore's concept.

> Singapore ... seeks to forge as many bilateral trade arrangements as possible in an effort to maximise gains from freer trade by becoming a 'hub' country regardless of criticisms from other ASEAN member nations for violating its unanimous and collective approach to non-members. Other ASEAN members do not seem to be satisfied with the limited gains from freer trade as a 'spoke' country. They appear not to want to open their markets unilaterally to non-members who are indirectly coming from the hub country (Lee and Park 2005, p. 23f).

This reluctance of Singapore's neighbours is understandable. If they had the intention to liberalize their import regime, they could do so without being aided by the small city state. In particular, important ASEAN countries (Malaysia, Indonesia, Thailand, the Philippines) have been negatively affected by the Asian crisis and are, therefore, reluctant to liberalize trade in services in general, and financial services, in particular (Thangavelu and Toh 2005, p. 1218). Those countries fear that Singapore's FTA strategy will open their economies to foreign competition, and that assumption is dampening further integration in ASEAN.

Besides, not only is the hierarchy between hub and spoke disturbing to Singapore's neighbouring countries, but in reality, the concept of a bridge in international relations, and even more so in economic relations, is fundamentally flawed. In history, there have been many countries thinking foolishly that they could function as a bridge between two other countries. What is the additional benefit for the two countries that are using Singapore as a bridge? Even the technical side of Singapore's hub-and-spoke concept does not work well. Singapore's bilateral FTA with, say, the United States, requires substantial local content in order to qualify for duty free trade. Products that have received most of their value added in other ASEAN countries do not qualify for duty free access to the American market. Where there is no substantial American import duty, there is no need to use the detour via Singapore.

Consequently, Singapore's concept of establishing itself as the free trade hub in the region does not make sense. The country tries to punch way above its weight. In order to be attractive as a hub, an economy ought to have a sizeable internal market, and Singapore does not have that. The United States or the European Union can try to establish themselves as hubs, but that function differs sharply from the entrepot trader role that Singapore had in the past.

THAILAND'S PREFERENTIAL AGREEMENTS: STRENUOUS NEGOTIATIONS WITH THE UNITED STATES

On 1 September 2005, Thailand concluded a free trade agreement with Japan. This deal is another example of the lack of free trade in the bilateral agreements in the Asia-Pacific. Rather than liberalizing comprehensively, even if it is limited to bilateral trade, Japan and Thailand agreed not to hurt each other too badly. Thailand's automobile industry, which developed relatively well in recent years, continues to be protected against Japanese competition. For example, the tariff for cars with more than 3,000 cc engine capacity has been reduced from 80 to 60 per cent, whereas the level of protection for cars with smaller engines, that is, the majority of cars, remains unchanged. Japanese steel producers will not get duty free access to the Thai market before 2015. As to be expected, Japan has wanted to protect its agricultural sector. Rice, beef, wheat, dairy products, and fish are excluded from the free trade agreement.

Bilateral free trade agreements with such characteristics do not have much to do with the concept of free trade. Rather than increasing competition exactly in those areas where the producers in one country are less competitive than in the other, these sectors are excluded. Consequently, the largest gains potentially of the free trade agreement are left out. Furthermore, such agreements are a violation of Article XXIV of the GATT, which permits free trade areas and customs unions only if they cover "substantially all trade". Agreements that exclude agriculture, cars, and steel violate this regulation. Pointing to very low levels of trade in these sectors prior to the creation of the FTA does not help because the dynamic effects of trade liberalization ought to be considered.

Thailand and the United States have been negotiating a free trade agreement since 2004. Again, these negotiations demonstrate that free trade is not the main objective in many bilateral agreements. There are two main sectoral sensibilities, and both parties anxiously defend their respective industries. The negotiations have exposed both the weakness of traditional industries in the United States and the strength of American services industries. The two disputed sectors are motor vehicles and financial services (*Wall Street Journal*, 3 October 2005, p. 1).

Thailand is today the world's second largest producer of light commercial vehicles, also called light trucks. Japanese and Korean manufacturers have been using Thailand's strong competitive position in manufacturing to export light trucks from Thailand to the rapidly expanding Asian markets as well as to OECD countries, for example, Australia. However, there are virtually no exports of light trucks to the United States. The reason for that is the high tariff of 25 per cent that the United States is applying on light trucks since the German-American chicken war of 1962–63. Although this rather bizarre trade conflict between then West Germany and the United States is virtually forgotten today, it resulted in an increase in the tariff for imported light trucks from 8.5 per cent to 25 per cent.

The important point is that this tariff continues to be applied despite various initiatives to reduce it or abandon it all together. For the American car industry, this high tariff provided (temporary) shelter against foreign competition. In recent years, half of the cars sold in the United States have been light trucks, and for several years, the two best-selling vehicles have been pickup trucks. Without foreign competition, American car producers were able to secure profits in this segment of the market.[9] Whereas General Motors, Ford, and Chrysler have had difficulties in competing with European, Japanese, and other producers in passenger vehicles, there was an oligopoly in light trucks. Today, with oil prices reaching all-time highs, the demand for these gas-guzzling trucks is comparatively low, and American producers are not able to satisfy the demand for small, stylish, and efficient cars.

Unsurprisingly, the Thai government is asking for free trade in light trucks, but the American government is well aware that General Motors and Ford might become insolvent if competition dramatically increased. The chief economist of General Motors, Mustafa Mohatarem, has claimed that Thailand would become an "aircraft carrier" for foreign producers if free trade were permitted between the two countries (*Financial Times*, 18 February 2005. p. 2). Consequently, there is very limited willingness of the U.S. Trade Representative to yield concessions in this sector. At the same time, the Thai government is trying to protect its financial sector. The country suffered a severe blow when the financial crisis hit Thailand and other countries in the region in 1997. Since then the government has tried to strengthen the domestic financial sector. The American side is asking for a complete opening of the Thai market for financial services, which is understandable considering the good competitive position of the American financial sectors.

The bottom line is simple: The American government fears Thai competition in trucks, and the Thai government fears American competition in financial services. If either of the two sides wished to increase competition in those sectors, they could do that unilaterally. Since both sides are apparently unwilling to make concessions, there will either be no agreement, or the deal will be incomprehensive. More precisely, an agreement excluding both light trucks and services is a violation of both the letter and the spirit of the GATT, General Agreement on Trade in Services (GATS), and the WTO.

WHAT ARE THE CONSEQUENCES OF BILATERAL TRADE AGREEMENTS FOR COMPETITIVENESS?

The trend in bilateral trade agreements in the Asia-Pacific is difficult to comprehend. These preferential agreements are often not liberalizing trade comprehensively, they cause great administrative burdens to producers, and they undermine the multilateral regime. Nevertheless, many countries are moving in that direction. What are their motivations?

The cases examined in this chapter offer a range of explanations. In Australia's case, a major motive was probably the desire to forge close links with the United States and use this allegedly close relationship in the 2004 election campaign. Singapore's government — striving for modernity as ever — attempted to give the country the advantage of being the first economy that established bilateral agreements. Systemic consequences were ignored. Thailand is joining the bilateral wave, but it has not conceded many preferences in its existing bilateral agreement with Japan and is unlikely to allow extensive competition in the agreement currently being negotiated with the United States.

There is, however, one case in which bilateralism could be a wise strategy. If the old multilateral trading regime is going to collapse — an unlikely event at this stage but not entirely impossible — then bilateral trade agreements would be a safeguard measure to avoid the breakdown of international trade. The irony is that bilateralism — despite many declarations that it is supposed to strengthen the WTO — actively contributes to the downfall of the multilateral order.

In the medium term, there are three potential developments in global trade relations, although it is unclear which of these will prevail:

• All relevant players continue to engage in bilateral trade agreements. Additionally, at an unidentifiable stage, one of the larger countries leaves the WTO or ignores vital commitments, for instance, it does not accept a ruling in the dispute settlement mechanism.

- The WTO and its member countries manage to clarify the rules on FTAs and turn them into true stepping stones for the multilateral regime. A potential remedy would be to limit the use of free trade agreements to the non-OECD world.
- Asian countries, the European Union and the United States return to multilateralism and abandon bilateral trade agreements.

Ultimately, bilateral trade agreements can negatively affect the competitiveness of companies in a region. Companies have to spend resources on documenting origin, and in the absence of diagonal cumulation of origin in the entire Asia-Pacific region, the bilateral trend is potentially welfare reducing. The administrative burden of certificates of origin results in an increase in costs to producers. Overall, too much emphasis on these preferential agreements deters manufacturers from remaining competitive in world markets.

Notes

1. Although the GATT Secretariat does no longer exist and has been replaced by the WTO, the GATT treaty — in its 1994 version — continues to be the legal basis for the multilateral trading regime. The General Agreement on Trade in Services (GATS) regulates services, including financial services.
2. Assuming a scenario in which all WTO member countries would have implemented a free trade agreement with the United States, the utility of such an agreement — compared with the multilateral alternative — would not be large. Only if the United States would have a protectionist trade regime under WTO regulations and a significantly more open bilateral regime, would there be some continuing advantage.
3. Similar regulations will be used in the ASEAN-China free trade agreement (Tongzon 2005, p. 193).
4. See Dieter (2004) for a detailed discussion.
5. For example, tariffs on cars with more than 3,000 cc continue to be as high as eighty per cent, with only marginally lower rates under the Thai-Japanese Free Trade Agreement (Dieter 2006, p. 29).
6. See the text of the treaty at <http://www.ustr.gov/assets/Trade_Agreements/ Bilateral/ Singapore_FTA/Final_Texts/asset_upload_file708_4036.pdf>, p. 10.
7. It is true that restrictions on current account may cause difficulties for international trade, but the same does not apply to restrictions on capital account. The need to have few restrictions on trade-related importation and exportation of capital is probably a useful measure. To reduce restrictions on capital flows is not necessary for unrestricted international trade. Just look at the

Chinese example: The country is the world's third largest trader, yet implements rather comprehensive restrictions on capital account.

8. See the text of the treaty, pp. 158ff.
9. For a detailed discussion, see Dieter (2005), pp. 174–82.

References

Baldwin, Richard. *Managing the Noodle Bowl:* "The Fragility of East Asian Regionalism". Centre for Economic Policy Research Working Paper No. 5561, March 2006 <http://www.cepr.org/pubs/dps/DP5561.asp>.

Capling, Ann. *All the Way with the USA. Australia, the US and Free Trade.* Sydney: University of New South Wales Press, 2005.

Dacquila, Teofilo C. and Le Huu Huy. "Singapore and ASEAN in the Global Economy. The Case of Free Trade Agreements". *Asian Survey* 43, no. 6 (2003): 908–28.

Dicken, Peter. *Tangled Webs: Transnational Production Networks and Regional Integration*, SPACES (Spatial Aspects Concerning Economic Structures). Marburg: Faculty of Geography, Philipps-University of Marburg, April 2005. <http://www.geographie.uni-marburg.de/spaces/SPACES%202005-04%20Dicken.pdf>. Accessed 20 June 2006.

Dieter, Heribert. *Abschied vom Multilateralismus? Der neue Regionalismus in der Handels- und Finanzpolitik.* Berlin: Stiftung Wissenschaft und Politik (February 2003): 4/03.

———. "Präferenzielle Ursprungsregeln in Freihandelszonen: Hemmnisse für den internationalen Handel?" *Aussenwirtschaft. Schweizerische Zeitschrift für internationale Wirtschaftsbeziehungen.* 59. Jg., Heft III (September 2004): 273–303.

———. *Die Zukunft der Globalisierung. Zwischen Krise und Neugestaltung.* Baden-Baden: Nomos-Verlagsgesellschaft, 2005.

Dieter, Heribert and Richard Higgott. "Exploring Alternative Theories of Economic Regionalism: From Trade to Finance in Asian Co-operation?". *Review of International Political Economy* 10, no. 3 (2003): 430–55.

Estevadeordal, Antoni and Kati Suominen. "Rules of Origin: A World Map and Trade Effects". Paper prepared for the workshop on The Origin of Goods: A Conceptual and Empirical Assessment of Origin in PTAs, Paris, 23–24 May 2003. <www.inra.fr/Internet/Departements/ESR/UR/lea/actualites/ROO2003/articles/estevadeordal.pdf> (accessed 17 November 2003).

Freyssenet, Michel and Yannick Lung. "Multinational Carmakers' Regional Strategies". In *Cars, Carriers of Regionalism?* edited by Jorge Carillo, Yannick Lung and Rob van Tulder, pp. 23–41. Houndmills, Basingstoke and New York: Palgrave Macmillan, 2004.

Inama, Stefan. "The Association of Southeast Asian Nations — People's Republic of China Free Trade Area: Negotiating Beyond Eternity With Little

Trade Liberalization?". *Journal of World Trade* 39, no. 3 (June 2005): 559–79.

Lee, Jong-Wha and Innwon Park. "Free Trade Areas in East Asia: Discriminatory or Non-discriminatory?". *World Economy* 28, no. 1 (January 2005): 21–48.

Meade, James E. *The Theory of Customs Unions*. Amsterdam: North-Holland, 1955.

Montes, Manuel F. and Swarnim Wagle. "Why Asia Needs to Trade Smarter". *Far Eastern Economic Review*, June 2006, pp. 45–48.

Priess, Hans-Joachim and Ralph Pethke. "The Pan-European Rules of Origin: The Beginning of a New Era in European Free Trade". *Common Market Law Review* 34, no. 4 (1997): 773–809.

Shimokawa, Koichi. "ASEAN: Developing a Division of Labour in a Developing Region". In *Cars, Carriers of Regionalism?*, edited by Jorge Carillo, Yannick Lung and Rob van Tulder, pp. 139–56. Houndmills, Basingstoke and New York: Palgrave Macmillan, 2004.

Thangavelu, S.M. and Toh Muh-Heng. "Bilateral 'WTO-Plus' Free Trade Agreements: The WTO Trade Policy Review of Singapore 2004". *World Economy* 28, no. 9 (September 2005): 1211–28.

Tongzon, Jose I. "ASEAN-China Free Trade Area: A Bane or Boon for ASEAN Countries?". *World Economy* 28, no. 2 (February 2005): 191–210.

Viner, Jakob. *The Customs Union Issue*. London: Stevens & Sons, 1950.

Weiss, Linda, Elisabeth Thurnbon, and John Mathews. *How to Kill a Country: Australia's Devastating Trade Deal with the United States*. Sydney: Allen & Unwin, 2004.

Woolcock, Stephen. "Rules of Origin". In *Regionalism and its Place in the Multilateral Trading System*, pp. 195–212. Paris: OECD, 1996.

World Trade Organization. *The Future of the WTO: Addressing Institutional Challenges in the New Millennium*. Geneva: WTO, 2004.

Yoshimatsu, Hidetaka. "The State, MNCs, and the Car Industry in ASEAN". *Journal of Contemporary Asia* 29, no. 4 (1999): 495–515.

Yun, Chunji. "Japanese Multinational Corporations in East Asia: Status Quo or Sign of Changes?". *Berichte aus dem Weltwirtschaftlichen Colloquium der Universität Bremen*, edited by Andreas Knorr et al. No. 95 (February 2005): 1–57. <http://www.iwim.uni-bremen.de/publikationen/pdf/b095.pdf>. Accessed 20 June 2006.

5

TECHNOLOGICAL INTENSITIES AND NETWORK STRENGTH
Electronics Firms in East Asia and Southeast Asia Compared

Rajah Rasiah

INTRODUCTION[1]

There is now recognition that firms' conduct and performance depend considerably on critical embedding institutions, connectivity, and coordination — what evolutionary economists refer to as the institutional and systemic features of the national innovation system (NIS). The theoretical basis to its role in stimulating innovation and competitiveness has its roots in Hamilton (1791) and List (1885), but efforts to examine it as a system of learning and innovation was articulated lucidly by Nelson and Winter (1982), Freeman (1989), and Lundvall (1988). Reinert (1994) traces its role, albeit from the lenses of industrial policy instruments, to 1485 Britain. The significance of taxonomies and trajectories in understanding firms' participation in innovation was emphasized by Dosi (1982) and Pavitt (1984).

While extensive work on issues related to network strength (NS) exists, little work has been done to compare its effect on firm-level technological capabilities across economies, including on foreign and local firms. Past work on multinationals have tended to address their superiority over national firms owing to efforts to internalize their superior tangible and intangibale assets

(Hymer 1960; Dunning 1974). Little work exists on the impact of NIS on the capabilities and conduct of foreign firms compared with local firms. It is, of course, extremely difficult to address this issue given the openness and vagueness of the concept and the strength and relationships involving institutions. The NS embedding firms in Korea and Taiwan are generally superior to those in Malaysia, Thailand, the Philippines, and Indonesia. All these economies were underdeveloped by most measures in the 1960s. Korea and Taiwan embarked on a process of building their science and technology infrastructure from the late 1960s and 1970s, managing to raise their levels of R&D personnel systematically in the population, and R&D investment in Gross National Investment (GNI) respectively by the 1990s.

Malaysia and Thailand made strong efforts from the late 1980s, but their R&D personnel and R&D investment endowments have remained significantly lower than developed economies' levels even in 2000. The Philippines fairly strong human capital endowments placed it in the same category as Malaysia and Thailand. Although the overall national basic infrastructure institutions in Malaysia and Thailand are superior to the ones in the Philippines and Indonesia, the location of several of the electronics firms examined in export-processing zones, where most of these services are concentrated, is likely to reduce these differences. Nevertheless, differences in network strength (NS) — a variable that captures the institutional and systemic effects — across the six economies offer the opportunity to test its influence on firm-level technological capabilities. The exercise also allows the partial testing of the hypothesis that firms rely on home-site more than host-site NS to drive their R&D activities (Lall 1992).

Because of the relentless movement of Korea and Taiwan in the value added chain, this chapter attempts to locate technological intensities of electronics firms in Malaysia, Indonesia, the Philippines, and Thailand against these economies. Since foreign ownership has been important in the electronics industries of the Southeast Asian economies examined, the chapter also addresses the question of ownership. Drawing from a survey sample of 223 electronics firms, the chapter seeks to examine first, differences in technological intensities between foreign and local firms facing different levels of NS; second, the relationship of NS on firm-level technological intensities; and third, whether foreign firms enjoy a lower propensity of technological intensities with host-site NS than local firms. The electronics industry is a key export-oriented industry in all six economies, and its exposure to intense competition, shortening product cycles, and continued miniaturization requiring strong technological support either from home or host sites, make it a unique laboratory for analysis.

Following this introduction, the next section documents the state of basic and high-tech support in the six economies. The discussion next presents the methodology and data, with the chapter turning next to an examination of the statistical differences involving technological indicators between foreign and local firms, and the statistical relationships involving these variables. The NS is introduced in the regression models in place of country dummies to examine the effects of the embedding institutional and systemic influences.

LITERATURE REVIEW

The theory of foreign direct investment posits that multinationals enjoy asset-specific (tangible and intangible) technological advantages over local firms (Hymer 1972; Dunning 1974). Access to superior resources in parent plants abroad is considered to explain this advantage. The relocation of such an activity to developing economies allows multinationals to internalize such resources. However, existing work on ownership and technological levels has hardly broached effectively the question of why technological intensity levels between foreign and local firms differ across industries and countries. This chapter seeks to address this question by examining firms in an economy endowed with fairly strong effective demand and high-tech infrastructure.

Neoclassical Models

Neoclassical models originate from the assumption that markets coordinate demand-supply functions effectively so that natural economy-wide equilibrium is achieved through optimal allocation of resources. Before the works of Romer (1986), Lucas (1988), Krugman (1986), Helpman and Krugman (1987), and Grossman and Helpman (1990), neoclassical analysis was anchored on Solow's (1956, 1957) production function accounting framework that reduced technology to an exogenous black box. Despite the introduction of elegantly constructed models demonstrating that in the presence of increasing returns, markets no longer generate Pareto optimal solutions, these new growth models did not enter neoclassical policy analysis owing to the belief that government failure was far more serious than market failure. Hence, the World Bank (1993), while conceding that government intervention was extensive in Korea and Taiwan, argued that it was neither necessary nor possible to pursue such policies to engender rapid economic growth.

The relative price theory as the basis of resource allocation and the choice of technology can be seen in the dynamics of foreign direct investment

(FDI) from the use of the production function and the technology gap. Caves (1974) had initiated these models to examine spillover effects by adapting the growth accounting model originally advanced by Solow (1956). Empirical works using refinements of this model produced mixed results (for example, Blomstrom 1986; Blomstrom and Sjoholm 1999; Aitken, Hansen and Haddad 1997; Aitken and Harrison 1999; Sjoholm 1999). However, Romer (1987*a*, 1987*b*, 1990, 1991, 1994), Nelson (1994), and Vaitsos (2003) provided a devastating critique of neoclassical growth models explaining technical change. These criticisms question the very foundation of production function approaches to understanding productivity growth and technical change. Likewise, Lall (1992) and Rasiah (1995) have argued that spillovers, being external to firms, cannot be measured exhaustively. Besides, spillover has both pecuniary and non-pecuniary, and positive and negative, dimensions so that its empirical investigation cannot be carried out exhaustively (Rasiah 1995, Chapter 2).

There has, however, been one largely consistent finding by neoclassical analysts, namely that the technological gap is inversely correlated with spillovers from foreign to local firms. The rationale is that the lower the technological gap, the easier is the diffusion from foreign to local firms. Just as the very fundamentals of the production function model have been argued to be shaky, the logic, and hence the evidence, adduced to defend the technology gap argument, is also fraught with problems. Firstly, the typical measure of technological gap — the difference in the values of machinery and equipment of foreign and local firms — does not really capture technological differences effectively, and also, given the wide dispersion in technology within ISIS 5 digit industries reduces it to a spurious proxy.[2] Hirschman (1958, 1970) had argued convincingly that the wider the gap, the greater the potential for learning, and that it is in the interest of local institutions and firms to learn to substitute imports with domestic production. Indeed, Hirschman emphasized the focus on backward rather than forward linkages, as export markets would raise the scale for expanding supplier links. *Ceteris paribus*, while it is easier to learn something one almost knows than to grasp something far more sophisticated, such a sequencing of learning does not take into account the dynamics of the "S" curve, where the rate of absorption rises sharply once a certain critical mass of knowledge is attained until the technology frontier is reached as indicated when the rate of absorption is considered to slow down again owing to the difficulty associated with producing new knowledge. Besides, it is the potential rather than the actual that sets the limits on learning, and hence planning and effort can be targeted to raise the rate of diffusion closer to the potential. Such a dynamic argument clearly undermines the very need to examine if diffusion will be higher when technological gaps are higher or lower between foreign and local firms.

An Alternative Framework: The Evolutionary Approach

In light of problems associated with the above approaches, this chapter borrows extensively from technological capability literature and case studies to construct an alternative framework to examine the differences and determinants of labour productivity, wages, and export, skills, and technological intensities between foreign and local firms in South Africa. The chapter employs indices measured using related proxies to compare and examine technological capabilities — human resource, process technology, and R&D (see also Rasiah 2004*a*, 2004*b*). The use of capability indices in examining the capacity of firms to compete can be traced to Lall (1992), Bell and Pavitt (1995), Westphal et al. (1990), Wignaraja (2002) and Figueiredo (2002). Wignaraja (2002) adapted the Ernst, Mytelka, and Ganiatsos (1998) taxonomy of capabilities to fit the narrow range of data available to examine upgrading in Mauritius' firms. Rasiah (1994, 1995) had identified a number of firm-level technological capabilities to examine their role in knowledge diffusion from foreign to local firms.

Like all industrial organization measures of concentration where estimations of market power only refer to its potential, technological intensities also only refer to potential, that is, the extent of learning-diffusion that can occur in a locality. Although the capacity to absorb new knowledge is easier when the gap between the leader and learner is small, there is neither a rigorous argument nor empirical evidence that convincingly substantiates this point. As Hirschman (1958, 1970) has argued, the bigger the gap, the larger will be the potential for learning and catch-up. Marx (1853) had established the basis for rapid technological transformation when he argued about the positive role of colonialism, pointing to how pre-capitalist modes of production give way to capitalist production. Despite the destruction and dislocation that accompany capitalist integration, the phase did quicken technical change in India (Kumar and Desai 1983). Unlike under colonialism when the objectives of the regime in power targeted policies primarily for accumulation within the borders of the colonial grandmaster, post-colonial governments have enjoyed relative autonomy to engender technical change to generate domestic accumulation (Warren 1973, 1980).

Hence, this chapter seeks to use an alternative methodology where the focus is directly on embodied technology. By using technological intensities, the assessment can be focused simply on the potential spillovers that can arise at host-sites.[3] Although higher technological intensities need not translate into commensurate levels of absorption by local economic agents — including firms — it is a more reliable indicator to examine than spillovers when the data collected come only from individual firms. A better method of examining spillovers would be to study the firms as a network of interconnected economic agents (for example, Rasiah 1994, 1995). However, this methodology is too expensive and requires enormous sacrifice by researchers to construct a national database.

To examine differences in technological intensities between foreign and local firms, it is also important to establish the institutional base within which these firms are operating. As Dosi (1982) and Pavitt (1984) have argued, taxonomies and trajectories are important when examining technological capabilities and demands in firms. Foreign firms with access to sophisticated technology from their plants at developed parent sites will tend to show higher overall technological intensities than local firms facing underdeveloped support domestically (Rasiah 2004).

However, the pattern of differences would vary between human resource (HR) practices, process technology, and R&D. Foreign firms are likely to show higher intensity levels than local firms in the easy-to-move internalized practices associated with HR, and machinery and equipment, and process technology associated with it. Industry differences matter here as most garment firms are likely to enjoy similar labour-intensive technologies owing to the abundant supply of labour in South Africa. Owing to South Africa's fairly developed high-tech infrastructure, the conduct of firms in undertaking R&D essentially at parent sites (Vernon 1983; OECD 1998, cited in Amsden, Tschang and Goto 2001),[4] and the risks associated with intellectual property rights, we can expect R&D intensities in local firms to be higher than in foreign firms. However, foreign pharmaceutical firms use South Africa as an important base for undertaking R&D and hence are expected to show higher R&D intensities than local firms. Overall, however, foreign firms enjoy higher product technologies as they have access to the know-how and brand name from their plants abroad.

THE EMBEDDING ENVIRONMENT AND FOREIGN DIRECT INVESTMENT

This section presents a brief account of the state of infrastructure and foreign ownership in Korea, Taiwan, Malaysia, Thailand, the Philippines, and Indonesia. Because the degree of connectivity and coordination involving embedding institutions is examined from firms (see next section), this section is confined to a discussion of basic and high-tech infrastructure.

The state of the basic infrastructure (BI) among the six economies generally followed their ranking against per capita incomes. BI was estimated using three proxies (see note for Table 5.1). Taiwan and Korea enjoyed a high BI score of 0.61 and 0.54 respectively, followed by 0.42 and 0.30 for Malaysia and Thailand respectively, and 0.12 and 0.10 for Philippines and Indonesia respectively in 2000 (Table 5.1). The Netherlands and Sweden had the highest scores of 0.84 and 0.82 respectively, while Niger and Cameroon were ranked the lowest among the ninety-six countries ranked in 2000, with both having a figure of 0.01.

High-tech infrastructure (HTI) was also strongest in Taiwan and Korea. R&D investment in Gross National Investment (GNI) in Taiwan and Korea were 2.7 per cent and 2.02 per cent respectively in 2000 (World Bank 2003; Lin 2003, p. 74). R&D scientists and engineers per million population in Korea reached 2,140 persons in 2000 (World Bank 2003), while R&D researchers reached 3,930 per million people in Taiwan in 2000 (Lin 2003, p. 74). HTI was measured using two proxies (see note for Table 5.1). The HTI figures for Taiwan and Korea were 0.490 and 0.446 respectively in 2000 (Table 5.1). The commensurate figures for Malaysia, Thailand, and the Philippines were 0.029, 0.019, and 0.023 respectively in 2000. Not only is the gap involving HTI between Taiwan and Korea, and the other economies much wider than the BI figures, the Philippines enjoyed a higher HTI score than Thailand. Malaysia, Thailand, the Philippines, and Indonesia enjoyed R&D expenditure in Gross Domestic Investment of 0.45 per cent, 0.11 per cent, 0.21 per cent, and 0.07 per cent respectively in 2000. R&D scientists and engineers per million people in Malaysia, Thailand, and the Philippines were 155, 101, and 156 respectively in 2000. Data for Indonesia were not available. Data on R&D investment were not available to compute the figure for Indonesia. Japan had the highest HTI score of 0.999, while Burkina Faso had the lowest score of 0.001 out of the fifty-five countries on which data were available in 2000.

Unlike in Korea and Taiwan where local firms figured prominently following deliberate national policies from the late 1960s and 1970, export-oriented foreign firms were targeted aggressively for generating investment, employment, and exports since 1971 in Malaysia, 1986 in Thailand, 1990 in Indonesia, and initially in 1971 but especially since 1995, in the Philippines. Foreign ownership has traditionally been high in Malaysia, although net FDI in gross capital formation (GCF) fell in the period 1994–99 whereas it became important in Thailand following the financial crisis. There was also

TABLE 5.1
Basic and High-Tech Infrastructure Index, 2000

	BI	*HTI*
Korea	0.544	0.446
Taiwan	0.613	0.490
Malaysia	0.416	0.029
Thailand	0.296	0.019
Philippines	0.117	0.021
Indonesia	0.109	0.012

Note: BI is calculated using the proxies of adult literacy rate (education), doctors per thousand people (health), and main telephone lines per thousand people (communication) using the normalization formula in model (4) below and the ninety-six countries where data were available from World Bank (2003). The same approach was used to calculate HTI using the proxies of R&D scientists and engineers per million people, and R&D investment in Gross Domestic Investment and fifty-five countries where the data were available from World Bank (2003) and national ministries. Both the BI and HTI scores were eventually divided by the highest score in the respective categories so that the leading country achieved a score of one, while that of the remaining countries fell in the range $0 \leq X \leq 1$.

Source: Computed from World Bank (2003); Taiwan (2004); Malaysia (2004); Thailand (2004).

a significant rise in net FDI in gross capital formation (GCF) in Korea and Taiwan primarily from mergers and acquisitions after 1998 (see Figure 5.1). Net FDI levels fell in Malaysia from 1993 until 2000 while the figures have been in the negative in Indonesia following the financial crisis and subsequent political fallout in 1997–98.

Despite an ostensible decline in FDI in Malaysia and Indonesia, foreign ownership remained significant in the electronics industry, as can be seen from the sample compiled. In fact, FDI ownership accounted for 83.1 per cent of fixed assets ownership in the electrical and electronics industry in Malaysia in 1999 (Malaysia 2000). The rise in net FDI levels after 1998 in Thailand was mainly the result of falling asset values and costs arising from a severe depreciation in the baht. In addition, despite higher levels of local participation compared with Malaysia, the largest electronics firms in Thailand in the 1990s until 2000 were foreign owned — for example, Seagate and Advanced Micro Devices. Despite falling FDI levels in GCF, labour-intensive

FIGURE 5.1
FDI in Gross Capital Formation, 1976–2000

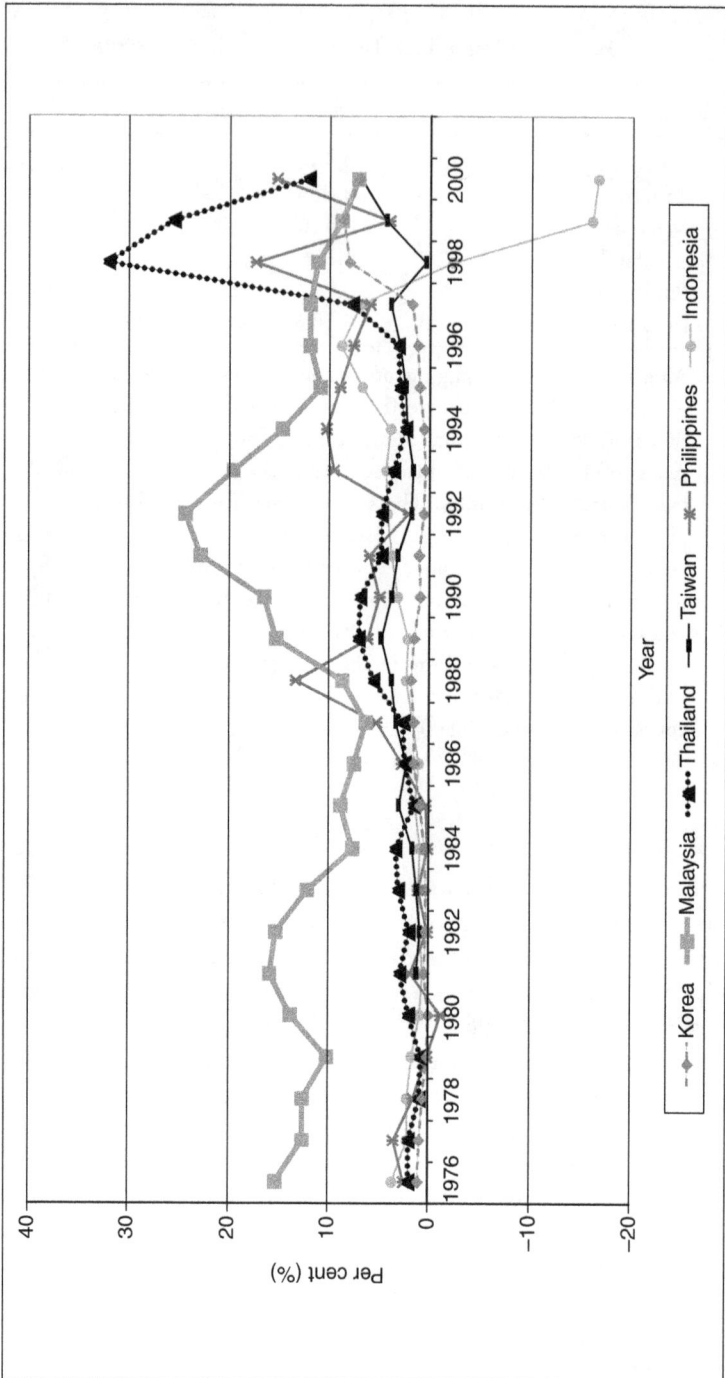

Source: World Bank (2002); Taiwan (2004).

consumer electronics firms such as Sony have significant assembly operations in Indonesia. Semiconductor and other foreign electronics component firms have expanded strongly in the Philippines especially in the late 1990s.

Overall, Korea and Taiwan show significantly stronger basic and high-tech institutions than the other four economies. Malaysia and Thailand enjoyed stronger basic institutions than the Philippines and Indonesia. The gap in the basic infrastructure scores between these economies was smaller. However, the gap involving the high-tech infrastructure was wider as Taiwan and Korea enjoyed far higher scores than the other economies. In addition, the Philippines enjoyed a high-tech infrastructure score only slightly lower than Malaysia, but higher than Thailand.

The rest of this chapter examines the impact of these instruments on the technological intensities of electronics firms. Despite lower FDI levels in Taiwan, Korea, and Indonesia, data on sufficient numbers of foreign firms were collected for examining the impact of network strength on the technological intensity variables in these countries.

METHODOLOGY AND DATA

This section introduces the methodology that will be used to examine the statistical differences and relationships involving NS and technological intensities. The chapter employs indices measured using related proxies to compare and examine technological capabilities.

The use of technological capability indices in examining the capacity of firms to compete can be traced to Lall (1992), Bell and Pavitt (1995), Westphal et al. (1990), Wignaraja (2002), Figueiredo (2002, 2003), and Ariffin and Figueiredo (2003). Wignaraja (2002) adapted the Ernst, Ganiatsos, and Mytelka (1998) taxonomy of capabilities to fit the narrow range of data available to examine upgrading in Mauritius' firms. Rasiah (1994) had identified a number of firm-level technological capabilities to examine their role in knowledge diffusion from foreign to local firms. Lall (1992), Bell and Pavitt (1995), and Ernst, Ganiatsos, and Mytelka presented a detailed conceptual and methodological framework to examine sources of learning and innovation, sequencing these processes and their role in capability building. Figueiredo (2002, 2003) refined this methodology and found these instruments extremely useful in defining learning activities in the steel industry in Brazil.

While the technological capability framework has become popular lately, it has yet to be applied seriously to compare foreign and local firms. The exceptions include Ariffin and Figueiredo (2003), who made simple comparisons of capabilities in Malaysia and Manaus, Brazil. Ariffin and Figueiredo used simple two-way correlations to show that there was no obvious differences in technological levels between foreign and local consumer electronics firms in Manaus, but that foreign firms enjoyed higher technological levels than local firms in the electronics firms in Malaysia.

The methodology developed here extracts elements from all the above, but adapts them further to obtain a simpler set of variables with common specifications for statistical analysis. As a result, it lacks some of the rich explorations undertaken by the above studies. In addition, because cross-firm quantitative approximation is essential for running regressions, only proxies referring to the same variable are normalized here. In addition, institutional and systemic variables were included in the chapter to facilitate cross-country effects of NS. No attempt is made to trace causation owing to the lack of panel data, and the simultaneity of relationships between institutional and systemic, and firm-level variables over the long run, as well as the cross-sectional data used. Smith (1776) and Young (1928) had argued that the dictum, "the division of labour is determined by the size of the market" works both ways (see also Best 1990, 2001). In addition, there are also dynamic influences such as increasing returns, structural interdependence, and complementarity (see Abramovitz 1956; Kaldor 1957).

Methodologically, this chapter seeks to use similar, but two-tail t-tests, to examine if statistical differences existed between foreign and local firms in all six countries, and to go beyond to examine the statistical relationships between technological intensity, and the explanatory variables of export incidence, network strength (NS), their elasticity differences by ownership, while controlling for size, age, management type, and union incidence. In addition to the usual comparison of technological capabilities between foreign and local firms, the results are expected to offer implications on whether the institutional and systemic strength of embedding firms influence technological intensities, and whether differences exist between foreign and local firms.

Specification of Variables

The variables used in the chapter are specified in this subsection, which along with the components, sources of data and, where relevant, their relationships with NS, are shown in Table 5.2. The firm-level variables defined refer to related effort or conduct demonstrated within each of the selected firms. Hence, a local firm undertaking R&D, but engaged in product technology, would show greater R&D intensity than a foreign firm that accesses it from its parent plant abroad. Yet, the foreign firm may be engaged in product

TABLE 5.2

Variables, Proxies and Expected Relationships with Network Strength

Variables and proxies	Acronym	Measure	Source of data	Expected Relationship with NS
Basic infrastructure	BI	$1/3[H, E, T]$	World Bank (2003) & National Ministries	
Health	H	Doctors/'000 people	World Bank (2003)	
Education	E	Literacy rate	World Bank (2003)	
Transport and telecom.	T	Tel. Lines/'000 people	World Bank (2003)	
High-tech infrastructure	HTI	$½[RD_I, RD_{SE}]$	World Bank (2003) & National Min	
R&D investment	RD_I	R&D investment/GNI	World Bank (2003)	
R&D scientists and engineers	RD_{SE}	R&D scientists and engineers/ million population	World Bank (2003) & National Min	
Network strength	NS	$NS_{BI} + NS_{HTI}$	ADB-UNU/INTECH survey	
Network strength with BI	NS_{BI}	$1/3[HH+EE+TT]$	ADB-UNU/INTECH survey	
Capacity and quality of health support	H	Likert scale (1..5)	ADB-UNU/INTECH survey	
Standard and quality of education	E	Likert scale (1..5)	ADB-UNU/INTECH survey	
Capacity and quality of transport and telecom.	T	Likert scale (1..5)	ADB-UNU/INTECH survey	
Network strength with HTI	NS_{HTI}	$1/3[RDu+RD_L+ RD_{IG}]$	ADB-UNU/INTECH survey	
Capacity and quality of R&D support from universities	U	Likert scale (1..5)	ADB-UNU/INTECH survey	
Capacity and quality of R&D support from R&D labs	RD_L	Likert scale (1..5)	ADB-UNU/INTECH survey	

TABLE 5.2 (continued)

Variables and proxies	Acronym	Measure	Source of data	Expected Relationship with NS
Capacity and quality of R&D incentives and grants from government	RD_{IG}	Likert scale (1..5)	ADB-UNU/INTECH survey	
Technology index	TI	HR+ PT+ RD	ADB-UNU/INTECH survey	Positive and significant
Human Resource	HR	1/3[TM, TE, CHR]	ADB-UNU/INTECH survey	Unclear
Process technology	PT	1/3[EM, ITC, QC]	ADB-UNU/INTECH survey	Unclear
R&D	RD	½[Rdexp, RDemp]	ADB-UNU/INTECH survey	Positive and significant
Foreign ownership	FO	Dummy (FO=1,0)	ADB-UNU/INTECH survey	Unclear
Size	S	Dummy (S=1,0)	ADB-UNU/INTECH survey	Unclear
Union	U	Dummy (U=1,0)	ADB-UNU/INTECH survey	Unclear
Age	A	Absolute years	ADB-UNU/INTECH survey	Unclear
Management type	OM	Dummy (OM=1,0)	ADB-UNU/INTECH survey	Unclear
Quality control methods	QC	Dummy (QC=1,0)	ADB-UNU/INTECH survey	
IT components	ITC	Likert scale (1…5)	ADB-UNU/INTECH survey	
Cutting edge HR practices	CHR	Absolute number used	ADB-UNU/INTECH survey	
Equipment and machinery	EM		ADB-UNU/INTECH survey	
Training expense	TE	% in payroll	ADB-UNU/INTECH survey	
Training mode	TM		ADB-UNU/INTECH survey	
R&D expenditure	Rdexp	R&D expenditure in sales	ADB-UNU/INTECH survey	
R&D employees	RDemp	R&D employees in workforce	ADB-UNU/INTECH survey	

technologies superior to the local firm. Nevertheless, the use of conduct variables — largely referring to cutting edge practices — allows the estimation of process and HR technology on the basis of their closeness to the technology frontier.

NS was computed by estimating selected proxies where data were available on the strength of basic and high-tech infrastructure from the firms' assessment of their capacity and degree of connectivity and coordination with firms. Technological capabilities were computed by estimating the strength or value of human resource, process technology, and R&D intensities.

Firm-level technologies include human resource practices, machinery and equipment, inventory and quality control systems, and R&D expenditure. Since a number of characteristics have overlapping objectives and effects, it is methodologically better to integrate related proxies into a composition of indices, which will not only help minimize double counting, but also avert collinearity problems in statistical analysis. In addition, adjusting firms' responses with related proxies, for example, R&D, will offer a better approximation of its intensity than just any one proxy — for example, R&D sales as a percentage of sales, and the proportion of R&D staff in the workforce. Because there are no *a priori* reasons to attach greater significance to any of the proxies used, the normalization procedure was not weighted. However, the indirect effects of these proxies would still remain as the hiring of a key R&D scientist or engineer by one firm from another would inevitably have a bearing on its R&D capability.

The following broad capabilities and related composition of proxies were specified:

Human Resource Capability

Because of the fairly developed nature of electronics manufacturing in all six economies, and the fact that competition is intense and the knowledge intensity in electronics assembly and testing is high, HR techniques in the sample can be expected to be strong in all of them. Indeed, HR technologies even in foreign semiconductor firms diffuse horizontally and simultaneously between plants (Rasiah 1994). Hence, there are unlikely to be statistically significant differences between foreign and local firms in the countries, and the relationship between HR and NS is unlikely to be statistically significant.

HR practices were measured as:

$$HR_i = 1/3[TM_i, TE_i, CHR_i] \tag{1}$$

where TM, TE and CHR refer to training mode, training expense as a share of payroll, and cutting edge HR practices respectively of firm i. TM was measured as a multinomial logistic variable of (1) when staff are sent out to external organizations for training; (2) when external staff are used to train employees; (3) when staff with training responsibilities are on payroll; (4) when a separate training department is used; (5) when a separate training centre is used, and 0, when no formal training is undertaken. CHR was measured by a score of one for each of the practices. The firms were asked if it was their policy to encourage (1) team-working, (2) small group activities to stimulate innovation, (3) multiskilling, (4) interaction with marketing, customer service, and R&D department, (5) lifelong learning, and (6) upward mobility.

Because all the proxies were evenly weighted, HR was divided by three. The proxies were normalized using the following formula:

$$\text{Normalization Score} = (X_i - X_{min})/(X_{max} - X_{min}) \qquad (2)$$

X_i, X_{min} and X_{max} refer to the ith, minimum, and maximum values of the proxy, X. The normalization procedure raises the highest observation among the six countries to one and the lowest to zero. Caution must be placed in the interpretation of the normalized means as they represent relative values against the highest and lowest observations, rather than absolute values.

Process Technology Capability

Owing to industry-specific characteristics of process technology in electronics firms where competitors require similar intensities to compete, there is unlikely to be significant differences between foreign and local firms, and the relationship between PT and NS is unlikely to be statistically significant. However, differences between foreign and local firms may exist in countries where the nature of participation of either one may just be emerging.

Data on three proxies facilitated the computation of PT, which was calculated using the formula:

$$PT_i = 1/3[EM_i, ITC_i, QC_i] \qquad (3)$$

EM, ITC, and QC refer to equipment and machinery, information technology components, and quality control instruments, respectively, of firm i. EM was computed as a multinomial logistic variable with average age of over five years = 0, five years = 1, four years = 2, three years = 3, two years = 4, and one year and less = 5. Likert scale scores ranging from 1–5 (least to strong) were used to measure ITC. QC was measured as a dummy variable (QC=1, if cutting edge methods were used, QC=0 otherwise). Because all the proxies were evenly weighted, PT was divided by three.

R&D Capability

With the exception of funding of public labs and universities, firms seldom participate in basic research. Hence, firm-level R&D is largely focused on process technology and product development — especially diversification of use and proliferation. Because Korea and Taiwan have a more advanced NS than Malaysia, Thailand, the Philippines, and Indonesia, it is hypothesized in the chapter that R&D will produce a statistically significant and positive relationship with NS.

The data collected enabled the computation of two R&D proxies, namely, R&D expenditure as a percentage of sales, and R&D personnel as a share of employment. It was not possible from the sample data to disentangle investment in process and product R&D, and hence this proxy was assumed to relate to both product and process R&D and was measured as:

$$RD_i = 1/2[RDexp_i, RDemp_i] \tag{4}$$

where RD_{exp} and RD_{emp} refer to R&D expenditure as a share of sales, and R&D personnel as a proportion of the workforce respectively of firm i. Because the proxies were evenly weighted, RD was divided by two.

Overall Technology Intensity

The overall technology intensity (TI) is specified to take stock of all the three proxies specified above — that is, HR, PT, and RD. TI is hypothesized to have a positive and statistically significant relationship with NS owing to the influence of RD. It is measured as follows:

$$TI_i = HR_i + PT_i + RD_i \tag{5}$$

Owing to the absence of *a priori* reasons, all three TI components above were weighted equally, which explains why the formulas used earlier to estimate these variables were divided with the number of proxies used.

Network Strength

Network strength (NS) is the key explanatory variable used in the analysis. Because of the stronger NS in Korea and Taiwan, firms there are likely to participate more in R&D activities than those in Malaysia, Thailand, the Philippines, and Indonesia. Firms have access to stocks of knowledge from foreign national innovation systems — for example, publications, education, licensing arrangements, and foreign affiliates. However, owing to proprietary obligations and greater support often given to national firms, firms tend to rely more on their own national innovation systems to participate in R&D activities (Vernon 1971). In addition, foreign firms tend to retain new product development at parent sites — preferring to participate largely in process and product adaptation activities at host-sites. Hence, local firms are likely to show a higher propensity to use NS for R&D activities than foreign firms. Hence, it is hypothesized that NS is likely to show higher impact on TI and RD in the sample of local firms than in the sample of foreign firms.

The NS computed here only takes cognizance of BI, HTI, and network cohesion (NC) between firms and these institutions. The information gathered for Korea, Taiwan, and Thailand prevented the inclusion of interfirm links and relationship with other institutions such as industry associations.

Using the firms' assessment, network strength (NS) involving basic infrastructure institutions was measured as follows:

$$NS_{BIi} = 1/3([HH_i, EE_i, TT_i]) \qquad (6)$$

where NS_{BI}, HH, EE, and TT refer to network strength involving basic infrastructure institutions, and capacity and strength of firm i's connections and coordination involving health institutions, basic education institutions, and transport and telecommunication institutions. Likert scale scores of 1–5 were used to measure the strength. The NS_{BI} was divided by three because of the number of proxies used.

Using the firms' assessment, network cohesion (NC) involving high-tech infrastructure institutions was measured as follows:

$$NS_{HTIi} = 1/3[RD_{Ui}, RD_{Li}, RD_{IGi}] \qquad (7)$$

where NS_{HTI}, RD_U, RD_L, and RD_{IG} refer to network strength involving high-tech infrastructure, and capacity and strength of firm i's connections and coordination involving R&D support from universities, R&D labs, and government R&D incentives and programmes. Likert scale scores of 1–5 were used to measure the strength. NS_{HTI} was divided by the number of proxies used (that is, three). Although most firms considered effective legal intellectual property rights (IPRs) as an important influence on their participation in R&D activities, it was excluded from the analysis as its influence was largely similar within individual economies.

NS was measured simply by adding the strength of basic and high-tech support faced by firms as follows:

$$NS_i = NS_{Bli} + NS_{HTli} \qquad (8)$$

The use of NS_{BI} and NS_{HTI} can have both positive and negative implications. On the positive side it helps draw the firms' assessments of the quality of connections and coordination with the relevant institutions involved, including explaining the geographical dispersion in institutional support across individual economies. On the negative side it could introduce perceptive biases.

Six Other Critical Firm-Level Variables

Six other important firm-level variables were included in the analysis (see Table 5.3). Ownership is the key differentiating variable used in the chapter. Export incidence is considered to influence the choice of technology. Size — depending on firms' specialization on the basis of scale or scope — brings different implications on technological capabilities. The other control variables introduced in the regression models are union, management type, and age.

a. Export Incidence

In the absence of sufficient responses on gross output and exports for Korea, Taiwan, Thailand, the Philippines, and Indonesia, export-incidence rather than the more important export-intensity was used as a proxy for capturing export market influences. However, this variable is unlikely to capture much significance, given the high incidence of exporting (90.1 per cent) of firms (Table 5.3). All firms enjoyed export experience in Thailand and the Philippines, and the share was also very high in Taiwan (97.4 per cent), Korea (95.3 per cent), and Malaysia (93.5 per cent). Only in Indonesia were there significant numbers of totally inward-oriented firms (42.1 per cent). Nevertheless participation in export markets helps firms enjoy greater scale effects and competition. Hence, where significant, the relationship between technology and export incidence can be expected to be positive.

$$X_i = 1 \text{ if firms have export experience; } X_i = 0 \text{ if otherwise.}$$

where X refers to export incidence of firm i.

TABLE 5.3
Breakdown of Sampled Firms, 2000

	Ownership		Export Experience		Size		Owner Managed		Union		Total
	Foreign	Local	Yes	No	SMI	Large	Yes	No	Yes	No	
Korea	15 (34.9)	28(65.1)	41 (95.3)	2 (4.7)	34(79.1)	9(20.9)	28(65.1)	15(34.9)	19(44.2)	24(55.8)	43(100)
Taiwan	13 (34.2)	25(65.8)	37 (97.4)	1 (2.6)	32(84.2)	6(15.8)	27(71.1)	11(28.9)	14(36.8)	24(63.2)	38(100)
Malaysia	36 (78.3)	10(21.7)	43 (93.5)	3 (6.5)	20(56.5)	26(43.5)	15(32.6)	31(67.4)	6(13.0)	40(87.0)	46(100)
Thailand	14 (45.2)	17(54.8)	31(100.0)	0 (0.0)	22(71.0)	9(29.0)	14(45.2)	17(54.8)	13(41.9)	18(58.1)	31(100)
Philippines	18 (66.7)	9(33.3)	27(100.0)	0 (0.0)	6(22.2)	21(77.8)	6(22.2)	21(77.8)	5(18.5)	22(81.5)	27(100)
Indonesia	13 (34.2)	25(65.8)	22 (57.9)	16(42.1)	23(60.5)	15(39.5)	18(47.4)	20(52.6)	23(60.5)	15(39.5)	38(100)
Total	109 (48.9)	114(51.1)	201 (90.1)	22 (9.9)	137(61.4)	86(38.6)	108(48.4)	115(51.6)	80(35.9)	143(64.1)	223(100)

Note: Figures in parentheses refer to percentages.
Source: Compiled from ADB Survey (2002); UNU-INTECH Survey (2002) using Stata 7.0 Package.

b. Union

Owing to collinearity problems between wages and NS, union was used to represent labour market conditions. Given the lack of strong institutional representation through electronics workers' unions in the countries selected, the relationship between union and the technological intensity variables can be expected to be insignificant even when union incidence is high. Union was measured as a dummy variable:

U_i = 1 when the firm enjoys unionized workers; U_i = 0 otherwise.

where U refers to unionization status of firm i. Using this criterion, the incidence of unionization was highest in Indonesia (60.5 per cent), which is a consequence of political freedom enjoyed by unions following democratization since 1998. Korea (44.2 per cent), Thailand (41.9 per cent), Taiwan (36.8 per cent), the Philippines (18.5 per cent), and Malaysia (13 per cent) followed next.

c. Size

There is a long-standing debate on the importance of size on firms' productivity and technology levels. Typical industrial organization arguments posit that firms achieve competitiveness with a certain minimum efficiency scale (MES), which varies with industries (Scherer 1980, 1992; Pratten 1971). The electronics industry is a diverse one in which some subsectors are scale-intensive (e.g. wafer fabrication and semiconductor and disk drive assembly), while some specialize on the basis of scope (e.g. capacitors, resistors, and diodes). Where scale is unimportant — for example, small-batch components — scope rather than scale is important (Piore and Sabel 1982; Rasiah 1994, 1995). Audretsh (2002) offered pervasive analysis of U.S. data to dispel arguments related to the significance of large size in efficiency and innovative activities. The increasing decomposition and dispersal of production involving electronics firms has made small size very efficient. Because of the controversy over the role of size in economic performance and the claims of industrial organization exponents over MES differences, a neutral hypothesis was framed — simply that size has a bearing on technological capabilities.

Two categories of size were chosen, *viz.*, small and medium, and large, and it was measured as a dummy variable:

S_i = 1 when employment size was 500 or more; S_i = 0 if otherwise.

where S refers to size of firm i. Based on this classification, small and medium firms dominated the samples of Taiwan (84.2 per cent), Korea (79.1 per cent), Thailand (71 per cent), and Indonesia (60.5 per cent) (see Table 5.3).

Large firms accounted for more than half the firms in the Philippines (77.8 per cent) and constituted 43.5 per cent of the Malaysian sample.

d. Ownership

The evidence on the influence of foreign ownership on technological capabilities is mixed. The OECD (1998, cited in Amsden, Tschang, and Goto 2001, p. 5) reported that not more than 12 per cent of total R&D expenditure is spent by firms outside home sites in developed economies. Lall (1992) argued that foreign firms transfer the innovation rather than the process itself abroad. Rasiah (2003) contributed empirical evidence to show that foreign firms generally participate only in process R&D in developing economies. However, Blomstrom and Persson (1983) and Blomstrom and Wolff (1994) provided evidence of positive spillovers from foreign firms to the local economy. Given the contradictory evidence produced, albeit the methodological approach used may explain the divergence, a neutral hypothesis was used. Foreign ownership was defined using equity share of 50 per cent or more, and was measured as:

FO_i = 1 if foreign equity ownership of firm i was 50 per cent or more;
FO = 0 otherwise.

where FO refers to the status of ownership of firm i. Using this criterion, foreign ownership in the sample was highest in Malaysia (78.3 per cent) and the Philippines (66.7 per cent), followed by Thailand (45.2 per cent), Korea (34.9 per cent), and Taiwan (34.2 per cent), and Indonesia (34.2 per cent) (see Table 5.3).

e. Owner-Managed Firms

There is sometimes a misconception that multinationals cannot be managed by owners, either fully or partially. Since the most common definition of a multinational corporation is a firm with assets in at least two countries, several foreign firms in the study met these conditions. It is often argued that owner managers impact both positively and negatively on firms' performance. On the one hand, owners are considered to have a greater drive to succeed because of lower agency costs and their availability to make quick decisions. On the other hand, owner-managers are considered to be less professional, especially when running big businesses, and hence may lack the instruments to succeed in export markets. Hence a neutral hypothesis with either a positive or negative sign is expected. OM is measured using a dummy variable as follows:

OM_i = 1 if firm is managed either partly or fully by the owner;
OM = 0 otherwise.

where OM refers to status of management of firm i. Using this criterion, there were more local owner-managed firms in Taiwan (71.1 per cent) and Korea (65.1 per cent) than in Malaysia (32.6 per cent), Thailand (45.2 per cent), the Philippines (22.2 per cent), and Indonesia (47.4 per cent) (see Table 5.3).

f. Age

Because firms with longer experience are considered to enjoy greater experiential and tacit knowledge, the age of the firm is considered to provide a positive relationship with exports and technological capabilities. However, the statistical relationship may not be positive if foreign firms, using superior technology from abroad and enjoying strong access to global markets, only started relocating their operations recently. Hence, a neutral relationship is assumed. The absolute age of the firm is used as an independent variable and was measured as:

A_i = years in operation of firm i.

where A refers to age of operation of firm i.

Overall 223 electronics firms responded to the survey (see Table 5.3). The national sampling frames of the six countries were not used owing to the difficulty of obtaining firm-level data. Case studies of three electronics firms in Korea, Taiwan, Thailand, and the Philippines were carried out by national consultants, while the author undertook similar interviews in the Indonesia and Malaysia study. The survey and the case studies constitute the basis for the results and analysis in this chapter. A correlation coefficient test was carried out to avert the use of variables causing multi-collinearity problems (see Appendix 5.I)

Statistical Models

This section presents the models specified to estimate the statistical relationships involving technological intensities. Tobit regressions were preferred because the technological intensity variables are censored both on the right and the left side of the data sets, and they take a maximum value of 1 and a minimum value of zero. NS is assumed to pick up country effects in models, and hence country dummies were not used in all the regressions.

Tobit: $TI = \alpha + \beta_1 X + \beta_2 NS + \beta_3 S + \beta_4 FO + \beta_5 OM + \beta_6 A + \mu$ (9)

Tobit: $HR = \alpha + \beta_1 X + \beta_2 NS + \beta_3 S + \beta_4 FO + \beta_5 OM + \beta_5 A + \mu$ (10)

Tobit: $PT = \alpha + \beta_1 X + \beta_2 NS + \beta_3 S + \beta_4 FO + \beta_5 OM + \beta_6 A + \mu$ (11)

Tobit: $RD = \alpha + \beta_1 X + \beta_2 NS + \beta_3 S + \beta_4 FO + \beta_5 OM + \beta_6 A + \mu$ (12)

All the regression models above were repeated using foreign and local firm samples separately. Individual country regressions by ownership were not carried out owing to low incidence of foreign ownership in Taiwan, and the small sample size involving Thailand and the Philippines.

RESULTS OF THE STATISTICAL ANALYSIS

This section uses statistical instruments and the variables specified in the previous section to examine differences in technological intensities between foreign and local firms in the six economies, and the relationship of technological variables with NS, including by separate samples of foreign and local firms.

Examination of Statistical Differences

The results of the analysis of statistical differences between foreign and local firms in wages and technological capabilities using two-tail t-tests of means are presented in Table 5.4.

Local firms enjoyed higher TI levels than foreign firms in Taiwan, the Philippines, and Thailand. The differences between foreign and local firms in Taiwan are mainly explained by differences in RD intensities, whereas in the Philippines and Thailand, they are largely due to differences in PT intensities. Local firms also enjoyed higher RD than foreign firms in the Philippines. However, the RD scores in the Philippines were extremely low. Foreign firms enjoyed higher PT and PT levels than local firms in Malaysia and Indonesia, which is linked to the participation of local firms as suppliers and in consumer electronics, and in Indonesia, also in simple computer assembly manufacturing for the local market. Foreign firms also enjoyed higher HR than local firms in Indonesia. The differences in Korea were not statistically significant.

All in all, except for RD involving firms in Taiwan, there were no obvious statistical differences between foreign and local firms in Korea and Taiwan. However, as mergers and acquisitions in Korea have expanded since 1998, it might very well be that foreign firms have absorbed the technological

TABLE 5.4

Two-tail t-tests of Technology Intensity Levels by Country and Ownership, 2000

TI	Foreign	Local	t		PT	Foreign	Local	t
Korea	0.945	0.850	1.10		Korea	0.358	0.357	0.08
Taiwan	1.195	1.536	-2.10**		Taiwan	0.452	0.505	-0.96
Malaysia	1.057	0.820	1.97***		Malaysia	0.479	0.333	2.29**
Thailand	0.651	0.852	-1.97***		Thailand	0.293	0.472	-3.73*
Philippines	0.807	1.001	-3.13*		Philippines	0.457	0.326	-2.57**
Indonesia	0.790	0.599	2.64*		Indonesia	0.310	0.235	1.97***
HR					**RD**			
Korea	0.361	0.288	1.21		Korea	0.225	0.205	0.48
Taiwan	0.319	0.421	-1.48		Taiwan	0.423	0.610	-2.38**
Malaysia	0.475	0.454	0.33		Malaysia	0.103	0.033	1.41
Thailand	0.334	0.349	-0.18		Thailand	0.024	0.031	-1.03
Philippines	0.445	0.458	-0.53		Philippines	0.036	0.087	-2.06**
Indonesia	0.429	0.305	2.81*		Indonesia	0.052	0.060	-0.31

Note: *, ** , and *** refer to significance levels of 1%, 5%, and 10% respectively; + – mean wages in US$100 per month.

Source: Computed from ADB (2002) and UNU-INTECH (2002) data using Stata 7.0 Package.

capabilities developed by local firms. Differences in HR levels only existed in Indonesia, which could be due to cutbacks faced by inward-oriented local firms from the financial crisis. Foreign firms enjoyed higher TI and PT levels than local firms in Malaysia and Indonesia, owing to the nascent status of local firms. Local firms dominated R&D capabilities in Taiwan. RD levels were also higher among local than foreign firms in Philippines, but the levels were extremely low.

Analysis of Statistical Relationships

This section examines the statistical relationships involving the technological intensity variables controlling for other variables. All the regressions in Table 5.5 passed the White test for heteroscedascity and the chi-square statistic of model fit was also statistically significant. The results generally confirm expectations. Country dummies were dropped when NS was used as they were subsumed and captured by the latter.

The explanatory variable NS was statistically highly significant and its coefficients were positive involving TI and RD — irrespective of ownership. However, the coefficients of NS in the sample of local firms for TI and RD were significantly stronger than those in the sample of foreign firms, confirming local firms' participation and higher reliance on national NS than foreign firms. NS was statistically insignificant against HR and PT in all the regressions, which is, as argued earlier, a consequence of similarities in processes and HR practices that are required of electronics firms engaged in export manufacturing. This finding confirms the hypothesis defined earlier that NS is unlikely to show statistical relationship with HR and PT owing to the need for firms to use similar technologies in the electronics industry.

Export incidence (X) was statistically significant and the coefficients positive in the TI, PT, and RD regressions in the overall sample and the sample of local firms. The lack of statistical significance involving the foreign firms' sample is invariably the consequence of too few firms lacking export experience.[5] Similarly, the inverse and statistically significant (10 per cent level) relationship in the HR regressions in the sample of foreign firms is likely to be spurious. The positive and strong coefficient involving the sample of local firms demonstrate that exporting both requires and drives higher technological levels.

Ownership was statistically insignificant in all the regressions, suggesting that technological capabilities in the aggregated samples were not significantly different between foreign and local firms once controlled for levels of NS and

TABLE 5.5
Statistical Relationships Involving Technological Intensities, 2000

	TI			HR			PT			RD		
	All	Foreign	Local	All	Foreign	Local	All	Foreign	Local	All	Foreign	Local
X	0.226	-0.163	0.307	0.030	-0.131	0.067	0.155	0.055	0.175	0.105	-0.056	0.132
	(2.83)*	(-1.09)	(3.09)*	(0.74)	(-1.69)***	(1.32)	(4.49)*	(0.67)	(4.75)*	(2.01)**	(-0.62)	(2.01)**
NS	0.833	0.513	1.000	0.071	-0.024	0.109	0.070	0.085	-0.002	0.795	0.530	0.980
	(5.87)*	(2.65)*	(4.48)*	(0.99)	(-0.24)	(0.95)	(1.14)	(0.81)	(-0.03)	(9.32)*	(4.78)*	(7.18)*
FO	-0.003			0.026			-0.008			-0.026		
	(-0.06)			(1.06)			(-0.38)			(-0.89)		
U	-0.040	0.037	-0.044	-0.035	-0.005	-0.043	-0.030	-0.012	-0.054	0.054	0.074	0.075
	(-0.82)	(0.58)	(-0.56)	(-1.44)	(-0.16)	(-1.09)	(-1.47)	(-0.35)	(-1.90)***	(1.87)***	(2.09)**	(1.57)
OM	0.112	0.087	0.121	0.016	0.024	0.006	0.041	0.020	0.065	0.068	0.049	0.063
	(2.34)**	(1.42)	(1.66)***	(0.67)	(0.76)	(0.15)	(1.97)**	(0.60)	(2.44)*	(2.31)**	(1.37)	(1.40)
A	0.006	0.002	0.008	-0.001	-0.002	-0.001	0.002	0.000	0.004	0.006	0.006	0.006
	(2.63)*	(0.67)	(2.29)**	(-0.98)	(-1.25)	(-0.61)	(2.40)**	(0.19)	(3.16)*	(4.60)*	(3.08)*	(3.00)*
S	0.149	0.173	0.106	0.127	0.136	0.114	0.057	0.098	0.028	-0.033	-0.039	-0.054
	(3.13)*	(2.98)*	(1.39)	(5.26)*	(4.52)*	(2.94)*	(2.77)*	(3.10)*	(1.01)	(-1.13)	(-1.15)	(-1.15)
μ	0.161	0.705	-0.011	-0.035	0.508	0.250	0.153	0.248	0.147	-0.460	-0.185	-0.573
	(1.66)***	(3.99)*	(-0.09)	(-1.44)	(5.54)*	(3.86)*	(3.66)*	(2.57)*	(3.15)*	(-7.16)*	(-1.70)***	(-6.77)*
N	223	109	114	223	109	114	223	109	114	223	109	114
LR χ²	79.61*	17.53*	62.56*	35.63*	22.92*	15.31**	52.39*	10.88***	52.92*	141.04*	50.39*	83.58*
LL	-73.97	-22.89	-45.88	76.22	47.55	28.59	104.20	29.88	58.69	4.90	12.57	-3.07

Note: *, **, and *** refer to 1%, 5%, and 10% levels of significance; NS is expected to capture country effects.
Source: Computed from ADB (2002) and UNU-INTECH (2002) survey data using Stata 7.0 Package.

other variables. However, the separate regressions by ownership show higher reliance on NS by local firms on TI and RD intensities than foreign firms. This is to be expected since foreign firms have access to superior technological support from their parent sites.

Size (S) had a positive sign consistently in all the regressions except those involving the RD regressions, that is, large firms show higher technological intensities than small firms. It was statistically insignificant only involving RD, and involving TI and PT in the sample of local firms. Clearly TI, HR, and PT in the overall sample and sample of foreign firms seem to be positively correlated with size — suggesting that scale is still important in HR and PT technologies in export-oriented assembly and testing activities. Although size was not statistically important, most firms with R&D activities are not involved in Original Brand Manufacturing (OBM) activities. Also, management type carried a positive coefficient in all the regressions, and was statistically significant in the overall sample and sample of local firms involving TI and PT, and overall sample involving RD. Age was statistically significant in all the RD regressions, suggesting that older firms enjoy higher R&D intensities than newer firms, although its influence was small. Union was statistically significant and the coefficient is positive in the RD regressions in the overall sample and sample of foreign firms. Either because of the weak position of unions, this relationship is likely to be spurious, or because of the fairly high incidence of unionization in Taiwan and Korea (only lower than in the Indonesian sample), the RD levels were the highest in the sample.

Taken together, it can be seen that NS has had a critical influence on TI and RD intensities in the countries examined. Although FO did not enjoy a statistically significant relationship with all the technological intensity variables, NS has had a greater impact on TI and RD in local firms than in foreign firms. The highly significant and positive coefficient of X in the sample of local firms showed that technological levels were higher in exporting than in inward-oriented local firms in these countries. The results involving the sample of foreign firms could not be interpreted owing to the dominance of only exporting firms in the sub-sample.

CONCLUSIONS

This chapter has produced some clear findings. Local firms enjoyed higher TI and RD capabilities than foreign firms in Taiwan and the Philippines. The latter is understandable given that foreign firms enjoyed access to their superior R&D capabilities abroad. As expected, there were no obvious differences in HR and PT capabilities between foreign and local firms in

Taiwan. There was also no obvious statistical difference between foreign and local firms involving all the technological indicators in Korea. Foreign firms in Malaysia and Indonesia enjoyed statistically superior TI and PT compared with local firms. Local firms enjoyed higher TI and PT capabilities than foreign firms in Thailand. Statistical differences involving HR was only obvious in Indonesia, where foreign firms enjoyed higher levels than local firms.

The results also showed that RD intensity of electronics firms in Indonesia, Malaysia, the Philippines, and Thailand was significantly lower than that of electronics firms in Taiwan and Korea. Quite clearly firms in Taiwan and Korea endowed with especially superior R&D capability enjoyed tremendous technological advantage over firms in Indonesia, Malaysia, the Philippines and Thailand. Hence, foreign-dominated operations in the Southeast Asian economies have tended to be limited to labour-intensive assembly and test operations whilst local-driven firms in Taiwan and Korea (foreign firms were largely acquired from local ownership) enjoyed integrated operations with strong participation in R&D. It can also be argued that with (for example, Malaysia) or without (for example, Indonesia and the Philippines) efforts to build high-tech institutions, the embedding institutional and systemic environment in Indonesia, Malaysia, the Philippines and Thailand has not evolved sufficiently to encourage R&D offshoring by foreign firms.

The econometric analysis showed that NS impacted strongly on TI and RD capabilities in all the regressions, demonstrating that network strength matters, especially with respect to the depth of R&D participation of both foreign and local firms. As expected network strength had a bigger impact on local TI and RD capability than that of foreign firms. Owing to the common parameters required in the electronics industry in assembly and test operations where the competition is intense, NS did not enjoy a statistically significant relationship with HR and PT in all the regressions. Export incidence enjoyed a strong and positive relationship with TI, PT, and RD in the sample of local firms, demonstrating its strong and positive influence on technological intensity. There were too few observations involving only inward-oriented foreign firms to interpret the sample of foreign firms.

Although local firms inexorably rely on domestic NS more than foreign firms do to support their R&D activities, it influences technological intensities in both sets of firms. Hence, the results indicate that there is a need to strengthen institutional and systemic support instruments to stimulate the participation of both local and foreign firms in technological activities, if electronics firms in Southeast Asia are to upgrade and compete for similar levels of value added as firms in Taiwan and Korea. The policy focus in the Southeast Asian economies should target strengthening the institutional and systemic environment facing firms, as it will enhance learning and innovation conduct in firms. The strategies for individual economies would obviously differ according to their specific endowments and technology trajectories.

APPENDIX TABLE 5.1

Correlation Matrix of Independent Variables, 2000

	NS	TI	HR	PT	RD	OM	FO	A	X	W	U	S
NS	1.000											
TI	0.410*	1.000										
HR	0.032	0.609*#	1.000									
PT	0.152	0.729*#	0.265	1.000								
RD	0.586*	0.755*#	0.078	0.371	1.000							
OM	0.101	0.192	−0.036	0.142	0.266	1.000						
FO	−0.116	−0.044	0.143	−0.003	−0.189	−0.283	1.000					
A	0.225	0.310	−0.047	0.248	0.409*	0.277	−0.201	1.000				
X	0.148	0.274	0.122	0.342	0.146	−0.041	0.203	0.156	1.000			
W	0.514*	0.432*	0.041	0.296	0.517*	0.111	−0.031	0.241	0.135	1.000		
U	−0.003	−0.006	−0.121	−0.060	0.127	0.080	−0.058	0.245	−0.035	−0.067	1.000	
S	−0.057	0.187	0.349	0.210	−0.099	−0.104	0.184	0.067	0.169	−0.153	−0.016	1.000

Note: * — refers to high correlation; # — refers to overlapping or sub-component variable.

Source: Computed from data collected from ADB (2002) and UNU-INTECH (2002) surveys using Stata 7.0 Package.

Notes

1. The data on Korea, Taiwan, and Thailand used in the chapter are drawn from an ADB (2001–02) survey, which this author contributed towards, and on Malaysia, from a UNU-INTECH (2002) survey. I am grateful especially to Sanjaya Lall and Shujiro Urata for encouraging me to use the quantitative methodology applied in the chapter, to Brahm Prakash, who allowed me to use the data for producing academic papers, and Rajiv Kumar, Yeo Lin, Doren Chadee, the late Linsu Kim, and Alice Amsden for their contribution to the questionnaire designed. The usual disclaimer applies.
2. For instance, PCB assembly in electronics is significantly different from wafer fabrication. The former is also associated with low margins and labour-intensive activities while the latter is a highly capital-intensive, high value added activity. Hence, industry dummies used do not actually control for such effects.
3. Using a range of economies, Rasiah (2004*a*, 2004*b*, 2004*c*) showed that differences in technological intensities between foreign and local firms also varied with the level of institutional and systemic strength embedding firms.
4. The OECD (1998, cited in Amsden, Goto and Tschang 2001) reported that only twelve per cent of R&D invested in OECD economies is undertaken outside parent locations.
5. The lack of export-intensity data prevented a statistically more rigorous analysis of the influence of exports on the technological variables.

References

Abramovitz, M. "Resource and Output Trends in the United States Since 1870". *American Economic Review* 46 (1956): 5–23.

ADB. "Survey Data on Asian Industrial Firms Competitiveness". Compiled by Asian Development Bank, Manila, 2002.

Amsden, A. "The Division of Labor Is Limited By the Rate of Growth of the Market: The Taiwanese Machine Tool Industry". *Cambridge Journal of Economics* 9, no. 4 (1985): 271–84.

──────. *Asia's Next Giant: South Korea and Late Industrialization*. New York: Oxford University Press, 1989.

Amsden, A., T. Tschang and A. Goto. "Do Foreign Companies Conduct R&D in Developing Countries". ADBI Working Paper No. 14, Tokyo, Asian Development Bank Institute, 2001.

Audretsch, D. "The Dynamic Role of Small Firms: Evidence from U.S.". *Small Business Economics* 18, nos. 1–3 (2002): 13–40.

Bell, M. and K. Pavitt. "The Development of Technological Capabilities". In *Trade, Technology and International Competitiveness*, edited by I.U. Haque. Washington, D.C.: World Bank, 1995.

Best, M. *The New Competitive Advantage*. Oxford: Oxford University Press, 2001.

Blomstrom, M. and H. Persson. "Foreign Investment and Spillover Efficiency in an Undedeveloped Economy: Evidence from Mexican Manufacturing Industry". *World Development* 11, no. 6 (1983): 493–501.

Blomstrom, M. and E. Wolff. "Multinational Corporations and Productivity Convergence in Mexico". In *Convergence of Productivity: Cross-national Studies and Historical Evidence*, edited by W. Baumol, R. Nelson and E. Wolff. Oxford: Oxford University Press, 1994.

Brimble, P. "Foreign Direct Investment, Technology and Competitiveness in Thailand". In *Competitiveness, FDI and Technological Activity in East Asia*, edited by S. Lall and S. Urata. Cheltenham: Edward Elgar, 2003.

Dalhman, C. and C. Frischtak. "National Systems Supporting Technical Advance in Industry: The Brazilian Experience". In *National Innovation Systems: A Comparative Analysis*, edited by R.R. Nelson. New York: Oxford University Press, 1993.

Dosi, G. "Technological Paradigms and Technological Trajectories". *Research Policy* 11, no. 3 (1982): 147–62.

Dunning J. *Economic Analysis and the Multinational Enterprise*. London: Allen & Unwin, 1974.

Ernst, D., T. Ganiatsos, and L. Mytelka. *Technological Capabilities and Export Success: Lessons from East Asia*, edited by D. Ernst, T. Ganiatsos, and L. Mytelka. London: Routledge, 1998.

Figueiredo, P.N. "Learning Processes Features and Technological Capability Accumulation: Explaining Inter-firm Differences". *Technovation* 22 (2002): 685–98.

———. "Learning, Capability Accumulation and Firms Differences: Evidence From Latecomer Steel". *Industrial and Corporate Change* 12, no. 3 (2003): 607–43.

Fransman, M. "International Competitiveness, Technical Change and the State: The Machine Tool Industries in Taiwan and Japan". *World Development* 14, no. 12 (1985): 1375–96.

Freeman, C. "New Technology and Catching-Up". *European Journal of Development Research* 1, no. 1 (1989): 85–99.

Hobday, M. *Innovation in East Asia*. Cheltenham: Edward Elgar, 1995.

Hymer S. "The International Operations of National Firms: A Study of Direct Foreign Investment". Doctoral thesis submitted to MIT in 1960. Cambridge, MA: The MIT Press, 1976.

Kaldor, N. "A Model of Economic Growth". *Economic Journal* 67 (1957): 591–624.

Katz, J. and N. Berkovich. "National Systems of Innovation Supporting Technical Advance in Industry: The Case of Argentina". In *National Innovation Systems: A Comparative Analysis*, edited by R.R. Nelson. New York: Oxford University Press, 1993.

Kim, L. "National System of Industrial Innovation: Dynamics of Capability Building in Korea". In *National Innovation Systems: A Comparative Analysis*, edited by R.R. Nelson. New York: Oxford University Press, 1993.

————. *From Imitation to Innovation*. Cambridge: Harvard Business School Press, 1997.

————. "The Dynamics of Technology Development: Lessons from the Korean Experience". In *Competitiveness, FDI and Technological Activity in East Asia*, edited by S. Lall and S. Urata. Cheltenham: Edward Elgar, 2003.

Kim, L. and R. Nelson. *Technology, Learning and Innovation: Experiences of Newly Industrializing Countries*, edited by L. Kim and R. Nelson. Cambridge: Cambridge University Press, 2001.

Lall, S. "Technological Capabilities and Industrialisation". *World Development* 20, no. 2 (1992): 165–86.

————. *Learning from the Asian Tigers*. Basingstoke: Macmillan, 1996.

————. *Competitiveness, Technology and Skills*. Cheltenham: Edward Elgar, 2001.

Lin, Y. "Industrial Structure and Market-Complementing Policies: Export Success of the Electronics and Information Industry in Taiwan". ADB Working paper series, Manila, 2003.

List, F. *The National System of Political Economy*. London: Longmans, Green & Company, 1885.

Lundvall, B.A. "Innovation as an Interactive Process: From User-producer Interaction to the National System of Innovation". In *Technical Change and Economic Geography*, edited by G. Dosi, C. Freeman, G. Silverberg and L. Soete. London: Frances Pinter, 1988.

————. *National Systems of Innovation: Towards a Theory of Innovation and Interactive Learning*. London: Frances Pinter, 1992.

Malaysia. "Science and Technology Data". Unpublished. Kuala Lumpur, Ministry of Science, Technology and Environment, 2004.

Mathews, J.A. and D.S. Cho. *Tiger Technology: The Creation of a Semiconductor Industry in East Asia*. Cambridge: Cambridge University Press, 2000.

Mytelka, L.K. *Competition, Innovation and Competitiveness in Developing Countries*, edited by L.K. Mytelka. Paris: OECD, 1999.

Mytelka, L.K. and L.A. Barclay. "Using Foreign Investment Strategically for Innovation". Paper presented at the International conference on FDI-Assisted Development", 2004. *European Journal of Development Research* (forthcoming).

Nelson, R.R. and S.G. Winter. *An Evolutionary Theory of Economic Change*. Cambridge: Harvard University Press, 1982.

Nelson, R. *National Innovation Systems*, edited by R. Nelson. New York: Oxford University Press, 1993.

Oyeyinka, B.O. "Human Capital and Systems of Innovation in Africa". In *Putting the Last First: Building Systems of Innovation in Africa*, edited by M. Muchie, B.A. Lundvall and P. Gammeltoft. Aalborg: Aalborg University Press, 2003.

Pavitt, K. "Sectoral Patterns of Technical Change: Towards a Taxonomy and a Theory". *Research Policy* 13, no. 6 (1984): 343–73.

Piore, M. and C. Sabel. *The Second Industrial Divide: Possibilities for Prosperity*. New York: Basic Books, 1982.

Phongpaichit, P. and C. Baker. *Thailand: Economy and Politics*. Singapore: Oxford University Press, 1994.

Pratten, C. *Economies of Scale in Manufacturing Industry*. Cambridge: Cambridge University Press, 1971.

Rasiah, R. "Flexible Production Systems and Local Machine Tool Subcontracting: Electronics Transnationals in Malaysia". *Cambridge Journal of Economics* 18, no. 3 (1994): 279–98.

———. *Foreign Capital and Industrialization in Malaysia*. Basingstoke: Macmillan, 1995.

———. "Malaysia's National Innovation System". In *Technology, Competitiveness, and the State: Malaysia's Industrial Technology Policies*, edited by K.S. Jomo and G. Felker. London: Routledge, 1999.

———. "Systemic Coordination and the Knowledge Economy: Human Capital Development in MNC-driven Electronics Clusters in Malaysia". *Transnational Corporations* 11, no. 3 (2002): 89–130.

———. "Foreign Ownership, Technology and Electronics Exports from Malaysia and Thailand". *Journal of Asian Economics* 14, no. 5 (2003): 785–811.

———. "Technological Capabilities in Korea, Taiwan, Malaysia and Thailand: Does Network Strength Matter?". *Oxford Development Studies* (forthcoming).

Reinert E.S. "'Catching-up From Way Behind: A Third World Perspective on First World History". *The Dynamics of Technology, Trade and Growth*, edited by J. Fagerberg, B. Verspagen and N.V. Tunzelmann. Aldershot: Hassocks, 1994.

Scherer, F.M. *Industrial Market Structure and Economic Performance*. Chicago: Rand McNally, 1980.

Scherer, F. *International High Technology Competition*. Cambridge: Harvard University Press, 1992.

Smith, A. *The Wealth of the Nations*. London: Strahan and Cadell, 1776.

Taiwan. *Investment Statistics*. Unpublished. Taipei, Central Bank of Taiwan, 2004.

Thailand. "Science and Technology Data". Unpublished. Bangkok, Ministry of Science and Technology, 2004.

UNU-INTECH. "Survey Data on Malaysian Industrial Firms". Compiled by the Institute for New Technologies (INTECH) and DCT, Penang, Malaysia, 2002.

Vernon, R. *Sovereignty at Bay: The Multinational Spread of U.S. Enterprises*. New York: Basic Books, 1971.

Wade, R. *Governing the Market: Economic Theory and the Role of Government in East Asia's Industrialization*. Princeton: Princeton University Press, 1990.

Westphal, L.E., K. Kritayakirana, K. Petchsuwan, H. Sutabutr and Y. Yuthavong. "The Development of Technological Capability in Manufacturing: A Macroscopic Approach to Policy Research". In *Science and Technology: Lessons for Development*

Policy, edited by R.E. Evenson and G. Ranis. London: Intermediate Technology Publications, 1990.

Wignaraja, G. "Firm Size, Technological Capabilities and Market-oriented Policies in Mauritius". *Oxford Development Studies* 30, no. 1 (2002): 87–104.

World Bank. *World Development Indicators*. Washington, D.C.: World Bank Institute, 2003.

Young, A. "Increasing Returns and Economic Progress". *Economic Journal* 38, no. 152 (1928): 527–42.

6

MANAGING LABOUR FOR COMPETITIVENESS IN SOUTHEAST ASIA

Chew Soon Beng and Rosalind Chew

INTRODUCTION

There are two types of trade unions, micro-focused and macro-focused. Micro-focused trade unions aim to protect the interests of their union members. Their union leaders are thus preoccupied with wages and other benefits for their union members. At the same time, they also demand employment stability for their union members. A typical result of micro-focused unions is that they use collective bargaining power to seek significant benefits and ignore unemployment in the economy. Macro-focused trade unions, on the other hand, aim to achieve full employment. They are prepared to allow wages to fluctuate to protect employment. Macro-based unions accept competition as a reality and do not object to capital outflows, as they are part and parcel of globalization. Consequently, such unions place significant emphasis on competition and training. In contrast, micro-focused trade unions object to capital outflows, which is seen as exporting jobs overseas. However, macro-focused unions face a free rider problem, which is not the case with micro-focused trade unions.

This chapter argues that macro-focused unions can help an economy compete in this era of globalization, which is especially important for the Southeast Asian countries as they are export-driven. As international competition becomes increasingly keen, the need for the labour movement to be macro-orientated becomes more urgent. The chapter shows that trade unions in Singapore are macro-focused and, therefore, act as a strategic partner to the government in enhancing the competitiveness of Singapore. Trade unions in Malaysia and Thailand, on the other hand, are not macro-focused and have not been a factor in attracting foreign investment to the respective countries. The labour movements in Indonesia and the Philippines have been a liability in government attempts to enhance labour competitiveness in these countries.

LABOUR AND COMPETITIVENESS

Few scholars have comprehensively studied the competitiveness and the overall development of countries in Southeast Asia in detail. One such scholar is Lim Chong Yah (2001), who applies his EGOIN Theory, Triple C Theory, and the S Curve to his assessment of the overall development of Southeast Asian countries and their competitiveness. Lim concludes that solutions to eradicate poverty must be country-specific and economy-specific. They include, among other things, "market-oriented economic policy and practice" (p. 349). In this chapter, we assess the competitiveness of five Southeast Asian countries — Singapore, Malaysia, Thailand, the Philippines, and Indonesia — through an examination of their labour market competitiveness. We are of the view that labour market competitiveness is a function of the overall competitiveness in each country.

Two possible approaches may be adopted to examine how labour is being managed for competitiveness. One is to take the labour market approach to see whether the rules governing employment are conducive to competitiveness. The other, the industrial relations approach, is to examine relations between the government and the labour movement. This chapter briefly discusses the labour market approach, but its focus is mainly on relations between the government and the labour movement in the area of industrial relations, which encompasses a range of rules governing employment.

The Labour Market Approach

The environment surrounding the labour market can affect the ability of a country to compete effectively in the international market. In this approach, the labour market must permit flexibility of hiring and the layoff of workers to enable firms to adjust to changing business requirements. For instance, if a firm experiences a fall in demand, it must be free to lay off workers or redeploy them to other areas of work in order to minimize losses and survive changes in demand. It must also be free to implement a wage payment system which is conducive to inducing higher productive effort from its workers. The conduciveness of the labour market environment to competitiveness is largely determined by institutional factors.

Employment protection can be one of the results of a certain type of relationship between the government and the labour movement, and it is one of the institutional factors which affects the conduciveness of the labour market milieu to competition. This is because employment protection makes it difficult for firms to redeploy or even lay off staff should there be a change in business conditions and business outlook. Firms would hesitate to hire new staff if they know that they cannot redeploy staff freely. This would not enhance competitiveness, and would result in high unemployment. Thus, in his (2005) study on the rules governing employment protection in Korea and other Organization for Economic Cooperation and Development (OECD) countries, Park finds that countries in which employment protection is too comprehensive experience higher unemployment rates, while OECD countries which have limited employment protection rules, such as Korea and the United States, register relatively lower unemployment rates.

The institutional environment is an important factor affecting the implementation of the wage system (Brown 2005). The environment in the United States, according to Brown, allows the firm to adopt a flexible wage system, which is more efficient as it promotes higher productivity among its workers and at the same time permits the firm to adjust labour costs to changing business conditions. In the case of firms in Germany, the centralized wage agreements and work councils restrict the firm, preventing it from adopting the flexible wage system.

Another institutional factor which is seen to affect competitiveness is the prevailing set of labour standards in a labour market. Higher labour standards protect the interests of workers, but undoubtedly impose higher costs on firms and make it more difficult for them to compete internationally. Developed countries and the International Labour Organization (ILO), however, have been pushing for higher labour standards in developing countries because the differential in unit labour costs between developed and developing countries, due to differences in labour standards, have been blamed for the decline in job creation in the developed countries, and also because of the desire to promote labour rights.

However, in their (1998) study, Raynauld and Vidal find that labour standards have not had any significant impact on the relative competitiveness of the countries covered in their study. This finding should allay the fear that differences in labour standards between developed and developing countries alone have contributed to the export of job opportunities out of the developed countries. Furthermore, it has been argued that as countries develop, the labour standards in their labour markets tend to improve. Therefore, many have argued that developing countries, including Southeast Asian countries, should be given the opportunity to develop their industries through appropriate wage levels, and have urged the ILO and the developed countries not to build obstacles to economic development. An article in *The Economist* states that "to build obstacles on the developing countries' paths out of poverty would be the crime of the century" (*The Economist*, 1 October 1994, p.16). As one researcher (Fields 1995) puts it in his appeal: "Don't push but pull them up through economic growth". Singapore provides the best example of this statement.

Other institutional factors that can affect competitiveness are minimum wage laws and unemployment insurance/benefits, which exist in many developed countries. For instance, OCED countries have a minimum wage law and also an unemployment benefits scheme for workers. However, countries in Western Europe have an unemployment rate of around 10 per cent. Even though per capita income in these countries is high, their labour-intensive industries have shrunk. While OECD countries may be able to afford strong employment protection rules, it is not wise for Southeast Asian countries to emulate this approach.

Based on the factors discussed above, Lawson and Bierhanzl (2004) have compiled the labour market freedom index for more than 100 countries. Table 6.1 presents the index for some OECD countries. This index shows that the United States has the most flexible labour market despite having high minimum wage laws. Denmark has flexible hiring and firing practices, but this advantage is overwhelmed by its high tax rate and unemployment benefits. Seifert and Massa-Wirth (2005) state that in Germany, pacts for employment and competitiveness effectively enable firms to adopt the flexible wage system. This new development will certainly bring the index up for Germany.

Among the East Asian countries, both Singapore and Hong Kong rank high in labour market flexibility (Table 6.2). While Singapore has a compulsory Central Provident Fund (CPF) scheme, the employers' CPF contribution rate has been reduced thrice over the past three decades to reduce labour costs (Chew and Chew 2004). We are not too sure that this aspect has been taken into account in arriving at the labour market freedom index for Singapore. Singapore also promotes the flexible wage system, which is not captured by the index,[1] and this might move Singapore's labour market index higher than Hong Kong's if it were taken into account.

TABLE 6.1
The Labour Market Freedom Index of Selected OECD Countries

OECD Countries	Marginal Tax Rate (Low Rate means High Index)	Min Wage (Low Min means High Index)	Hiring and Firing Practices (Easy means High Index)	Centralized Collective Bargaining (Less Rigid means High Index)	Unemployment Benefits (Low means High Index)	Labour Market Freedom Index
USA	7	3.8	6.7	8.4	7.0	6.6
U.K.	6	4.6	4.9	8.6	6.5	6.1
Japan	5	4	4.2	7.4	6.8	5.5
Denmark	2	4.8	6.5	4.9	4	4.4
France	2	4.5	1.7	5.5	3.2	3.4
Germany	2	4.6	1.8	2.3	2.5	2.7

Source: Lawson and Bierhanzl (2004).

TABLE 6.2

The Labour Market Freedom Index of Hong Kong, Taiwan, and Southeast Asian Countries

Hong Kong, Taiwan and Southeast Asian Countries	Marginal Tax Rate (Low Rate means High Index)	Min Wage (Low Min means High Index)	Hiring and Firing Practices (Easy means High Index)	Centralized Collective Bargaining (Less Rigid means High Index)	Unemployment Benefits (Low means High Index)	Labour Market Freedom Index
Hong Kong	10	4.3	7.6	9.0	7.7	7.7
Indonesia	7	4.6	3.2	6.2	5.8	5.4
Malaysia	8	4.5	4.0	7.5	7.0	6.2
Philippines	7	4.4	3.3	6.9	5.7	5.5
Singapore	9	4.6	7.2	8.4	7.5	7.3
Thailand	7	3.9	4.6	6.5	6.5	5.7
Taiwan	7	3.8	4.6	8.0	6.2	5.9

Source: Lawson and Bierhanzl (2004).

The marginal tax rate in Southeast Asian countries is low, which contributes positively to labour market flexibility. Singapore has no minimum wage law, although there is a foreign worker levy. Indonesia, on the other hand, has a minimum wage law. In fact, the index indicates that all Southeast Asian countries, apart from Singapore, have some form of minimum wage law. It is necessary to review whether such a law is useful, as it may introduce distortions into the labour market. With regard to rules governing retrenchment, in all countries in Southeast Asia, with the exception of Singapore, it is not easy to dismiss workers. There is a need for countries such as Indonesia, Malaysia, the Philippines, and Thailand, to look into employment laws to see whether the rules governing retrenchment can be eased according to the needs of the labour market (but that would depend on the state of industrial relations, which will be addressed below). Generally, the labour market freedom index for each of the five Southeast Asian countries is respectably high, ranging from 5.4 for Indonesia to 7.3 for Singapore.

On the whole, the labour market freedom index of each of the Southeast Asian countries is not much better than that of the OECD countries, which are more competitive. This raises the issue of whether the labour market freedom index is an important factor affecting competitiveness. Table 6.1 reveals that the United States has a much higher labour market freedom index than Germany. Despite this, Germany still exports to the United States on the basis of comparative advantage. It may, therefore, be argued that the fact that the United States has a higher growth in GDP could be attributed to factors other than the country's higher efficiency in the labour market. However, it should be noted that a significant difference between the two countries is that, unlike the United States, Germany has to cope with a 10 per cent unemployment rate due to its inefficient labour market. Some may also point to the fact that China has enjoyed trade surpluses with many countries despite the fact that the Chinese labour market has not been efficient, especially in the 1990s. Again, this may be countered with the possibility that the Chinese economy could have been even more competitive if the Chinese labour market had been more efficient.

We are, therefore, of the view that labour market flexibility is an important factor affecting competitiveness. If a country has an inefficient labour market, it has to cope with a high unemployment rate, as evidenced in both Germany and China. The fiscal and related resources that will be used to reduce unemployment will erode the competitiveness of the country. Southeast Asian countries are developing countries and hence these countries should try to increase their labour market flexibility so as to enhance their competitiveness in the international market. As labour unions generally contribute to the inefficiency of the labour market in many countries, we shall now discuss the industrial relations approach to competitiveness.

The Industrial Relations Approach

The labour market environment, which determines the degree of labour market flexibility discussed in the preceding section, is the outcome of the interplay of various factors in the industrial relations system. Hence, in this section, we present the industrial relations approach. The industrial relations systems of different countries generally differ owing to differences in culture, social, economic and political developments, and government policies. These differences are reflected in the behaviour of trade unions, employers' associations, and the government, which are the three key participants in the industrial relations system of a country.

The behaviour of the government is of paramount importance to the type of industrial relations system that develops, especially in developing economies. An active government not only sets the ground rules for participation in the industrial relations system, but can also affect the behaviour of both the employers' association and the trade union. The most extensive form of government intervention is in terms of regulation, which in the developing world defines the playing field for the labour movement. The behaviour of the employers' association is the least complicated. Firms maximize profit and are mobile. In other words, they go wherever they can maximize profits. In the short run, employers feel the need to speak with one voice when they are confronted with a militant union.

The industrial relations system of a country is, to a large extent, dictated by the orientation of the labour movement at the macro level. This is because unions are able to influence the rules of industrial relations and these influences also reflect the interdependence between the government and the labour movement, in general, and the nature of government intervention or lack of it, in particular. In the literature, Deyo (1989), for instance, categorizes state-union relations in Asia as state corporate, state exclusionary, and state collaborative. Singapore is state corporate as the state is strong and the union is suppressed, but allowed into the decision making process. Malaysia, Thailand, and Indonesia are state exclusionary, meaning that the state is strong and unions are excluded from decision making in the industrial relations process (see also Kaur 2004). However, the impact of suppression or subordination on competitiveness is not that clear. In this chapter, we focus on the impact of the orientation of the labour movement on competition in selected countries in Southeast Asia using an approach that is quite different from Deyo's.

TRADE UNION OBJECTIVES AND STRATEGIES

With increasingly widespread globalization and rapidly advancing technology, trade unions generally are concerned about their impact on employment. Cormier and Targ (2000) find that employment growth under the United States-Canada FTA and NAFTA has been limited. There have been substantial job dislocations in the United States, Canada, and Mexico; moreover, income inequality has also increased in these three countries. Trade unions, therefore, must find ways to cope with the new environment in terms of an appropriate political and economic role in the economy.[2]

The political role exists because trade unions are a form of democratic institution. They serve as a check and balance against government and big businesses. Before trade unions can play that political role, however, they must become established, efficient, and democratic institutions themselves. Only then can they influence the government into pursuing more balanced policies that will ultimately protect the interests of the workforce. This political role of the trade unions is a means towards achieving the goal of raising the standard of living for the workforce, especially in developing countries. Researchers such as Morris and Fosh (2000) have attempted to measure trade union democracy. Some researchers, such as Smith et al. (1993), for instance, discover that union policy does not reflect the views of union members, indicating an absence of union democracy. Recently, in countries in Central and Eastern Europe, the labour movement has been involved in political reform (ILO 2005). The political role of the labour movement in these countries outshines its trade union role. As a result, the policy of attracting foreign investment in Central and Eastern Europe has not been too fruitful. As will be discussed later, Indonesia faces similar obstacles.

The extent and means by which trade unions fulfill the economic role depend on the orientation of the trade unions concerned. Traditional trade unions aim to protect the interest of union members in terms of a wage premium, which is obtained at the expense of growth in employment or employment level. Using U.S. data, Budd and Na (2000) discover that the union wage premium is about 12 per cent. Deere and Tracy (1994) find that higher union coverage is associated with slower employment and sales growth, decreased productivity in non-manufacturing firms, lower profitability, and less investment in R&D. Freeman and Kleiner (1999) find that trade unions do seek higher wage growth that will retard growth in employment, but not to the point of forcing firms to close. The trade unions covered in the studies cited are characteristic of the traditional trade union. Such unions rely on the creation of a wage premium to induce workers to join unions. They, therefore, cause wages to rise in the unionized sector, inevitably bringing about the retrenchment of some workers.[3] Retrenched workers will move to the non-unionized sector, depressing wages there, and also forcing some of the retrenched workers to join the informal sector. Hence, traditional trade unions may be regarded as micro-focused as they protect union members at the expense of other workers.

Under increasing globalization, micro-focused unions can only achieve this rather narrow objective at increasing social costs. This threatens the survival of the firm and the security of jobs. As Booth (1995) implies, employers who face competitive pressure resent micro-focused unions more than those who have a technological lead over their competitors. This explains why micro-focused unions do not generally support trade agreements, as is evident in Lowie's (1997) analysis of the U.S. labour campaign against NAFTA on the basis of fear of job losses, unfair suppression of labour rights in Mexico, cross-border solidarity, and international labour rights.

At the other end of the spectrum, other kinds of trade unions aim to promote employment stability. This type of trade union is macro-focused; that is, such a trade union aims to set wages at levels that will maximize employment. Macro-focused trade unions work closely with the government and firms to enhance competitiveness. With trade unions that are macro-focused, the standard of living will rise as wages rise in tandem with the prosperity of the country. Because of their emphasis on competitiveness, macro-focused trade unions help to ensure the survival of the firm and the security, as well as creation, of jobs. Using standard labour demand and labour supply analysis, micro-focused trade unions are expected to raise wages by moving upward along the demand curve for labour. In the case of macro-focused trade unions, however, the wage rate is determined at the point of intersection of the labour demand and supply curves. Macro-focused trade unions can raise wages by helping firms to raise productivity, which shifts the demand curve for labour upwards.

Macro-focused trade unions, however, face a survival problem. Workers find no incentive to join them as they can free-ride. This is because workers can enjoy the benefits that are generated by the macro-focused trade unions without joining these unions. Although free-riding exists for micro-focused trade unions as well because employers do apply collective bargaining benefits to non-union members (Harbridge and Wilkinson 2001), the free-rider problem is far more serious for macro-focused trade unions.

Macro-focused trade unions, therefore, need to find other means in terms of non-collective bargaining benefits to induce workers to join them. In the micro-focused environment, workers still join the unions, instead of free-riding, because of the presence of non-contractual benefits (Booth 1985; Naylor 1989, 1990; Olson 1965). But in the macro-focused environment, non-collective bargaining benefits are expected to be, and indeed must be, much more substantial because there is no wage premium to serve as the main incentive for joining unions.

The Micro-foundations of the Macro-focused Labour Movement

Unions at the plant level are by their very existence micro-focused. As mentioned above, unions can attract membership through two avenues: by creating a wage premium or by providing non-contractual services to members only. By far the bigger incentive that attracts union membership is the creation of a wage premium, which Booth (1995) refers to as the "monopoly role of trade unions".

Micro-focused unions face the problem of free riders because the collective bargaining agreement is a form of public good, which is available to all workers regardless of union status. However, as Booth (1995, p. 73) argues:

> The free rider problem is generally not considered insurmountable in small groups, as the benefits will not be achieved at all without cooperation, and it is easy with small numbers to subject potential beneficiaries to surveillance and control to ensure that they do not cheat. The larger the number of potential beneficiaries, the more difficult it is to overcome the free rider problem, because of exclusion and surveillance difficulties, and the less likely is the collective good to be provided.

Hence, micro-focused unions rely mainly on the wage premium to attract members, and use non-contractual services to minimize the free rider problem. In other words, union members enjoy a wage premium even while the union tolerates a few free riders.

At the plant level, union leaders perceive that the union does not provide gains at all by being macro-focused. That is, the perception is that attainment of full employment does not benefit the plant-level union. At the same time, union leaders perceive that by creating a wage premium at their plant they will not affect the attainment of full employment because theirs is just one of many unions in the economy. Furthermore, if some unions in the economy are micro-focused, unions which are macro-focused will lose out. This is the standard argument for imposing an incomes policy (Meade 1982).[4] Hence, at the plant level, union leaders have the tendency to create a wage premium as the main incentive to attract union membership; moreover, they themselves benefit from it personally. Thus, they are by nature micro-focused. Similarly, at the affiliated level, union leaders tend to be micro-focused.

This tendency implies that if the leaders of a macro-focused labour movement want to pursue the policy of not creating a wage premium at the individual plant level, they either subject the union leaders at the plant level to tight surveillance control and/or provide the unions at the plant level with some specific private goods (non-collective bargaining benefits), which branch unions can use to induce workers to join unions, and reduce or remove the incentive to create a wage premium. The latter is consistent with Olson's (1965) observation that a large group can exist despite the free rider problem, provided the group offers private goods and services accessible only to its members, with ancillary provision of the collective good as a by-product. Olson (1998) further adds: "Organizations that use selective social incentives to mobilize a latent group interested in a collective good must be federations of smaller groups" (p. 46). As the labour movement is a large group, in order for union leaders at the national level to be macro-focused, they must offer selective incentives to union leaders at the branch level as well as union leaders of affiliated unions to forgo the use of a wage premium to induce workers to join the unions.

In summary, the union federation must apply the following three steps to ensure that unions at the plant level are macro-focused: First, institute surveillance control. This may not be as difficult as it appears. Next, provide non-collective bargaining benefits to union members, and also enable workers at non-unionized firms to access those benefits. Finally, impose some sort of incomes policy or wage-fixing mechanism to prevent unions at the plant level from being able to create a wage premium.[5]

The preceding discussion shows that the macro-focused trade union is a strategic partner to the government in the latter's task of competing for foreign investments and in ensuring that labour is managed for competitiveness. The discussion to follow discusses the Singapore case to show how the macro-focused trade union model works to the advantage of the Singapore economy. We will use this case as a benchmark to examine labour market issues and their implications for how labour is managed in each of the four selected countries in Southeast Asia, namely Indonesia, Malaysia, the Philippines, and Thailand.

SINGAPORE

The labour movement in Singapore is represented by the National Trades Union Congress (NTUC). NTUC is a macro-focused union for the following two reasons: a symbiotic relationship exists between NTUC and the ruling party (People's Action Party, PAP)) that has governed Singapore since 1959, and it has been the tradition that the top leader of NTUC is at least a minister in the Cabinet of the Singapore Government; For instance, the present Secretary-General of the NTUC, Lim Boon Heng, is also a Minister Without Portfolio in the current cabinet.

As a macro-focused union, the NTUC promotes employment and training. This strategy is, as expected, well-supported by the government and the employers. NTUC has also openly supported the government's policy of attracting foreign professional and scientific talent, as well as foreign production and other workers, as this policy will induce more foreign investment in Singapore and consequently generate more good jobs. As Singapore is a small-, open economy, its GDP and labour demand fluctuate in tandem with the state of the world economy. In the recessions that affected Singapore in 1985 and 1998, when Singapore registered negative GDP growth rates, the government had, with the support of the NTUC, used labour cost reductions as an effective solution to prevent retrenchment.

Thus, the industrial relations system in Singapore is employment-driven because the unions are macro-focused (Chew and Chew 1995). This means that the labour market bears the burden of adjustment in an economic downturn. The employment-driven industrial relations system has been effective in enabling Singapore to recover quickly from economic slowdowns. This explains why the labour market freedom index for Singapore is very high. Indeed, if the CPF scheme and the flexible wage system had been adequately captured in the calculation, the index for Singapore might be the highest amongst the economies studied. This has only been possible with NTUC being a macro-focused union. Using the Singapore case, the relationship between the orientation of the labour movement and competitiveness can now be summarized, as shown in Table 6.3.

In order to ensure competitiveness, wage increases should be based on market forces, rather than on collective bargaining tactics. Furthermore, if the industrial relations system is geared towards minimizing variation in employment, then the wage system would be sufficiently flexible and hiring

TABLE 6.3
Trade Union Regimes and Competitiveness

	Micro-focused	*Macro-focused*
Objective	Promote interests of union members	Full employment
Wage increase	Collective bargaining outcome	Outcome of increase in competitiveness
Effectiveness in solving unemployment	Poor	Effective
Hiring policy	Conservative	Needs of the economy
Free ridership	None	High
Real-in-time system for factory	Impossible	Able to implement
Social security scheme	Unemployment benefits scheme	Employment-based, such as the CPF scheme
Exchange rate regime	Seeks to allow the exchange rate to float more freely	Seeks to avoid appreciation of the currency to ensure employment growth

practices would also be demand determined. On these three counts, macro-focused trade unions do better than micro-focused trade unions.

If cordial industrial relations exist, then the real-in-time system, which is more efficient for competitiveness, can be implemented. Under micro-focused unions, however, it is not possible to apply this system as it is possible for unions to blackmail firms since there would be no inventory that could serve as a buffer for firms. In contrast, since macro-focused unions aim for greater efficiency in production in order to ensure higher demand for labour, firms can implement the real-in-time system, with complete assurance that the unions will not use the lack of an inventory to hold them to ransom. Where social security schemes are concerned, countries in which micro-focused unions operate have an unemployment benefits scheme that provides handouts to the unemployed. However, in countries where macro-focused unions operate, the social security scheme is employment-based, such as the CPF in Singapore. Because of this difference in the social security scheme, countries in which micro-focused unions operate can afford to permit the home currency to appreciate, which is not the case for countries in which macro-focused unions operate.

MALAYSIA

Malaysia was a Third World success story until the 1997 Asian financial crisis. For over two decades, Malaysia relied on both natural resources and export competitiveness to achieve high GDP growth. In the Malaysian industrial relations system, the government is quite powerful, and the labour movement is fragmented. The main labour federation is the Malaysian Trade Union Congress (MTUC), but there are other federations such as the National Union of Newspaper Workers and the Malaysian Labour Organization, which has the support of the government (Kuruvilla and Arudsothy 1995). Syed (1995) states that "union leaders tend to be oligarchic, controlling several unions simultaneously in an interlocking manner and not fully committed to serving the interests of workers" (p. 78).

Malaysian industrial relations are also overshadowed by political developments. Malaysia has three main ethnic races, namely Malays, Chinese, and Indians. In the 1960s, Malays constituted 54 per cent of the population, while Chinese and Indians accounted for 37 per cent and about 10 per cent, respectively. While the Chinese have done well economically in Malaysia, politics is in the control of the Malays. Following the communal violence after the 1969 elections, the Malaysian government, which is dominated by the ethnic Malay party, UMNO, implemented the New Economic Policy (NEP), which was designed to increase the Malay share of corporate ownership from 2.4 per cent in 1970 to 30 per cent by 1990. Norrizan (1999) points out that "the economic disparities between the Malay and Chinese communities in the early days of independence led to the formulation of New Economic Policy (NEP)" (p. 307).

The NEP formed the basis of the Bumiputra policy that accorded privileges to the Malays.[6] This policy (reformulated in 1990 as the National Development Policy, which also maintained privileges for ethnic Malays, though at a reduced level) has long been associated with ethnic-based regulations such as the following:

- An employment quota of 30 per cent for Malays, which allowed firms to qualify for import protection and tax holidays.
- Government contracts are reserved for Malay-owned firms, and all firms are required to set aside 30 per cent of their shares for ethnic Malays.
- In addition to the policy of sending Malays students on scholarship abroad to study, 55 per cent of public university enrolment is reserved for Malay students (these quotas no longer apply, at least officially).

As a result of policies such as these, labour market competitiveness has been affected. Moreover, Chinese and Indian employees are grossly under-represented in the public sector. Many Chinese and Indian professionals have also felt discriminated against and have emigrated, and many more work outside Malaysia, including the 200,000 Malaysians who work in Singapore. Due also to the high birth rate among ethnic Malays, the population composition has changed in favour of the Malays. It is now estimated that Malays account for over 65 per cent of the population, while the Chinese account for about 28 per cent or less.

The onslaught of globalization is likely to force the Malaysian government to modify such ethnic-based policies to place greater emphasis on meritocracy for the following three reasons: Firstly, to compete effectively with other countries, especially China, the best brains and the best workers are needed. Secondly, it is not possible to compete successfully if some of the workers are not trained, or worse, if the best workers are driven away to work in other countries that compete against Malaysia. Moreover, as the proportion of Malays in the population increases, the Bumiputra policy becomes less relevant.

In summary, it can be said that labour market flexibility in Malaysia is adversely affected by the fact that wage payments can be said to be influenced not only by collective bargaining tactics, but by political factors as well, rather than by market forces alone. Moreover, an employment policy based to a large extent on ethnic-based criteria such as the Bumiputra policy, can undermine labour competitiveness.

THAILAND

Thailand was also a Third World success story until the 1997 crisis. In Thailand's industrial relations arena, a serious problem confronting Thai labour unions has been the lack of leadership and solidarity. The labour movement is more fragmented compared to the Malaysian situation as there are eight labour congresses in the country. According to Levine (1997), leaders of the congresses work for their self-interests rather than for the labour movement.

Hence, unions in Thailand are not only micro-focused, but weak, divided, and fragmented (Brown 2004). In the 1990s, a few attempts were made to improve the effectiveness of the unions by focusing on, among other things, democratization of the unions to ensure transparency in decision-making and to ensure that leaders are more accountable to the rank-and-file, and emphasizing training and skills development programmes (*The Nation*, 28 January 1996). Brown (2004) argues that at the turn of the twenty-first century, the Thai labour movement, facing criticism, has undertaken a process of revaluation and reorganization and has also made concerted efforts to improve health and safety at the workplace.

Although multinational companies have been criticized in Thailand and in the West for exploiting Thai workers, they do comply with the labour laws of the country and offer good pay and pensions in Thailand. In fact, it is the owners of small firms who are the most common abusers of labour laws, with most of the hardship and privation falling on Thailand's 3.5 million women factory workers (Levine 1997).

With globalization, firms in Thailand face three options according to Levine: Relocate plants to China or other lower-cost regions; trim labour costs by using small firms that do not adhere to labour laws; and increase the skills level through training. Policymakers see the third as the only viable option for the country. The government and the labour movement need to work together with employers to find niches for Thai exports by educating Thais and training Thai workers effectively. However before this can be achieved, the quality of the Thai labour movement needs to be improved.

In summary, Thailand's labour market flexibility is adversely affected by (a) unions that are micro-focused, with union leaders more concerned with individual benefits than the labour movement or country; (b) wage payments that are affected by collective bargaining tactics, especially in the smaller firms; and (c) a lack of good training schemes to improve the skills of the Thai workforce.

INDONESIA

According to Soeprobo and Tjiptoherijanto (2001), the changes in government in Indonesia since the downfall of the Soeharto government in May 1998 led to more freedom in Indonesian economic and social life. The labour movement in Indonesia too benefited from these changes. Through the abolition of the one-union policy, the new government has provided more opportunities for unionists to establish free and independent organizations. Consequently, the number of unions and union members increased substantially since 1998.

Although the number of unions has increased, most of them are not well established and their quality is perceived to be low (Soeprobo and Tjiptoherijanto 2001). The labour movement has improved only in terms of quantity rather than quality and effectiveness. The FSPSI, formerly known as All Indonesia Workers Union Federation and the only workers' union endorsed by the government, is still superior to other unions, for instance, in the number of affiliates and provincial networking.

Currently, unions in Indonesia tend to be micro-focused in terms of getting more members, but their effectiveness is not high. They are more excited about enjoying the freedom of organizing. The unions are not democratically managed, and union orientation is dictated by leaders who may have micro interests in mind. The industrial relations system in Indonesia needs a stable political and economic environment before unions can play a significant role in the country.[7]

In the case of Indonesia, labour market flexibility is low because (a) the labour movement is fragmented and micro-focused and the unions are more concerned with labour rights than with competitiveness, and (b) the weak economic and political environment, including periods of social and political unrest and uncertainty, makes it difficult for firms to operate.

THE PHILIPPINES

The Philippines has the longest history of industrialization in Southeast Asia. But the Philippine economy has not been performing well (Sicat 1970; Ofreneo 1995). The Philippines' industrialization started with import substitution in the 1950s and switched to export-oriented industrialization in the 1970s. However, both phases of industrialization met with a balance of payments crisis. Consequently, an externally-imposed Structural Adjustment Programme (SAP) was adopted in the 1980s, which called for the wholesale liberalization of the economy and the removal of the remaining protection for import substitution industries. According to Ofreneo (1995), the timing of the SAP was a disaster. It coincided with the recession in 1980–83 and the depression in 1983–85. He concludes that both Export Orientation and Structural Adjustment Programme strategies failed to achieve the twin goals of greater industrialization and job creation for the Philippine economy.

At the same time, the Philippine trade union scene is badly divided. According to Ofreneo (1994), there are about eight labour centres and 140 labour federations and thousands of independent unions. Inter- and intra-union rivalry is the worst in the Philippines. One has to conclude that unions in the Philippines look after their own narrow interests and few have the macro interest at heart. West (1997) examines whether unions should agitate for bread and butter issues, or act as social movements, as agents of broad social change in the context of the most militant contemporary labour movement in the Philippines. She further states that "the US was great at exporting forms of political democracy to the Philippines, but it did not export economic democracy" (p. 202). But many countries in the region did enjoy economic democracy, and in the case of Singapore, with the aid of macro-focused unions.

In terms of human resource development, the Philippines has probably achieved the most in Southeast Asia. Also, because their professionals speak English, the Philippines has become the largest exporter of professionals to countries in Asia and beyond. The export of Filipino professionals in such large numbers suggests that the industrial relations system in the country does not operate to suit Philippine interest. With globalization and intensified competition, one would expect to see even more Philippine nationals working aboard. However, before the industrial relations climate can be reformed to attract foreign investment, better law and order in the country is needed. The recent spate of kidnappings involving business tycoons and their families does not help to promote the country as an attractive place for foreign investment.

In short, labour market flexibility in the Philippines is adversely affected by (a) micro-oriented unions and inter- and intra-union rivalry; (b) a weak legal and political environment; and (c) lack of a conducive environment for economic development and productivity enhancement.

CONCLUSION

As globalization spreads, there is a tendency worldwide for unions to become macro-based. However, for unions to be macro-based, a common interest must be arrived at between the government and the labour movement. Attempts to build a common interest, however, may be lacking in some countries. Singapore presents a classic example of a country in which unions are macro-based. In contrast, trade unions in Malaysia and Thailand are not macro-based. The labour movements in these countries have not functioned as a tool in enhancing the respective country's competitiveness and hence in enhancing job opportunities for workers. It is possible for Malaysian and Thai unions to evolve into macro-based institutions in the near future, provided a common interest between the government and the labour movement can be established. In the case of Indonesia and the Philippines, the labour movements in these two countries have been a liability in attracting foreign investment.

Notes

1. See Chew and Chew (2005) on the flexible wage system in Singapore.
2. See Lowie (1994) for an analysis of trade unions' objections to NAFTA.
3. See Disney and Gospel (1989) for the implications of the Seniority Model of Trade Unions.
4. See also Olson's (1965) examination of this issue concerning collective action.
5. See Chew and Chew (1998) for details on these issues.
6. Wad (1998) also discusses this issue.
7. For more discussion on trade unions and the new Indonesia, see Hadiz (1997).

References

Booth, A. "A Public Choice Model of Trade Union Behaviour and Membership". *Economic Journal* 94, no. 376 (1984).
———. "The Free Rider Problem and A Social Custom Theory of Trade Union Membership". *Quarterly Journal of Economics* 100 (1985): 253–61.
———. *The Economics of Trade Unions*. Cambridge: Cambridge University Press, 1995.
Brown, Andrew. *Labour, Politics and the State in Industrializing Thailand*. London: Routledge Curzon, 2004.
———. "The Wage Policy of Firms: Comparative Evidence for the US and Germany from Personnel Data". *International Journal of HRM* 16, no. 1 (2005): 104–19.

Budd, J. and I.G. Na. "The Union Membership Wage Premium for Employees Covered by Collective Bargaining Agreements". *Journal of Labour Economics* 18, no. 4 (2000): 783–807.

Chew, Rosalind. *Wage Policies In Singapore: A Key to Competitiveness*. International Labour Organization, Asian Pacific Project On Tripartism, 1996.

Chew Soon Beng. *Trade Unionism in Singapore*. Singapore: McGraw-Hill, 1991.

Chew Soon Beng and Rosalind Chew. "Industrial Relations in Singapore". *Singapore Economic Review*, Singapore 34, no. 2 (1989).

———. *Employment-Driven Industrial Relations Regimes: The Singapore Experience*. London: Avebury, 1995.

———. "Singapore's Responses to Globlisation and Regional Competition". In *Globalisation and World Economic Policies: Studies Highlighting Effects and Policy Responses of Nations and Country Groups*, edited by Clem Tisdell. Serials Publications, 2004.

———. "Wage Issues and Human Resources in Singapore". *Journal of Comparative Asian Development* 4, no. 2 (2005).

Chiu, Stephen and David Levin. "Stagnation or Revival of Hong Kong Trade Unionism? Implications of Recent Trends in Membership and External Union Structure". *Employment Relations Record* 1, no. 1 (2001).

Cormier, D. and H. Targ. "Globalization & the North American Worker". *Labour Studies* 26, no. 1 (2000): 42–59.

Crouch, Colin. *The Politics of Industrial Relations*. Glasgow: Fontana/Collins, 1979.

Dabscheck, Graham. "A Survey of Theories of Industrial Relations". In *Theories and Concepts in Comparative Industrial Relations*, edited by J. Barbash and K. Barbash. Columbia, Carolina: University of South Carolina Press, 1989.

Deyo, F.C. *Beneath the Miracle: Labour Subordination in the New Asian Industrialism*. Berkeley: University of California Press, 1989.

Dunlop, J. *Industrial Relations Systems*. Carbondale: Southern Illinois University Press, 1958.

Ferner, A. and R. Hyman. *Changing Industrial Relations in Europe*, edited by A. Ferner and R. Hyman. Oxford: Blackwell, 1998.

Fields, Gary. S. Trade *and Labur Standards: A Review of the Issues*. Paris: Organization for Economic Cooperation and Development, 1995.

Freeman, R. and M.M. Kleiner. "Do Unions Make Enterprises Insolvent?" *Industrial and Labour Relations Review* 52, no. 4 (1999): 510–27.

Hadiz, V.R. *Workers and the State in New Order Indonesia*. London: Routledge, 1997.

ILO Online. *New Social Dialogue in Central and Eastern Europe*. Geneva: ILO, 2005/9.

Harbridge, R. and D. Wilkinson. "Free riding: Trends in Collective Bargaining Coverage and Union Membership Levels in New Zealand". *Labour Studies Journal* 26, no. 3 (2001): 51–72.

Hodgkinson, A. and C. Nyland. "Space, Subjectivity and the Investment Location Decision: the Case of Illawarra". *Journal of Induistrial Relations* 43, no. 4 (2001): 438–61.

International labour Organization. *National Tripartite Consultative Mechanisms in Selected Asian Pacific Countries.* Asian Pacific Project on Tripartism, Geneva: ILO, 1994.

Kaur, Amarjit. *Wage Labour in Southeast Asia since 1840.* London: Palgrave, 2004.

Kuruvilla, S. and P. Arudsothy. "Economic Development Strategy, Government Labour Policy and Firm Level Industrial Relations Pratices in Malaysia". In *Employment Relations in the Growing Asian Economies*, edited by A. Verma, T. Kochan, and R. Lansbury, pp. 158–93. London: Routledge, 1995.

Lawson, R.A. and Bierhanzl. "Labour Market Flexibility: An Index Approach to Cross-Country Comparison". *Journal of Labour Research* 25, no. 1 (2004): 117–26.

Levine, D. *Workers' Rights and Labor Standards in Asia's Four New Tigers: A Comparative Perspective.* New York: Plengm Press, 1997.

Lim Chong Yah and Associates. *Policy Options for the Singapore Economy.* Singapore: Mcgraw-Hill, 1998.

Lim Chong Yah. *Southeast Asia: The Long Road Ahead.* Singapore: World Scientific, 2001.

Lowie, Jefferson. "National Struggles in a Transnational Economy: A Critical Analysis of US Campaign Against NAFTA". *Labour Studies Journal* 21, no. 4 (1994): 3–32.

Meade, J.E. *Wage-Fixing.* London: George Allen and Unwin, 1982.

Morris, H. and P. Fosh. "Measuring Trade Union Democracy: The Case of the UK". *Civil and Public Service Associated* 38, no. 1 (2000): 95–114.

Naylor, R. "Strikes, Free Riders and Social Customs". *Quarterly Journal of Economics* 104, no. 4 (1989): 771–86.

———. "A Social Custom Model of Collective Action". *European Journal of Political Economy* 6 (1990): 201–16.

Norrizan Razali. "Human Resource Development in Malaysia: The Government Role". *ASEAN Economic Bulletin* 16, no. 3 (1999): 307–29.

Ofreneo, E. Rene. "The Labour Market, Protective Labour Institutions and Economic Growth in the Philippines". In *Workers, Institutions and Economic Growth in Asia*, edited by Gerry Rodgers. Geneva: Intertional Zinstitute for Labour Studines, 1994.

———. "Philippine Industrialization and Industrial Relations". In *Employment Relations in the Growing Asian Economies*, edited by A. Verma, T. Kochan, and R. Lansbury, pp. 194–241. London: Routledge, 1995.

Olson, M. *The Logic of Collective Action.* Cambridge, MA: Harvard University Press, 1965.

———. "Group Size and Group Behavior". In *Managing the Commons*, edited by J.A. Baden and D.S. Noonan, pp. 39–50. Indiana: Indiana University Press, 1998.

Pan, Shih Wei. "Trade Union Movement in Taiwan: Struggling between Markets and Institutions". *Employment Relations Record* 1, no. 1 (2001).

Park, Young Bum. "Financial Crisis and Unions in Korea". *Employment Relations Record* 1, no. 1 (2001).

———. "A Comparative Study on Employment Protection in Korea and Other OECD Countries". Unpublished monograph, 2005.

Raynauld, Andre and Jean-Pierre Vidal. *Labour Standards and International Competitiveness*. Cheltenham: Edward Elgar, 1998.

Schmitter, P.C. "Still the Century of Corporatism". In *Trends Toward Corporatist Intermediation*, edited by P.C. Schmitter and G. Lehmbruch. Beverly Hills: Sage Publications, 1974.

Seifert, H. and H. Massa-Wirth. "Pacts for Employment and Competitiveness in Germany". *Industrial Relations Journal* 36, no. 3 (2005): 217–40.

Sicat, Gerardo P. *Economic Policy and Philippine Development*. Quezon City: University of the Philippines Press, 1972.

Smith, P., P. Fosh, R. Martin, H. Morris, and R. Undy. "Ballots and Union Government in the 1980s". *British Journal of Industrial Relations* 31, no. 3 (1993): 365–82.

Soeprobo, T. and P. Tjiptoherijanto. "Labour Union in Crisis: An Indonesian Experience". *Employment Relations Record* 1, no. 1 (2001).

Syed Hussein Ali. "Economic Take-off: Trade Unions in Malaysia". In *Globalization and Third World Trade Unions*, edited by Thomas Heck, pp. 63–79. London: Zed Books, 1995.

Verge, P. "How Does Canadian Labour Law Fare in a Global Economy". *Journal of Industrial Relations* 42, no. 2 (2000): 275–94.

Wad, Peter. "The Japanization of the Malaysian Trade Unions Movement". In *Trade Unions and the New Industrailization of the Third World*, edited by Roger Southha, pp. 210–29. University of Ottawa Press, 1988.

West, L.A. *Militant Labor in the Philippines*. Philadelphia: Temple University Press, 1997.

PART THREE

Competitiveness and the Social Dimension

7

LABOUR REGULATIONS IN SOUTHEAST ASIA
Boon or Bane for Competitiveness?

Carolina S. Guina

INTRODUCTION

Labour market policies are a critical element of national strategies for economic growth because of their potential to create employment and income opportunities that can ultimately help reduce poverty. Increasing competition in the global market place however, has raised the challenge of crafting labour market policies that are both socially responsive and economically viable. This suggests a precarious balance in the manner by which labour market policies should be formulated. In the context of global competition, labour regulations and standards have emerged as a critical factor in attracting foreign direct investments (FDI). They are generally associated with higher labour costs that could erode the competitiveness of firms. In their bid to attract foreign investments, countries could choose to relax labour standards and "race to the bottom", to the detriment of the labour force. Differences in labour regulations and their enforcement could thus provide a cost advantage in internationally traded goods.

This chapter reviews the empirical evidence on the impact of labour regulations on international competitiveness. It presents this review in the light of increasing pressure for countries to attract foreign investments and be competitive in exports as part of the strategy to sustain economic growth. The evidence suggests that carefully designed and well-implemented labour standards can generate long-term macroeconomic gains that far outweigh short-run cost adjustments for the firm. There is scope for crafting labour policies that protect workers rights without impinging on desired economic outcomes.

LABOUR MARKETS IN SOUTHEAST ASIA

Asia's labour force was estimated at about 1.75 billion in 2005, representing more than half of the world's labour force (Asian Development Bank (ADB) 2005). The People's Republic of China (PRC or China) and India account for more than 70 per cent of this market while the ASEAN countries comprise about 15 per cent. Asia's labour market is projected to reach 2.2 billion in 2015. Relatively high rates of unemployment and underemployment remain persistent in many Asian countries and are at higher levels than before the 1997 Asian financial crisis. Some ASEAN countries such as Indonesia, the Philippines, and Thailand have witnessed an expansion of employment in the informal sector despite increases in per capita incomes. In 2003, unemployment rates in China and India stood at 4.7 per cent and 7.9 per cent, respectively. Among the ASEAN countries, Indonesia and the Philippines have the highest unemployment rates (Table 7.1).

Asia's huge labour market and robust economic performance in recent years have made it an attractive destination for FDI. To lure foreign capital, Asian economies have adopted comprehensive policy reforms — dismantling trade barriers, privatizing state enterprises, and reforming labour markets. At the core of labour market reform is the call for increasing flexibility in labour regulation to reduce costs for firms so that they can become more competitive in world markets.

Many Asian countries fear that the entry of China into the global economy could adversely affect their ability to absorb an expanding domestic labour force. Since its entry into world markets, China has been one of the largest recipients of FDI, which amounted to $60.6 billion in 2004, or about a quarter of FDI flows to all developing countries. There is a widely held view that the surge of FDI flows to the PRC has been at the expense of Southeast Asian countries. It has been argued, however, that this may not necessarily be the case considering that FDI patterns of growth

TABLE 7.1
Labour Force Estimates of Selected Asian Countries
(in millions)

	2005	*2015*	*2030*
ASEAN	**270.3**	**315. 6**	**357.2**
Cambodia	7.0	8.8	11. 6
Indonesia	106.3	121.6	136.4
Lao PDR	2.8	3.6	5.0
Malaysia	10.7	13.2	15.7
Myanmar	26. 1	30.3	33.2
PRC	785.9	842.4	812.9
Philippines	34.1	42.5	52.3
Singapore	2.1	2.4	2.1
Thailand	37.1	40. 1	40.8
Vietnam	44.0	53. 0	60.0
PRC (China)	**785.9**	**842.4**	**812.9**
India	**460.2**	**550.8**	**654.3**
Total Asia & the Pacific	**1, 748.0**	**1,992.5**	**2,173.0**
% Share of ASEAN	15.4	15.8	16.4
% Share of PRC and India	71.3	70.0	68.0

Source: ADB Key Indicators (2005).

and decline for both China and ASEAN are similar, and that ASEAN's major investors, namely Japan, the United States and the European Union have consistently invested in ASEAN (Wu et al. 2002). The PRC has itself been posting substantial FDI outflows (mostly directed at other Asian developing countries), reaching $6.9 billion, $2.5 billion, and $1.8 billion, in 2001, 2002, and 2003, respectively. Notwithstanding these trends, the shift in the pattern of FDI flows in Asia is clearly evident. United Nations Conference on Trade and Development (UNCTAD)'s Inward Performance Index[1] indicates that Singapore, Malaysia, Thailand, the Philippines, and Indonesia were less able to attract FDI in the period 1998–2000 compared with the period 1988–90. The PRC, Hong Kong, and Vietnam have shown that they are increasingly able to do better in attracting FDI (Table 7.2).

TABLE 7.2
UNCTAD Inward FDI Performance Index

Country	1988–90		1998–2000	
	Value	Rank	Value	Rank
Singapore	13.8	1	2.2	18
Hong Kong	5.4	4	5.9	2
Malaysia	4.4	8	1.2	44
Thailand	2.6	26	1.3	41
Myanmar	1.9	36	0.6	82
Philippines	1.7	39	0.6	89
Vietnam	1.0	53	2.0	20
Taipei, China	0.9	58	0.3	112
PRC	0.9	61	1.2	47
Indonesia	0.8	63	–0.6	138
South Korea	0.5	93	0.6	87
Japan	0.0	128	0.1	131
ASIA	1.07		0.85	

Source: UNCTAD, *World Investment Report 2002.*

KEY CONCEPTS IN LABOUR MARKET POLICIES

The theory underlying interventions in labour markets is that free labour markets are imperfect, and that as a consequence, there are rents in the relationship between employers and workers (Botero et al. 2003). Governments intervene in labour markets to ensure that the market functions efficiently and fairly. Efficiency means that individuals willing to work are likely to find jobs that match their skills and educational qualifications, while fairness means that workers are paid a wage that is commensurate with his/her "worth" measured in terms of productivity. The nature and degree of government intervention in labour markets vary widely and are dependent on social, economic, and political considerations.

Government interventions in the labour market can be through active and passive policies and programmes. Active labour market policies are those that aim to put people to work, while passive labour market policies are those that extend protection to workers. Active labour market programmes include direct employment generation schemes, labour exchanges or employment services, and skills development programmes. Passive policies include interventions that relate to unemployment insurance, income support, and labour protection. (ADB 2003).

Active labour market policies are directed at enhancing employment although specific interventions can have different outcomes on the labour market and on labour productivity. For instance, Bechterman, Olivas, and Dar (2004) cite the positive impact of employment services (counseling, job market, and placement) on employment and earnings, but cites a more limited impact of training for the unemployed. Micro-enterprise and self-employment assistance can have some positive impact, but generally, only for educated workers. Bechterman, Olivas, and Dar conclude that for active labour market policies to be effective, they should be part of a comprehensive package, oriented to labour demand and linked to workplaces, and should be carefully targeted.

Passive labour policies are generally associated with labour regulations and standards aimed at protecting workers. They may be categorized into (i) core labour standards; (ii) employment-related standards; and (iii) standards related to social protection (Table 7.3). Core labour standards are the universally agreed

TABLE 7.3
Categories of Labour Protection Policies

Core Labour Standards	Terms of Employment	Social Protection for Labour
Prohibition from forced labour	Minimum wage	Protection from arbitrary dismissal
Prohibition of child labour	Standard work hours	Severance pay
Providing equal opportunity and prohibition against discrimination	Establishment of overtime hours and compensation	Disability benefits
Freedom to form associations for collective bargaining	Compensation for accident	Pension and retirement insurance
	Occupational health and safety	Survivor's compensation
	Alternative employment contracts	Unemployment benefits
	Maternity leave	

Sources: International Labour Organization (2003); Modified from Rodgers and Berik (2006).

minimum acceptable guarantees of human rights in the work place forged
by the international community acting through the International Labour
Organization (ILO). The four core labour standards include: (i) eliminating
all forms of forced or compulsory labour, (ii) abolishing child labour,
(iii) providing equal opportunity and non-discrimination in employment, and

TABLE 7.4
Some Basic Arguments for and against Labour Regulations

Arguments for Labour Regulation	*Arguments against Labour Regulation*
Prohibition against child labour supports the objective of investing in human capital through education, which could impact positively on FDI in the long run.	Prohibition against child labour will deprive families of additional sources of income and the opportunity to rise out of poverty.
Union rights and collective bargaining provide a platform for dialogue with workers that can promote workplace stability and industrial peace.	Industrial bargaining compresses the wage structure and can result in inefficiencies if increases in wages are not linked to productivity.
Setting minimum wages promotes decent jobs and reduces poverty among workers.	Minimum wages, unless linked to productivity, can distort the market price of labour and lead to inefficiencies in the labour market.
Regulatory interventions protect workers from arbitrary action and provide employment stability, promotes long-lasting work relationships, and encourages firms to invest in the long-term development of their workforce.	Restrictive legislation on hiring and firing can curtail business responsiveness to rapidly changing conditions, and could eventually result in a decline in investments.
Promoting health and safety conditions in the workplace, regulating working time, and encouraging paid leave can benefit workers in the formal sector and, by promoting better working conditions and motivation, can contribute to productivity.	Stringent job security measures can raise the cost of reorganizing the firm in times of economic downturns or when growth enhancing technologies are required.

(iv) ensuring freedom of association and the right to collective bargaining. The second set of policies pertains to terms of employment. They cover (i) minimum wages; (ii) standard work hours; (iii) overtime hours and compensation; (iv) compensation for accident; (v) occupational health and safety; (vi) alternative employment contracts; and (vii) maternity leave. The third set of policies relates to social protection, intended to protect workers against vulnerability and risks associated with the hazards of work interruption and loss of income. They include (i) provisions for job security (protection from arbitrary dismissal); (ii) pension and retirement compensation; (iii) survivor's compensation; and (iv) unemployment benefits.

The extent to which compliance with labour regulations and standards has affected FDI and exports has triggered much debate. The debate has basically centred on the extent to which labour market interventions affect competitiveness (that is, the impact of labour market interventions on costs and productivity). Micro-econmic theory argues that a highly regulated labour market has the potential to limit the demand for labour. As firms find it difficult to expand, the potential for job creation is reduced, thus limiting the opportunities for decent jobs made possible through protective legislation in the formal sector. A highly protective labour market regime is often associated with increasing employment in the informal sector, which is generally not covered by labour laws. At the macro level, it is argued that compliance with labour legislation and standards can enhance competitiveness through higher macroeconomic gains and long-run social benefits. In fact, there have been successful cases of export strategies that combine the enforcement of labour standards with higher productivity. Table 7.4 outlines some of the basic theoretical arguments for and against labour regulations.

THE IMPACT OF LABOUR REGULATIONS ON COMPETITIVENESS: A REVIEW OF THE EMPIRICAL EVIDENCE

A review of the literature seems to confirm the "divide" between the macro and micro arguments concerning the impact of labour standards. A study of the effects of labour standards on FDI location by Rodrik (1996) finds no evidence that FDI tends to locate in countries with lower labour standards and refutes the "conventional wisdom" that low labour-standard countries are a haven for foreign investors. Kucera (2001) similarly concludes that no solid evidence exists to support the widely held view that lower labour standards have an adverse impact on FDI flows. Kucera's study builds on the findings of Rodrik by using newly constructed measures of labour standards that focus on actual (as opposed to legislated) workers' rights and uses them in an econometric model of FDI flows and manufacturing wages for 127 countries. The macro perspective in these two studies contrasts with the views from a firm-level survey conducted by the World Bank, where labour regulations are generally perceived to be a major constraint to expansion and growth (World Bank 2005).[2]

The following sections examine the empirical evidence on the impact on FDI of specific labour regulations dealing with child labour, trade unions, minimum wages, and job security. In general, investigations on the impact of these variables indicate that compliance with labour regulations results in at least a neutral, if not a positive, efficiency gain at the macro level.

Child Labour

Although an increasing number of countries have signed the ILO convention on core labour standards in recent years, child labour and other forms of indiscriminate employment are still widespread in many developing countries.[3] It is estimated that one out of six children aged between five to seventeen years is at work in many developing economies (World Bank 2005). Children at work are basically deprived of education, and consequently, the opportunity for future earnings.

Evidence presented by Galli and Kucera (2002) has shown that a reduction in the levels of child labour creates a more positive environment for economic growth. Higher levels of investment are also associated with lower incidence of child labour. In Vietnam for example, increases in family income brought about by rapid economic growth and significant FDI inflows in recent years have led to a reduction in child labour. Foreign firms are generally discouraged from investing in countries with potentially low level of skills which is likely to be the case where child labour is tolerated or allowed. Investors are thus more likely to locate in countries that invest comprehensively in human capital through education, and adopt labour policies that allocate skills efficiently in the economy. Investment, in turn, increases the demand for human capital because as firms meet new opportunities and acquire better access to new technologies, their demand for skilled workers increases, thus allowing them to engage in growth-enhancing activities.

Trade Unions and Collective Bargaining

Trade unions are important platforms for representing the rights of workers. It is generally the norm that unionized workers enjoy higher wages, greater job security, and receive more training than non-unionized workers. Collective bargaining improves communication among workers, and with their employers, which could lead to a lower incidence of strikes (Adit and Tzannatos 2002). Trade unions' ability to negotiate for wage premiums may impact differently, depending on the conditions of the labour market and the socio-economic context of the countries in which they function. In recent years, the emergence of global networks and regional coalitions has also begun to influence and leverage the workings of trade unions.

The evidence linking trade union rights and economic growth is varied. It has been observed that the East Asian miracle during the first half of the 1990s happened in countries where the role of labour unions was largely suppressed, suggesting that restricting trade unions could be a factor contributing to economic growth (ADB 2005). Freeman (1993) has argued that there is no robust empirical evidence regarding the role of labour unions; the fact that they were suppressed during the 1980s does not necessarily imply that this restriction contributed to stability and economic growth. Other works indicate either a statistically insignificant relationship, or a positive net effect between trade unions and economic growth. In a study of over a hundred countries, Kucera (2001) found that higher labour costs, associated with freedom of association and collective bargaining, did not adversely affect FDI. Kucera thus argues that there is a need to take a broader view of workers' rights beyond that of the labour cost-productivity nexus.

One perspective is to view workers' rights as positively contributing to greater political and social stability through freedom of association, and to a better quality of human capital with respect to issues of child labour and gender inequality. In a recent cross-country analysis, Kucera and Sarna (2006) showed that neither trade openness nor export success could be attributed to the curtailing of union rights. In fact, the relationship between manufacturing exports and trade union rights is positive, suggesting that union rights offer greater stability and offset the negative effects associated with higher labour costs.

Minimum Wages

Minimum wages are set by governments to afford workers a decent pay and to reduce poverty among workers. Wage setting practices, either through collective bargaining or initated by the government, directly affect labour costs and consequently the decision of firms on the combination of factor inputs. As part of their competitive strategies, many countries are now assessing wage setting policies and moving into more flexible and pluralistic wage-setting practices such as linking minimum wages with firm performance, and having wider social representation in the wage setting process.

In many developing countries, non compliance with minimum wages is widespread and is linked with the capacity of enforcement mechanisms (ADB 2005). Its effectiveness as a policy tool has been questioned on the grounds of distorting the distribution of wages and productivity. A study by Bird and Manning (2002) concluded that higher and binding minimum wages led employers to hire fewer workers; relatedly, they raised the possibility that higher severance pay would make it more costly for firms to fire workers. However, Freeman (1993) claims that there is little evidence to the claim that an enforced minimum wage reduces employment, observing that in many developing countries, minimum wages are set too low to have much effect. He concludes that where unemployment rates are very high, minimum wages are not enforceable as both workers and employers will have an incentive not to comply with the law. Negotiated wages, on the other hand, could curtail employment growth if wages are above the market clearing rate. He observed that the sharp drop in real wages in a number of developing countries is an indication that wages could adapt when required.

Based on a study of 199 countries, Forteza and Rama (2002) conducted a regression analysis comparing economic growth and the rigidities in the labour market (as measured by minimum wages, cost on mandated benefits, strength of the labour market movement, and the size of government employment). The results of the regression analysis indicate, among other things, that minimum wages and mandated benefits do not appear to hinder economic growth. At the same time, they found that minimum wages and mandated benefits were irrelevant to the success of economic reform measures, and such being the case, it may be useful to concentrate reform efforts in other areas such as fiscal policy, the dismantling of trade barriers, and financial regulation.

Labour Protection: Job Security and Social Insurance

Labour protection measures are intended to safeguard the rights of workers from arbitrary dismissal (job security), and minimize the vulnerability and risks associated with the hazards of job interruption and loss of income (retirement compensation and pensions). Job security measures impact on the employment cycle by reducing the rate (and cost) of turnover to firms. On the other hand, strong job security policies can also limit workers' flexibility as well as the firm's in pursuing expansion, especially in new technology fields. Overly strict regulations can raise the cost of reorganizing the firm during economic slowdowns (Bertola 1999) or when growth-enhancing technologies are required. Rigidities in job security policies can, therefore, affect a firm's decision to invest or expand operations as it could potentially erode their competitive edge. Since new firms are often better at harnessing new technologies than incumbent firms, stringent regulations can reduce the potential for the entry of new investments (World Bank 2005).[4]

Freeman (1993) debunks this argument by citing that the negative impact of job security is not compelling or at most, uncertain. While he found evidence of countries realizing significant employment growth with the relaxation of job security regulations, there are also countries where such relaxation have not had much impact. OECD (1999) studies, in fact, indicate that there is a strong association between employment protection legislation and more stable employment regimes. Galli and Kucera (2004) studied both the short- and long-term effects of labour protection legislation and observed that if a country were to relax job security measures, the immediate impact would be an increase in worker dismissals with a subsequent increase in employment in the informal sector. However, as firms face relatively lower costs with worker dismissals, there could be a net gain in formal-sector employment as firms restructure the composition of their workforce.

The foregoing review of a variety of empirical studies suggests that compliance with labour regulations, in particular, those pertaining to child labour, trade unions, minimum wages, and job security, do not hinder economic growth and FDI, or at most, have neutral effects on these variables. While labour regulations may have short-term costs for the firm, the long-run gains in terms of a more stable investment environment far outweigh the adjustment costs. This reinforces the importance of looking at labour market policies in the context of broader strategies, including efforts to foster a more skilled and adaptable workforce. Well-crafted labour regulations, within the context of wide economic reforms, will have the potential to bring about positive benefits for the economy in the long run.

LABOUR REGULATIONS IN SOUTHEAST ASIA: A COMPARATIVE VIEW

A look at how selected Southeast Asia countries fare in terms of their labour protection policies can be made based on the worker protection scorecard developed in the study of Botero et al. (2003), which compared labour laws of eighty-five countries across Asia, Latin America, and Africa, as well as those of the industrialized countries. The Botero study codified data on employment laws (for individual employment contracts), industrial, and labour relations laws (that relate to collective bargaining), and social security laws (those that involve social response to the needs of, and conditions pertaining to, quality of life, such as maternity leave, unemployment pay, etc.) A higher score was assigned when a regulation was seemingly more protective to workers.

Based on Botero's data set, regional comparisons between Asia, Latin America, Africa, and the industrialized countries were summarized in the ADB Key Indicators Report (2005). The regional comparisons indicate that in terms of employment laws, Asia is not markedly different from the other regions except in severance pay and the cost of firing workers, where it scored as more restrictive. With respect to collective bargaining, Asia is also not very different from the other regions except for strikes, which are not considered illegal even when there are collective bargaining agreements. For social security laws, Asia is also not markedly different from the other regions. Most Asian countries have mandatory minimum wages. Asia has the same union density (proportion of workers affiliated) as in the Latin America and African regions, and about half that of the industrial countries.

Details of the data for five ASEAN countries, as well as Hong Kong, Taipei, and Korea are reflected in Table 7.5. For employment laws, the ASEAN countries differed in terms of the number of days of paid leave and the cost of increasing hours worked. The cost of firing workers is lowest in Malaysia and Hong Kong and about the same for the rest of the Asian countries. Malaysia has the highest duration of fixed-term contracts, followed by Singapore. Third party approval prior to a dismissal of a redundant employee is required only in the Philippines and Indonesia. In terms of paid mandatory holidays and the maximum number of hours worked per week, the scores for all countries are about the same.

Collective or industrial relations in ASEAN countries are generally reflected in the restrictions on the right to strike. These include prohibiting strikes while a dispute is under conciliation, mediation, or arbitration, and the prohibition of strikes for political purposes and in essential industries. To promote workplace flexibility and efficiency, there has been a movement towards adoption of enterprise-based unions (as opposed to national level unions). What is common across these kinds of strategies is the focus on national level stability and workplace-level flexibility, both of which are key ingredients from the perspective of the foreign investor. The methods for reaching these goals, however, vary among the ASEAN countries (Kuruvilla, Gibson, and Osborne 1998).[5]

In Table 7.5, collective relations laws are reflected in two dimensions: labour union power and collective disputes.[6] A score of 1 indicates a pro-

TABLE 7.5
Scores on Worker Protection in Selected Asian Countries

Variables	ASEAN					Other Asian		
	Sin	Mal	Thai	Phil	Ind	HK	Tpe	Korea
Employment Laws								
Part-time workers are not excluded from mandatory benefits of full-time workers (no. 1)	1	1	1	1	1	1	1	1
It is not easier or less costly to terminate part-time workers than full-time workers (no. 2)	1	1	1	1	0	1	1	1
Fixed-term contracts are only allowed for fixed-term tasks (no. 3)	1	0	0	0	0	0.0	0	0
Maximum duration of fixed-term contracts (no. 4)	0.63	0.88	0.00	0.00	0.00	0.00	0.00	0.63
Days of annual leave with pay in manufacturing (no. 5)	14	16	6	5	10	10	24	28
Paid mandatory holidays (no. 6)	11	10	13	12	12	11	10	12
Maximum number of hours per week (no. 7)	44	48	48	48	40	48	48	44
Cost of increasing hours worked (no. 8)	0.14	0.06	0.03	0.01	0.42	0.00	0.09	0.19
Legally mandated severance payment (redundancy) (no. 9)	12.90	2.14	25.70	12.9	25.8	8.60	12.9	12.8
Cost of firing workers (no. 10)	0.60	0.19	0.63	0.57	0.68	0.18	0.61	0.62
The employer needs the approval of a third party prior to a collective dismissal (no. 11)	0	0	0	1	1	0	0	0
The employer needs the approval of a third party to dismiss one redundant worker (no. 12)	0	0	0	1	1	0	0	0

TABLE 7.5 (continued)

Variables	ASEAN					Other Asian		
	Sin	Mal	Thai	Phil	Ind	HK	Tpe	Korea
Collective Relations Laws								
Labour Union Power								
Right to unionization (no. 13)	0	0	1	1	0	1	0	1
Right to collective bargaining (no. 14)	0	0	1	1	0	0	1	1
Employers have the legal duty to bargain with unions (no. 15)	1	0	1	1	1	0	0	1
Workers' councils are mandated by law (no. 16)	0	0	0	0	0	0	1	1
Collective Disputes								
Wildcat strikes are legal (no. 17)	1	0	0	1	1	1	0	0
A strike is not illegal even if there is a collective agreement in force (no. 18)	1	1	1	0	1	1	0	0
Compulsory third-party arbitration during a labour dispute is mandated by law (no. 19)	1	1	0	1	1	0	1	1
Employers are not allowed to fire or replace striking workers (no. 20)	1	1	1	1	1	0	1	1
Civil Rights								
Mandatory minimum wage (no. 21)	0	0	1	1	1	0	1	1
Political Variable								
Union density (no. 22)	0.24	0.10	0.10	0.12	0.01	0.22	0.35	0.14

Source: Botero et al. (2003), as cited in ADB Key Indicators (2005).

worker regime. In terms of labour union power, Korea's labour unions are most powerful when it comes to protecting workers' rights, the Philippines and Thailand come in as close seconds. Malaysia is the least pro-worker, scoring zero for all four variables, followed by Indonesia which scored zero in three variables. As regards collective disputes, the laws of Indonesia and Singapore reflect a pro-worker bias scoring 1 in all four variables. Malaysia and the Philippines are next with a score of one in three variables. Among the five ASEAN countries, Singapore has the highest union density while Indonesia has the lowest.

In Table 7.6, the scores on worker protection in ASEAN and three other Asian countries are compared with the Inward FDI Performance Index and the 2003 unemployment rates to determine whether certain patterns emerge with respect to worker protection regimes, FDI attraction, and labour market outcomes (unemployment rates). On the basis of the worker protection scores, Singapore and Malaysia seem to combine both institutional and market-oriented approaches to labour protection. Thailand, the Philippines, and Indonesia have followed a more institution-oriented approach.

Based on Table 7.6, there seems to be no clear pattern linking worker protection to labour market outcomes. Unemployment rates in Singapore and Malaysia increased slightly over the period 1999 to 2003; while those for the Philippines and Indonesia experienced significant deterioration. One reason for this could be the relatively weak institutional capacities in these two countries to implement the reform process. Hence, it is possible that regulations are either not binding, or compliance is weak. As regards the impact on inward FDI, Singapore and Malaysia's ranking as FDI destinations improved significantly compared with other Asian economies with a similar mix of labour market structures. It would seem that some countries with different experiences in terms of labour outcomes have similar labour market policies and vice versa. Hence, it would not be easy to make generalizations about ASEAN's labour policies.

Taking a historical perspective, Kuruvilla, Gibson, and Osborne (1998) observe that despite variations among countries, certain patterns of industrial relations seem to emerge over time. Three primary factors account for this development: (a) the similarity between ASEAN nations in terms of the linkage between industrial relations and economic development; (b) the similarity of their current labour relations systems on critical dimensions such as workplace flexibility and union voice; and (c) the similarity and the complementary nature of the economic development strategies undertaken in the region. He observes that industrial relations policies during the stage of import substitution strategies were pluralistic for many ASEAN countries.

TABLE 7.6
Worker Protection Scores, Unemployment and FDI

Country	EL	LUP	CD	MMW	UD	Inward FDI Performance Index 1988–90	1998–2000	Unemployment Rate (%) 1999	2003
ASEAN									
Singapore	3	1	4	0	0.24	13.8	2.2	3.6	4.6
Malaysia	2	0	3	0	0.10	4.4	1.2	3.4	3.6
Thailand	2	3	2	1	0.10	2.6	1.3	3.0	1.8
Philippines	4	3	4	1	0.12	1.7	0.6	9.4	10.2
Indonesia	3	1	4	1	0.01	0.8	−0.6	6.4	9.5
Other Asia									
Hong Kong	2	1	2	0	0.22	5.4	5.9	—	7.9
Taipei	2	2	2	1	0.35	0.9	5.0	—	5.0
Korea	2	4	2	1	0.14	0.5	3.4	—	3.4

Notes:

EL — Employment Laws. For employment laws, five variables with 0 to 1 scores were selected from Botero's data. These are variables 1, 2, 3, 11, and 12 in Table 7.5. The score ranges from 5 to 0, depending on the number of variables for which a country scored 1 (pro-worker). Five (5) thus represents a pro-worker orientation (maximum protection) and 0 indicates least protection (most market-oriented).

LUP — Labour Union Power. For this item, a similar approach was followed as in employment laws. Variables 13, 14, 15, and 16 were taken from Table 7.5.

CD — Collective Disputes. The same approach for EL and LUP was applied. Variables 17, 18, 19, and 20 were taken from Table 7.5.

MMW — Mandatory Minimum Wage. Variable 21 in Table 7.5. The score of 1 indicates the presence of minimum wage legislation, which is pro-worker. Zero indicates the absence of minimum wage laws.

UD — Union density. Variable 22 in Table 7.5. Number of workers affiliated with unions over number employed.

Sources:

Worker Protection Scores: Botero et al (2003) in *ADB Key Indicators 2005*;
Inward FDI Performance Index: UNCTAD, *World Investment Report 2002*;
Unemployment Rates of ASEAN Countries: *ASEAN Statistical Yearbook, 2004*;
Unemployment Rates of other Asian countries: *ADB Key Indicators 2005*

During the period of low-cost, export-oriented industrialization, policies tended to be more restrictive of workers rights. As the ASEAN economies moved up the ladder of competition, the strategy for industrial relations began to focus more heavily on skills development. With the exception of Singapore, however, the influence of labour has not improved with this transition since restrictions on labour union rights seem to have continued. Even in cases where they have been eased, labour has not been able to adapt easily to strengthen its voice.

The wide variations in ASEAN labour policies could possibly explain why no labour market harmonization initiative has emerged under the ASEAN Free Trade Area (AFTA), unlike in the North American Free Trade Agreement (NAFTA)[7] and the European Union. The capacity to enforce labour laws in ASEAN countries also varies widely. Moreover, labour laws in the new ASEAN member countries (Cambodia, Laos, Myanmar, and Vietnam) are still in the rudimentary stage. For instance, Vietnam has only recently enacted its labour code, and Laos and Cambodia have codes that do not yet approximate the standards of the more advanced nations in ASEAN.

The concept of labour markets in Vietnam, being a transition economy, is relatively new. It was not until the *Doi Moi* (modernization) in 1986 that Vietnam had a "labour market". Labour market reforms were gradually initiated until a Labour Code was passed in 1994. Although comprehensive on paper, the Labour Code suffers from limited coverage (only labourers who have a signed labour contract are covered), uneven applicability (resulting from the proliferation of other laws), and weak compliance (especially in four key areas — labour contracts, social insurance, minimum wages, and labour unions). As the Labour Code is fairly recent, and because Vietnam is still in the process of learning to become a market economy, a more rigorous assessment of its labour market policies is in order. To improve its labour markets further, future policies should focus on enhancing opportunities for non-farm employment, building human capital, and strategies for industrial restructuring.

Case studies of Indonesia and the Philippines (ADB 2005*b*) serve to illustrate how factors beyond labour market policies could impinge on labour market outcomes as well as the operations of firms. In Indonesia, labour market policies following the 1997 crisis and the shift to democratically elected governments have moved sharply in the direction of stronger workers' rights, raising concerns about their possible adverse effects on investments. A survey of manufacturing firms revealed 23 per cent of the managers interviewed reporting labour market policies to be a constraint on their operations (ADB 2005*a*). Two elements of the country's new labour policies were particularly contentious — increases in the minimum wage and severance pay. Compounding the impact of higher minimum wages is the fact that under the policy of decentralization, minimum wages are set by the regional governments, which could result in arbitrariness. Apart from labour policies, the case study reports other key factors constraining the growth of formal-sector employment in Indonesia. Based on a survey of manufacturing enterprises, these factors include political uncertainty, macroeconomic instability, tax rates, and the cost of finance. In addition, business regulations in Indonesia are among the most cumbersome in Asia (World Bank 2004a) — a disincentive for investors and a limiting factor for the growth of employment in the formal sector.

The Philippines represents a classic case of "jobless growth". Despite a GDP growth rate of 6.1 per cent in 2004, unemployment was very high at 12 per cent of the labour force, and underemployment was 17 per cent of the total employed. The fundamental problem is that the labour supply is growing faster than the number of jobs created. Three elements in the Labour Code are perceived to be creating difficulties for employers, namely: (i) labour relations and the protection of permanent and unionized workers; (ii) laws relating to labour contracts, in particular, restrictions to subcontracting arrangements, and security of tenure; and (iii) minimum wages. With respect to minimum wages, in particular, the wage setting process is considered to be complex and cumbersome. Minimum wages are differentiated by sector and by region, encouraging labour migration to urban areas where wages are generally higher. Wage adjustments also tend to maintain the level of real wages, and disregard the fact that relative wages may have changed. The perceived rigidities in the Labour Code, however, may not be the sole factor constraining employment creation considering the high incidence of Labour Code violations, and the increase in the number of non-regular workers.

THE CHALLENGES AHEAD

The foregoing discussion suggests that the impact of labour market reforms on employment and FDI is based on the interplay of a wider set of factors. There is little argument that social protection in the labour sector in terms of guaranteed wages, freedom of association, freedom from compulsory work, prohibition against child labour, and prevention of gender discrimination, are beneficial. The extent, however, to which these interventions will translate into long-term macroeconomic gains will depend on the country's larger development agenda as well as the economic, social, and political milieu in which these policies operate.

Policy Challenges at the National Level

Policymakers generally face three major challenges in further improving their labour market policies, namely: (i) ensuring the sustainability of labour regulations and social protection measures in the wake of increased pressures for competition; (ii) enhancing governance aspects as they affect the structure and processes of labour market reforms; and (iii) linking labour market policies with a wider human development strategy.

The first challenge arises from the intense competition for FDI. The evidence reviewed in this chapter suggests that lower labour costs and the absence of rigid regulations do not necessarily affect the potential of a country to attract FDI. Therefore, the "race to the bottom" that is commonly feared need not take place. Labour market reforms that tend to weaken social protection through inferior wages and working conditions could result in social inequities and low levels of human capital that could ultimately discourage investors. From the perspective of improving the investment climate, labour market reforms should provide opportunities and incentives for firms to invest productively, create jobs, and expand.

Governments can take the following three steps to ensure labour market interventions benefit all workers: (i) encourage wage adaptability and ensure workers are properly compensated for their work; (ii) ensure that workplace regulations reflect a good institutional fit; and (iii) balance workers' preference for employment stability with firms' need to adjust to the market (World Bank 2005). Admittedly, striking a balance between promoting job creation and protecting existing jobs or workers is not easy, particularly during periods of economic slowdown when the long-term benefits of increased employment and wages are often clouded by short-term concerns for jobs and wage security. Thus, alongside policies to promote employment in the formal sector, extending social protection policies for those employed in the informal sector should also be promoted. Well-targeted social protection programmes such as micro-finance and micro-insurance schemes have been found to be beneficial and should be developed. Ultimately, successful reforms should be able to bring about higher wages and better working conditions — as well as higher employment and lower unemployment and informality in the long run.

The second challenge pertains to the need to strengthen the structures and processes of governance. Weak institutions can undermine labour regulations and could result in weak compliance. When compliance is weak, as it is in many developing countries, stringent regulations do not reduce the size of labour reallocation, but they do change its nature and reduce its effectiveness

(World Bank 2005). Decentralized implementation at the local levels can further exacerbate the problem because of the risk of uneven application of labour regulations as well as the lack of implementation capacity of the local units. Governance mechanisms should take into account the political economy of trade unions and collective bargaining mechanisms as dynamic factors influencing labour market outcomes. Nascent private sector and business associations, as well as civil society organizations, especially in the transition economies, could also influence the outcome of labour market policies.

A third and very important challenge is the need to complement labour market policies with a strategy for human capital development. Building a country's comparative advantage on low wage costs could result in a low-productivity, low-skills feature, which has proven to be a disincentive to investors. Today's globalized world requires skills-intensive and innovative approaches to production, since high product quality has become the norm. The level of competencies, or the quality of the workforce, rather than labour cost, has now become a major determinant of the type and level of investments in a country. The level of knowledge, skills, and attitudes of the workforce are in turn shaped fundamentally by education policies and the overall strategy for human development.

Implications for ASEAN Cooperation

Global and regional institutions and networks are likely to have a pervasive influence on national policies. For ASEAN in particular, the goal of economic integration compels an assessment of ASEAN labour markets from the perspective of regional production in key priority sectors. Wage differentials in the input and output markets, mutual recognition and skills certification, and harmonized social insurance schemes are some of the key issues that would need to be addressed.

The present trends in labour movements within ASEAN attest to the still strong historical links between the countries as well as the differences in their pace of economic growth. The faster growing economies such as Singapore and Malaysia have tended to attract greater numbers of migrant labour from the other ASEAN countries. There are also patterns of migration to Thailand from Laos, Myanmar, and Cambodia, mostly in the unskilled labour categories. However, as the ASEAN countries move up the value chain, and with the current initiative to promote mobility of professional and skilled labour within ASEAN, new patterns of intra-ASEAN migration are likely to emerge. A closer look at the FDI-labour migration nexus would be increasingly important. Present attempts to develop indicators of ASEAN labour market integration will be initially useful in this regard.

Recognizing fully the potential social risks of economic integration, ASEAN has adopted a comprehensive social agenda — the ASEAN Socio-Cultural Plan of Action — centred on the need to manage the social impacts of economic integration.[8] The agenda consists of: (i) enhancing human resource development through the networking of skills, training institutions, and the development of regional assessments and training programmes; (ii) strengthening the capacity of governments to monitor labour markets and monitor human resource indicators; and (iii) promoting social protection and social risk management systems. The inclusion of health services as one of the eleven priority sectors for vertical integration will also require strategies to address the impact of liberalization in the health sector. In addition, the development of mutual recognition arrangements could facilitate labour mobility in the region, and will support the realization of the ASEAN Economic Community.

While ASEAN cooperation has vigorously pursued an active and comprehensive agenda in liberalizing the movement of goods and capital flows (that is, FDI, and more recently, financial integration) it has proceeded more cautiously in the area of labour market cooperation. The Vientiane Plan of Action sets the direction for promoting social protection systems and social risk management systems, but concrete plans of action in these areas are still evolving. A specific regional initiative that is emerging is the development of mutual recognition arrangements for professional credentials as a means to foster regional mobility of labour. Other ASEAN initiatives in the labour sector are in the nature of networking arrangements for occupational health and safety, and joint projects in skills training and exchanges. The ASEAN countries are also considering the formulation of a regional framework of collabouration for sound and harmonious industrial relations, addressing priorities such as labour management, wages, and productivity in the light of globalization and trade liberalization.[9] Whether this regional framework will ultimately lead to a harmonized framework for labour market interventions remains to be seen.

Notes

1. The Inward FDI Performance Index, as presented by UNCTAD in *World Investment Report 2002*, compares the relative performance of countries in attracting FDI. An index of >1 implies that a country is receiving more FDI, while an index of <1 may indicate that the business environment may be protectionist or technologically backward.

2. Based on the World Bank's World Business Environment Survey of seventy-three firms as cited in the World Development Report, 2005, pp. 147–49.
3. Even if an ILO Convention is ratified, the degree to which it is enforced is uncertain, since ILO does not have the power to enforce these conventions. Moreover, in many cases, national legislation is required to implement the provisions of these conventions.
4. The World Bank Development Report 2005 (p. 149) cites data for nineteen developed and developing economies which indicate that countries with more flexible hiring and firing rules experience significantly higher entry rates of small firms (but not microenterprises, often exempt from such regulations or managing to avoid them). Stringent rules also tend to discourage foreign direct investment (FDI), especially in countries where rules are opaque and enforcement is uncertain.
5. Kuruvilla, Gibson, and Osborne (1998) cite Singapore as perhaps the only ASEAN country where the goals of stability and flexibility have been achieved without significant erosion of workers' voice in decision making. While Singapore's unions have relatively little voice at the workplace (given the restrictions on the subjects of bargaining), the tripartite framework in Singapore ensures that unions have considerable voice at the national level.
6. The union densities for Cambodia, Lao PDR, and Vietnam are not reflected in Table 5. Kuruvilla, Gibson, and Osborne (1998) observe that the union densities for these countries are rather high; however, implementation may have been compromised by weak implementation and state opposition.
7. In NAFTA for example, there is a "Supplemental Agreement on Labour Cooperation", which avoids setting standards, but encourages members to promote many areas of labour market policies and enforce laws and regulations pertaining to such areas as: (i) freedom of association and protection of the right to organize; (ii) the right to bargain collectively; (iii) the right to strike; (iv) prohibition of forced labour; (v) labour protection of children and young persons; (vi) adherence to minimum employment standards; (vii) elimination of employment discrimination; (vii) no gender discrimination for pay; (ix) safeguards for prevention of occupational injuries and illnesses; and (x) compensation in cases of occupational injuries and illnesses.
8. The Tenth ASEAN Summit held in Vientiane, Lao PDR in November 2004 agreed on a comprehensive social agenda — the ASEAN Socio-Cultural Plan of Action — as part of the Vientiane Action Plan.
9. Joint Communique. 18th ASEAN Labour Ministers Meeting, 18–24 May 2004, Bandar Seri Begawan, Brunei Darrusalam.

References

Adit, T. and Z. Tzannatos. *Unions and Collective Bargaining: Economic Effects in a Global Environment.* Washington, D.C.: World Bank, 2002.

ASEAN Labour Ministers Meeting (ALMM). Joint Communique of the 18th ALMM, Bandar Seri Begawan, Brunei Darrusalam, 18–24 May 2004.

Ashwani Saith. "Social Protection, Decent Work and Development". *DP/152/2004*, Institute of International Labour Studies, Geneva, 2004.

Asian Development Bank (ADB). *Social Protection*. Manila: ADB, 2003.

————. *Key Indicators. Special Chapter on Labour Markets in Asia*. Manila: ADB, 2005*a*.

————. *Asian Development Outlook 2005*. Special Chapter on Labour Markets in Asia: Promoting Full, Productive and Decent Employment. Manila: ADB, 2005*b*.

Betcherman, Gordon, Amy Luinstra, and Makoto Ogawa. "Labour Market Regulation: International Experience in Promoting Employment and Social Protection". Social Protection Discussion Paper Series No. 0128, Washington D.C., November 2001, pp. 28–29.

Betcherman, Gordon, Karina Olivas, and Amit Dar. "Impacts of Active Labour Market Programs: New Evidence from Evaluations with Particular Attention to Developing and Transition Countries". Social Protection Discussion Paper 0402, Washington, D.C., January 2004, pp. 58–59.

Bertola, Guiseppe. "Microeconmic Perspective on Aggregate Labour Markets." In *Handbook of Labour Economics*, Vol. 3B, edited by O. Ashenfelter and D. Card, pp. 2985–3028. Amsterdam: North Holland Publishers, 1999.

Bird, Kelly and Chris Manning. "Impact of Minimum Wage Policy on Employment and Earning in the Informal Sector: The Case of Indonesia". Paper presented at the 8th Convention of the East Asian Economic Association, Kuala Lumpur, 4–5 November 2002.

Botero, Juan, Simeon Djankov, Rafael La Porta, Florencio Lopez de Silanes, and Andrei Shliefer. "The Regulation of Labour". *NBER Working Paper No. 9756*. June 2003.

Busse M. and S. Braun. "Trade and Investment Effects of Forced Labour: An Empirical Assessment". *International Labour Review* 142, no 1 (2003): 49–71

Dar, Amit and P. Zafiris Tzannatos. "Active Labour Market Programs: A Review of the Evidence from Evaluations". Social Protection Discussion Paper no. 9901, Washington, D.C., January 1999.

De Neubourg, Chris. "Incentives and the Role of Institutions in the Provision of Social Safety Nets". Social Protection Discussion Paper No. 0226, The World Bank, Washington. D.C., January 2004, pp. 11–17.

Dennis, David J. and Zainal Aznam Yusof. "Developing Indicators of ASEAN Integration: A Preliminary Survey for a Roadmap (Final Report)". REPSF Project 02/001. ASEAN Secretariat, August 2003.

Forteza, Alvaro and Martin Rama. "Labour Market 'Rigidity' and the Success of Economic Reforms Across More than One Hundred Countries". Unpublished. August 2002.

Freeman R. "Labour Market Institutions and Policies: Help or Hindrance to Economic Development". World Bank Annual Conference on Development Economics 1992, World Bank, Washington, D.C, 1993, pp. 117–44.

Henk, Thomas. "Trade Unions and Development". DP/100/1999. Institute of International Labour Studies. Geneva, 1999.

International Labour Organization (ILO). *Towards an Integrated Market in Southeast Asia: The Trade Union Agenda*. Labour Education No 117. Geneva: ILO, 1999.

————. *Every Child Counts: New Global Estimates on Child Labour*. Geneva: ILO, 2002.

————. *Key Indicators of the Labour Market*. 3rd ed. Geneva: ILO, 2003.

Kucera, David. "The Effects of Core Workers Rights on Labour Costs and Foreign Direct Investment: Evaluating the 'Conventional Wisdom'". DP/130/2001. Institute of International Labour Studies. Geneva, 2001.

Kuruvilla, Sarosh, Bryan Gibson, and Corrine Osborne. "Regional Integration and Industrial Relations in AFTA". Cornell University, 1998.

Organization for Economic Cooperation and Development (OECD). *Employment Outlook*. Paris: OECD, 1989.

————. *Employment Outlook*. Paris: OECD, 1999.

Rodrik, Dani. "A Labour Standards in International Trade: Do They Matter and What Do We Do About Them?". In *Emerging Agenda for Global Trade: High Stakes for Developing Countries*, edited by Robert Lawrence, Dani Rodrik, and John Whalley. Washington, D.C.: Overseas Development Council, 1996.

Susangkarn, Chalongphob. "ASEAN Beyond AFTA: Initiatives in Labour Market Cooperation and Integration". Thailand, *TDRI Quarterly Review*, 12, no. 2 (September, 1997): 3–8.

UNCTAD. *World Investment Report 2002*. UNCTAD: Geneva, 2002.

Van der Meulen Rodgers, Yana and Günseli Berik. "Asia's Race to Capture Post-MFA Markets: Snapshot of Labour Standards, Compliance, and Impacts on Competitiveness". *Asian Development Review* 23, no. 1 (2006): 55–88.

World Bank. *Doing Business in 2004: Understanding Regulation*. Washington, D.C.: World Bank, 2004.

————. "Workers and Labour Markets". In *World Development Report*, Ch. 7, pp. 136–156. Washington, D.C.: World Bank, 2005.

Wu, Friedrich, Poa Tiong Siaw, Yeo Hn Sia, and Puah Kok Keong. "Foreign Direct Investments to China and Southeast Asia: Has ASEAN Been Losing Out?". *Economic Survey of Singapore*, 3rd Quarter 2002, pp. 96–115.

Yussof, Ishak and Rahmah Ismail. "Human Resource Competitiveness and Inflows of Foreign Direct Investments into the ASEAN Region". *Asia Pacific Development Journal* 9, no. 1 (2002).

8

SOCIAL SECURITY POLICY IN AN ERA OF GLOBALIZATION
Challenges for Southeast Asia

Mukul G. Asher and Amarendu Nandy

INTRODUCTION

Globalization is a multi-faceted phenomenon covering the economic, political, social, and cultural dimensions. It is not a new phenomenon, and does not have a standard definition. In economic terms, globalization may be broadly defined as the shrinkage of economic distances, that is, the ease with which each element in the production-distribution-information-communication process and trade flows can be located over large geographical distances. Three broad trends comprise the current phase of globalization. First, advances in transportation, information, and communication technologies, including the internet; second, a strong tendency towards global, regional, bilateral, and unilateral economic liberalization;[1] and third, the rebalancing of the state-market mix towards the latter, and greater recognition of the complementary role each plays.

Most countries, including those in Southeast Asia, have concluded that globalization is an irreversible process, which they need to manage with the objective of emerging as net winners. In particular, as China and India continue to pursue greater integration with the world economy, the Southeast Asian countries are experiencing increased competition for markets, foreign capital, and manpower. Simultaneously, these two potential economic giants also offer considerable opportunities for the Southeast Asian countries to participate in their economic growth.

It is generally accepted that globalization has made safety nets even more essential for at least three reasons. First, for cushioning the burden of restructuring; second, for increasing the political legitimacy of economic reforms; and third, for enabling risk-taking by individuals and firms by providing a floor level income in the event that rewards from risk-taking do not materialize. As they have embraced globalization, it is, therefore, not surprising that social security reform has become an important public policy issue in the Southeast Asian countries in recent years. The 1997 East Asian crisis underscored the need for adequate social safety nets (World Bank 2000). Demographic trends manifested in rapid individual and population ageing,[2] globalization and associated changes, urbanization, industrialization, and changing family structures and attitudes all suggest that formal social security systems will become necessary in Southeast Asia (Asher 2002). As these systems have long lead times before they can provide adequate retirement income support in a sustainable manner, there is considerable urgency in initiating the reform process.

This is, therefore, an appropriate juncture to assess recent social security reforms in Southeast Asia, and suggest future directions. To make the discussion manageable, this chapter takes a narrower view of social security, focusing only on retirement financing.[3] It thus excludes other elements usually considered to be part of social security such as health care, unemployment compensation, workmen compensation, food and fuel subsidies, disaster relief and others. The importance of these other areas of social security should not be underestimated.

The rest of the chapter is organized as follows. The next section discusses the objectives of a social security system and outlines a possible framework for social security reforms that are particularly relevant for countries in Southeast Asia. Following this, the discussion focuses on the wide divergences in the philosophy of social security systems in Southeast Asia, and the extent to which the core functions of the relevant social security organizations are being performed satisfactorily. The chapter next turns to outlining the main challenges facing Southeast Asian policymakers in reforming their respective social security systems in an era of globalization and competition, which will likely involve complex trade-offs. In particular, the issues of coverage, adequacy, administrative efficiency and transparency, and governance and regulatory matters pertaining to provident and pension funds in selected Southeast Asian countries, will be discussed before some concluding thoughts on this topic are offered.

OBJECTIVES OF SOCIAL SECURITY SYSTEMS AND THE FIVE PILLAR FRAMEWORK

The core objectives of any social security system, for both individuals and government, are to smooth consumption over a lifetime, through insurance (particularly against longevity and inflation risks),[4] income redistribution, and poverty relief. However, these have to be traded off against economic growth, labour market efficiency and flexibility, and against other needs such as health, education, and infrastructure. Individual, fiscal, and societal affordability should also be kept in mind when reforms to social security systems are considered. This implies, therefore, that benefits promised must evolve over time as affordability grows.

There are five core functions which any social security organization must perform (Ross 2000): (a) reliable collection of contributions, taxes, and other receipts, including any loan payments; (b) payment of benefits for each of the schemes in a timely and correct way; (c) securing financial management and productive investment of provident and pension fund assets; (d) maintaining an effective communication network, including development of accurate data and record keeping mechanisms to support collection, payment, and financial activities; and (e) production of financial statements and reports that are tied to providing effective and reliable governance, fiduciary responsibility, transparency, and accountability. In most developing countries, organizational reforms aimed at performing the above five tasks in a more professional and effective manner are a prerequisite for broader systemic reform.

At the systemic level, a well-designed social security system should be broad based, that is, it has to be *adequate* both in terms of coverage and the range of risks covered; it needs to be *affordable* from the individual, business, fiscal, and macroeconomic perspectives; it must be actuarially sound and *sustainable* for a period of seventy years or more; it needs to be *robust* to withstand macroeconomic and other shocks; and it must be able to provide reasonable levels of post-retirement income[5] (as determined by a considered evaluation of alternatives and trade-offs within society), coupled with a *safety net* for the elderly poor.

As for a pension system, its main role is to pay out pensions to the retired. However, the impact of pension arrangements on economic efficiency, incentives to work and save, achieving fiscal consolidation and flexibility, international competitiveness, lowering labour market distortions, as well as on financial and capital markets, should also be considered. As social security reform is a process that spans a decade or more, sequencing and scalability

TABLE 8.1

Multi-Pillar Pension Taxonomy of the World Bank

Pillar	Target Groups			Characteristics	Main Criteria	
	Lifetime Poor	Informal Sector	Formal Sector		Participation	Funding/Collateral
0	X	x	x	"Basic or "Social pension", at least social assistance, universal or means-tested.	Universal or Residual	Budget/general revenues
1			X	Public pension plan, publicly managed, defined-benefit or notional defined-contribution.	Mandated	Contributions, perhaps with financial reserves
2			X	Occupational or personal pension plans, funded defined-benefit or funded, defined-contribution.	Mandated	Financial assets
3			X	Occupational or personal pension plans, funded defined-benefit or funded, defined contribution.	Voluntary	Financial assets
4	x	X	X	Personal savings, homeownership, and other individual financial and non-financial assets.	Voluntary	Financial assets

Note: The size of x or X denotes the importance of each pillar for each target group.
Source: Holzmann and Hinz (2005).

are also important. Effective reform needs to be directed towards better organizational effectiveness and broader, system design issues.[6]

There has been considerable debate and experience with different social security reforms, but no single idea, system, or model has emerged, including among Asian countries.[7] There has, however, been appreciation that from a practical policy point of view, a multi-tier framework is better able to address various social security risks than reliance on a single tier. The World Bank, in an early 1994 report (World Bank 1994), suggested a three pillar/tier framework, but accumulated evidence and rethinking led the Bank to endorse a five pillar/tier framework subsequently (Table 8.1) (Holzmann and Hinz 2005).

This system recognizes that different target groups require different combinations of pillars, and that a basic pension or, at least, social assistance financed from general budgetary revenues (Pillar Zero) is essential for the lifetime poor. This group may constitute as high as 30 per cent of the total population in some developing countries. It also recognizes that private management, investment allocation among a wide variety of physical and financial asset classes, and international diversification may not be suitable for all countries. There is also less insistence on private management of pension assets and recognition that accumulation of large assets is not always optimal. The role of family, community, physical assets (such as housing), and labour market activity after retirement (Pillar 4) also receive emphasis. In this model, the context of each country must be given substantive consideration in provident and pension fund design and governance.

NATURE AND PHILOSOPHY OF SOCIAL SECURITY SYSTEMS IN SOUTHEAST ASIA

Southeast Asian countries exhibit considerable divergence in their social security systems and philosophies (Table 8.2). Each country has a separate pension and provident fund organization for the private and government sectors respectively. The systems for these two sectors are also not integrated.

The nature of the formal social security systems in Southeast Asia reflects both continuity and adaptation. Among the Southeast Asian countries, Singapore and Malaysia essentially rely on a single mandatory savings pillar (Pillar 2 in Table 8.1) for retirement financing. In these two countries, civil service pensions are of the defined-benefit type, based on a formula incorporating years of service, salary level, and other factors.[8] There is, however, no automatic indexation. In Singapore, only top civil servants

TABLE 8.2
Key Provident and Pension Fund Indicators in Southeast Asia

Country	Organizations	Contributors as Percentage of Labour Force[a]	Contribution Rate (2004)	Wage Ceiling (2004)	Member Balances (US$ Billion), Percentage of GDP
Malaysia	Employees Provident Fund (EPF)	48.7[b]	23.0	No	68.0, 51.2 (early 2005)
	Government Pension Fund, Malaysia (GPF)	NA	NA	No	NA
Philippines	Social Security System (SSS)	20–25[c] (2003)	8.4 (5.07/3.33)	P 15,000 per month	3.3, 3.8 (2004)
	Government Service Insurance System (GSIS)	4.5 (2003)	21.0 (12/9)	No wage ceiling	3.7, 4.3 (early 2005)
Singapore	Central Provident Fund (CPF)	60.0[d] (March 2004)	30.0[f]	$4,500 month (2006)	66.4, 61.9 (2004)
	Government Pension Fund, Singapore (GPF)	NA	NA	NA	NA
Thailand	Social Security Organization (SSO)	21.2[e] (2003)	6.0	B15,000 month	20.0, 11 (early 2005)
	Government Pension Fund, Thailand (GPF)	3.5 (2003)	6.0	Yes	NA

Notes:

NA: Not Available.

a. Figures in brackets refer to year to which data refer.

b. Includes 4,017 foreign workers.

c. Membership in the SSS is 23 million but the active contributors are 6 to 8 million.

d. Foreign workers are around 25 per cent of the labour force and are excluded.

e. The SSO coverage is overstated as the figure refers to members rather than active contributors. If the provident funds of SOE's are included, the coverage rate may be as high as 25 per cent.

f. This rate applies to those below fifty-five years of age. Lower rates apply to those above fifty-five years.

Sources: Information obtained from official sources in each country.

are covered by the pension scheme, while in Malaysia all civil servants are covered. Malaysia is considering requiring civil servants to contribute to their pensions, but it is unlikely to alter the defined benefit nature of the scheme. Malaysia's method of financing its civil service pensions (through the budget) is, therefore, likely to come under strain unless some substantive prefunding provisions are made. Malaysia and Singapore, however, do not accept the defined benefit and social risk pooling method for private sector employees. The mandatory savings pillar provides individual security, but not social security; and leaves individuals open to longevity and inflation risks. It also does not de-link retirement provision from macroeconomic and other shocks (Diamond 2004).

Indonesia in 2004 passed a law on a National Social Security System (SJSN Act No. 40/2004), which aims to apply the social insurance principle on a comprehensive basis. It covers health insurance, work injury, old age (provident fund), pensions, and death benefits. The law further stipulates that the government will develop social assistance programmes. This corresponds to the zero pillar in the five-pillar framework discussed in the previous section. There are, however, concerns that there is a serious mismatch between the objectives of the law on the one hand, and financial, institutional, organizational, and regulatory capacities to implement the law on the other. The impact of this law on employment growth also needs to be considered. Therefore, careful sequencing and planning are needed before the social security law can be implemented in the country.

The Philippines and Thailand have both accepted the principle of social insurance and the defined benefit method for both the private sector and the government employees. In the Philippines, the Social Security System (SSS) and the Government Service Insurance System (GSIS) provide comprehensive sets of benefits to covered workers. The Philippines is also planning to introduce a mandatory savings pillar, but no firm decision has been taken on this thus far.

Thailand decided to introduce social insurance based pensions for private sector workers in the midst of the 1997 crisis. The first pensions to private sector employees, however, will not be paid until 2013. Thailand has thus scaled its system to keep affordability in mind. In addition to unfunded defined benefit pensions, civil servants in Thailand also compulsorily belong to a provident fund called Government Pension Fund (GPF). Under the 1987 Act, Thailand requires all firms listed on the stock exchange to operate provident funds, but does not require employees to join them. Thailand's Social Security Organization (SSO) provides comprehensive coverage of various short-term and long-term risks, including old age pension, disability, sickness, and maternity, work injury, health benefits, survivors' benefits, and unemployment. Since 2004, Thailand has also introduced unemployment insurance. It is unusual in providing such an array of benefits under a single organization, the SSO.

Among the countries in Southeast Asia, Thailand, therefore, has made relatively more progress towards a multi-pillar system than the other sample countries. The Philippines has been planning to introduce a mandatory savings pillar, but no firm decision has been made so far. It should be noted that in countries such as the Philippines and Thailand, which have accepted the social insurance principle, the accumulation of balances in the mandated programmes is likely to be relatively low. In the two countries, the accumulated balances to GDP ratio is about 10 per cent (Table 8.2). In contrast, in countries that rely on mandatory savings as the primary pillar, the accumulated balances to GDP ratio is likely to be high. In Malaysia, this ratio is over 50 per cent, while in Singapore it is over 60 per cent (Table 8.2). In none of the countries discussed does the zero-pillar, involving social pension financed from budgetary revenues, play a significant role. For the lifetime poor, this is among the most important pillar. In affluent Singapore, social assistance is deliberately kept at below even the bare subsistence level. To receive even this meager amount, extremely stringent criteria are applied (Asher 2004). Singapore has thus scarcely progressed beyond the philosophy of the poor laws in historical England, which held the poor solely responsible for their poverty.

The above discussion suggests significant divergence in social security philosophy among the five countries surveyed. There are also wide differences in the effectiveness with which the core functions are being performed by various provident and pension fund organizations in Southeast Asia. The two countries with higher per capita income, that is, Singapore and Malaysia, have persisted with a single-tier system, while Thailand is making efforts to develop a multi-tier system on a gradual and sustainable basis. Examining the reasons for such fundamental differences in the philosophy of social security systems among Southeast Asian countries is beyond the scope of this chapter. Some analysts have, however, argued that political systems and regime autonomy are important elements of the explanation (Ramesh with Asher 2000).

CHALLENGES FACING SOCIAL SECURITY SYSTEMS IN SOUTHEAST ASIA

The social security arrangements in Southeast Asia face many challenges. These may be grouped under coverage, adequacy, administrative efficiency and transparency, and governance and regulation. Each is discussed in turn.

Coverage

Table 8.2 provides coverage (ratio of contributors to total labour force) in four Southeast Asian countries — Malaysia, the Philippines, Singapore, and Thailand. The coverage has been relatively low (about a quarter of the labour force) in countries such as the Philippines and Thailand, where the formal sector is relatively small. In Malaysia, the Employees Provident Fund (EPF) covers one in two workers. In Singapore, three fourths of the labour force is covered. But as about a quarter of the labour force comprises foreigners, and these workers are statutorily not included in the Central Provident Fund (CPF), the coverage of eligible workers may be regarded as high.

The above suggests that in any employer-employee relationship-based systems, the level of formal sector employment acts as a constraint on coverage. Two implications emerge from this. First, formal sector employment needs to be increased through domestic reforms (for example, labour market reforms), and through increasing employment elasticity with respect to GDP. Clear rules about who is covered are essential. Good management systems should be developed to ensure that wages reported are consistent with actual wages paid to members. Formal sector coverage can also be expanded through improved administration and compliance. For this purpose, unique identification numbers for members and strong IT support are essential.

Second, the needs of informal sector workers must be addressed.[9] This, however, poses difficult challenges, particularly as such workers are found in both urban and rural areas, and the informal sector tends to be extremely heterogeneous in terms of income levels, types of occupation, and asset ownership, among other things. Therefore, the informal sector is more difficult to cover and has high administrative costs. Thus, evidence-based public policies to target particular types of persons for coverage are essential, as is designing specific schemes to reach these persons. In most Southeast Asian countries, there are identifiable occupations which employ large number of people. These may include fishermen from a particular area, small tobacco growers, and handicraft workers concentrated in a small area. Specialized coverage schemes, including possible livelihood insurance, could be devised for such identifiable large groups to sustain their incomes and to organize them in cooperative bodies.

In Southeast Asia, coverage of foreign workers is also an important issue. The Philippines, Malaysia, Thailand, and Myanmar are major labour-exporting countries, while Malaysia and Thailand, along with Singapore, are major importers of foreign labour from the region. Addressing the social security needs of these workers, therefore, requires a regional agreement. The ASEAN Social Security Association (ASSA), formed in 1998, might be an appropriate forum to discuss the possibility of a regional agreement on minimum social security coverage standards and reciprocal arrangements.

Adequacy

A pension system needs to address not only the poverty alleviation objective, but should also permit maintenance of an accustomed standard of living. Pension experts usually recommend a replacement rate (that is, the ratio of retirement income over pre-retirement income) of between two-thirds to three-fourths of income, which is then maintained throughout the retirement period by addressing longevity and inflation risks.[10] It should be stressed that the requisite replacement rates should be derived from different pillars and not from one pillar alone.

The dual nature of the social security systems in the four countries under consideration means that, in general, civil servants (including armed forces personnel) have obtained reasonably high replacement rates, with longevity and inflation risks protection. The methods used to ensure high replacement rates across these countries, however, vary. Thus in Malaysia, when government salaries are revised, a similar revision is also undertaken for the pensions of retired civil servants. This suggests that the main challenge of adequacy concerns private sector employees. As already noted above, social assistance or basic pensions financed through the budget are essential for the lifetime poor (Table 8.1). In none of the four countries does the zero-pillar play a significant role. Fiscal constraints are *not* a factor in explaining why the zero-pillar has not been adopted in these countries. With the exception of the Philippines, the fiscal position of other countries is, in fact, comfortable. The main constraint, instead, comes from prevailing socio-political norms, which do not regard provision of a floor level of income as an essential element of a good society.

In Malaysia and Singapore, private sector workers are covered under mandatory savings schemes. There are two phases in such schemes, the accumulation phase and the payout phase (Figure 8.1). In the accumulation phase, the balances at retirement depend on the contribution rate, the wage base, the extent of pre-retirement withdrawals, and the real interest rate credited to members' accounts. At the time of retirement, arrangements must be made for a phased payout. This is because a lump sum payment

FIGURE 8.1
Accumulation and Payout Phases of DC Schemes

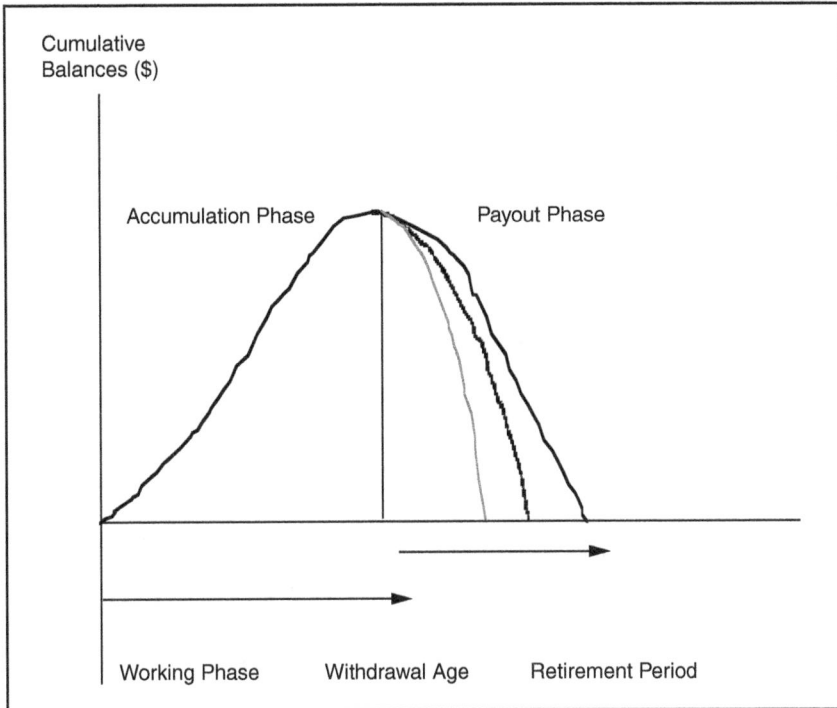

Notes:
Cumulative Balances = Net contributions (contributions minus withdrawals), plus interest credited on accumulated balances.
Payout phase: The funds accumulated can be spent rapidly or slowly. Death may occur before the funds are exhausted or the reverse is also a possibility. Hence the need to protect against longevity risk. As it is the purchasing power of the funds that is relevant, protection against inflation risk is also desirable.
Source: Authors.

is not consistent with the primary rationale of mandated savings, which is that people are essentially myopic with respect to their future. As people become older, they do not necessarily become wiser. The variables studied in behavioral finance, such as lack of self-control, inadequate pension finance literacy, and herd mentality, among others, are said to reflect retirement savings behaviour of both the elderly as well as the young (Holzmann and Hinz 2005; Asher 2004).

In Malaysia and Singapore, substantial pre-retirement withdrawals have tended to have severe impacts on the accumulation of balances, even though contribution rates and wage growth have been high (Asher 2002). Such withdrawals, as a proportion of contributions, averaged around 40 per cent in Malaysia, and around 70 per cent in Singapore for a prolonged period (Asher 2002). Moreover, Singapore's CPF members have not benefited from the power of compound interest to expand their accumulated savings. We have estimated that the real rate of return credited to CPF members was only 1.2 per cent per annum during the 1987–2004 period. In contrast, the corresponding rate credited to Malaysia's EPF members was nearly three times that in Singapore.[11] Malaysia's EPF did much better in harnessing the power of compound interest over a longer run than the Singapore CPF. In contrast, the real rates of return in Latin American countries have been substantially higher, but more volatile (Gill, Packard, and Yermo 2005). The decentralized nature of the pensions system in Latin America meant that the net real rates of return (gross rates — administration and investment management costs) are likely to be lower (about 5 per cent per annum) than the gross rates (about 10 per cent) (Gill, Packard, and Yermo 2005).

While EPF balances are wholly invested domestically in Malaysia, some consideration is now being given to investing these abroad. This is because at current accumulation rates, the EPF balances will soon outstrip the stock market capitalization. Nevertheless, EPF investments are well diversified among domestic asset classes (Figure 8.2). It is particularly noteworthy that since 1991, the share of Malaysian Government Securities (MGS) has declined significantly while the share of equity investments has correspondingly increased. The size of the domestic capital markets is acting as an increasing constraint on EPF investments.[12] The Malaysian government has, consequently, permitted EPF to invest up to RM1 billion (out of total balances of nearly RM250 billion) abroad. The EPF is in the process of operationalizing such investments.

Similarly in the Philippines and Thailand, provident and pension fund assets are currently wholly invested domestically. As of September 2003, the SSS in the Philippines had total assets of P171.3 billion (4 per cent of GDP), and total investments of P155.4 billion (3.6 per cent of GDP). The allocation was 29.1 per cent in equities; 26.3 per cent in housing loans; 19.6 per cent in salary loans; and 5 per cent in real estate. As of 30 June 2003, GSIS had total assets of P245.9 billion (5.7 per cent of the GDP), substantially higher than for the SSS. The SSS membership as of 3 September 2003 was P24.9 million (assets of P6,880 per member). In contrast, the GSIS membership was P1.4 million (assets of P175,643 per member). For

FIGURE 8.2
Malaysia: Investment Allocation of EPF: 1990–2004

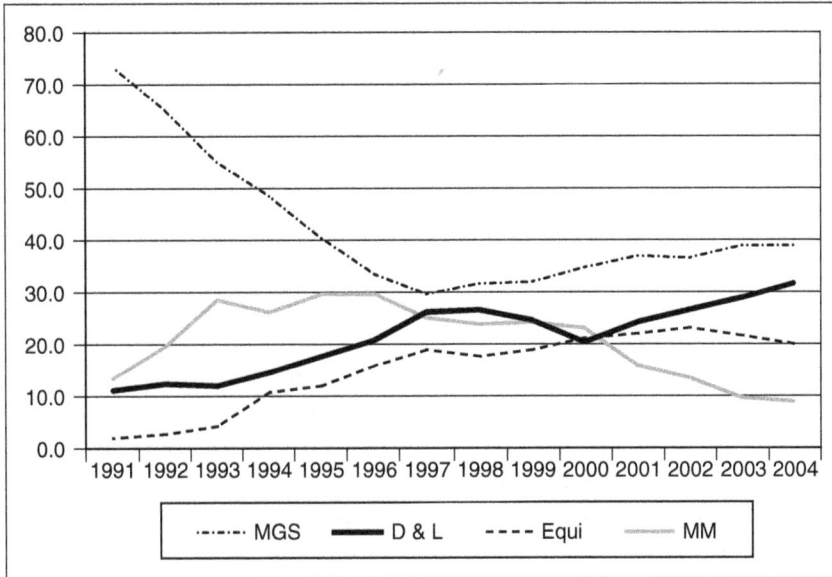

Notes:
MGS — Malaysian Government Securities
D & L — Debentures and Loans
Equi — Equities
MM — Money Market
Source: Calculated from the Annual Reports of the EPF.

the January–September 2003 period, the average monthly pension paid by the SSS was P2,526 (US$45), about half of the per capita income.

In Thailand, in 2003, the GPF's portfolio of 230 billion baht (US$5.5 billion) was 80 per cent in fixed income instruments; 15 per cent in equities; 3 per cent in real estate, and 2 per cent in others (Kanjanaphoomin 2005). There has been considerable pressure on the GPF under the current government to support the Thai stock market and invest in projects deemed of national importance by the government. Thailand is considering investing a small proportion of GPF balances abroad.

In the case of Singapore, the CPF's balance sheet shows that all the balances are invested in non-marketable government securities. The interest on these securities are determined retrospectively as a weighted average of one-year fixed deposit rates and savings account rates of the four domestic banks. The interest rate credited to members is, therefore, an administered rate. As the Singapore government has exhibited budgetary surpluses for many years, the bond proceeds are, in effect, handed over to the Singapore Government Investment Corporation (GIC) and other holding companies. Statutory provisions protect these SGIC and others from disclosing their investment portfolio and performance. Thus, CPF members do not know the ultimate deployment of their savings. Besides the potential implicit tax (difference between returns obtained by SGIC and others and returns actually credited to members), the above arrangement also carries high political risk and is not conducive to transparency and accountability.

A simulation study by McCarthy, Mitchell, and Piggott (2001) suggests that for a representative CPF member who began contributing in the year 2000 under then prevailing rules, about three-fourths of the total CPF wealth will be in the form of housing in the base case and the replacement rate will be 28 per cent. The rate will decline to 17 per cent if the contribution ceiling of S$6,000 per month is held constant in nominal terms. The rate will be lowered to 14 per cent if the contribution rate is reduced from 40 per cent to 30 per cent. Even if the real rate of return of 5 per cent is credited to members, the replacement rate increases to only 34 per cent. These rates are clearly inadequate. Following the simulation study, the nominal wage ceiling has been lowered substantially (it is currently S$4,500), and so has the contribution rate. This suggests that if the proportion of housing wealth in total CPF wealth remains at the base case level, the replacement rates will be in the early teens. This shows the danger of relying on the mandatory savings scheme alone to finance retirement.

The EPF authorities in Malaysia have not published the replacement rate for its members. While the replacement rate is expected to be somewhat higher than that of Singapore in spite of the lower contribution rates, it is unlikely to exceed 25–30 per cent for the middle income workers. This is also clearly inadequate and calls for a multi-tier system. The replacement rate of SSS in the Philippines and SSO in Thailand are not available. Pensions under Thailand's SSO when they commence in 2013 are likely to be quite modest. This is because of the low contribution rates and conservative investment management practices (Kanjanaphoomin 2005). The current plan is to provide 15 per cent of the average wage of the last sixty months of members who have contributed for fifteen years. For those contributing for a longer period, the benefit will increase by one percentage point for every twelve months of contribution. Thus, a person contributing to Thailand's SSO for thirty years will be entitled to a replacement rate of 30 per cent, assuming the base is the average wage for the last sixty months. There are no plans for inflation indexation, but longevity protection is provided.

The Payout Phase

In Malaysia, one-third of EPF balances can be withdrawn at age fifty and the rest at age fifty-five. Given the life expectancy at birth of seventy for men and seventy-five for women (life expectancy at age fifty-five is likely to be higher), the withdrawal age is clearly too low. Moreover, the withdrawals are in a lump sum. The EPF did attempt to organize a deferred annuity scheme under which a member can purchase a desired amount of monthly annuity income anytime during his working years. A member could make annuity purchases in small amounts throughout the working career. As Malaysia does not have long-term assets such as bonds in which insurance companies providing such annuities could invest, they naturally took a very conservative view of the risks involved. As a result, the rate of return offered on the deferred annuities was significantly lower than the dividend paid by the EPF. Hence, this scheme was not successful. The government is, however, considering issuing special bonds for pensioners. Whether these will help provide at least partial inflation protection will depend on the terms and conditions of such bonds.

In Singapore, the withdrawal age for the CPF is fifty-five years. However, a minimum sum (S$90,000 since 1 July 2005, 50 per cent of which may be pledged in the form of property) must be put aside, and income from it cannot be used until age sixty-two. This effectively increases the withdrawal age for a portion of the accumulated balances. However, the proportion of members buying annuities is quite small. Most deposit it with the approved bank or keep it with the CPF Board. The longevity and inflation risks are, therefore, not addressed. The tax treatment of the annuities and other pension products should also be made more neutral, both with respect to various instruments designed to provide an income flow during retirement, and with respect to providers (Asher 2004).[13]

The challenge in the Philippines is to make the SSS benefits financially sustainable. The essence of the challenge is that the political system in the Philippines has the tendency to expand the benefits provided by the SSS, but without increases in contribution rates, or permitting better investment management and diversification (Asher 2002; Templo 2002). While the GSIS is well funded and, therefore, civil servants are likely to obtain an adequate replacement rate,[14] if current policies continue, then the SSS is unlikely to be able to sustain the promised benefits financially. This suggests an urgent need to base the operations of the SSS on sound actuarial principles. If this is not done, then either the shortfall will have to be made up from the budget, or sharp reductions in benefits or increases in contributions will become necessary in the future. The former will adversely impact fiscal consolidation and flexibility, while the later option will incur political costs. In Thailand, the provident funds permit a lump sum withdrawal. Therefore its members are not protected against longevity and inflation risks.

Administrative Efficiency and Transparency

There are several reasons a high level of administrative and compliance efficiency is essential. First, any real cost savings from administrative efficiency translate into higher rates of return to members. Similar savings in compliance costs to both employers and employees will result in a positive impact on labour markets as these reduce the real burden of statutory levies. Second, compliance costs may affect the default rate by employers and the willingness of employees to cooperate with employers to circumvent statutory provident and pension fund contributions. These will indirectly impact on the effective coverage of social security schemes. Third, a high degree of administrative and compliance efficiency is essential for sustaining the legitimacy of social security arrangements.

How provident and pension fund schemes are designed have an important bearing on administrative costs. In general, decentralized employer or individual-based systems exhibit higher administrative costs, although these may be offset by potentially higher rates of return on investments (Gill, Packard, and Yermo 2005). The investment management costs need to be separated from the administrative costs, which involve the operations of provident and pension fund organizations. Both these aspects, however, have been under-researched in the four countries. As a result only some broad comments are possible in this chapter.

In general, administrative efficiency as measured by conventional indicators is fairly high in Malaysia and Singapore.[15] Table 8.3 reveals that operating costs as a percentage of contributions in Malaysia are larger than in Singapore (1.68 per cent compared with 0.88 per cent) due to lower contribution rates (23 per cent compared with 33 per cent in Singapore), and the country's larger physical size requiring substantial coordination across large distances. Administrative costs as a proportion of Funds under Management (FUM) were substantially smaller in Singapore compared with Malaysia (0.11 per cent for Singapore and 0.15 per cent for Malaysia), due to the large asset base of their provident funds (Table 8.2). The efficiency indicators for employees of the EPF are somewhat better than those of Singapore's CPF.

TABLE 8.3
Indicators of Administrative Efficiency in Malaysia and Singapore, 2004

Variable	Central Provident Fund (CPF), Singapore	Employees Provident Fund (EPF), Malaysia
Operating cost as % of income	3.52	3.11
Operating cost as % of Funds Under Management (FUM)	0.11	0.15
Operating cost as % of contributions	0.88	1.68
Number of employers registered per employee	55.7	78.4
Number of members registered per employee	2,156	2,124
Number of active contributors per employee	946	1,067

Source: Authors' calculations based on official data.

Data along similar lines of analysis for the Philippines and Thailand were not available for 2004. In 2000 in the Philippines, administrative costs as a proportion of contributions and as a proportion of assets of the SSS were 13.9 per cent and 2.3 per cent respectively (Asher 2002).[16] These are substantially higher than the corresponding values for Malaysia and Singapore. The 1999 data for Thailand's SSO suggest that the respective ratios were 3.9 per cent and 1 per cent (Asher 2002). While these ratios are substantially better than those of the Philippines, they are still much higher than those for Malaysia and Singapore. The Philippines and Thailand, therefore, need to consider ways to bring about real costs savings in their administration of social security schemes. There are no studies as yet on compliance costs for employers and employees of the provident and pension funds in the four countries. This area deserves much greater research emphasis.

Governance and Regulation

The importance of good governance in both private and public sector organizations has been increasingly recognized. In the case of provident and pension funds, the areas where good governance are important include:

(a) the composition of the Board and its access to expertise; (b) fiduciary responsibility, transparency, and accountability; and (c) disclosure norms; and (d) actuarial analysis (Asher and Nandy 2006). Individual, account-based savings schemes, whether mandatory or voluntary, require a sophisticated regulatory regime as well as sophisticated financial and capital markets (Munnell and Sunden 2004; Holzmann and Hinz 2005; Gill, Packard, and Yermo 2005).

Provident and pension funds require Board members who are independent-minded and competent. They should be highly conscious of their fiduciary responsibilities. The relevant laws and regulations should give high priority to such responsibilities. In all four countries, there is tripartite representation on the Board (government, employees, and employers), and provision is made for the presence of experts. The provident and pension fund organizations, however, are closely tied to their respective government ministries. In Malaysia, the EPF is under the Ministry of Finance; Singapore's CPF is under the Ministry of Manpower; the SSS and the GSIS in the Philippines are under the Office of the President; Thailand's SSO is under the Ministry of Labour and Welfare, while the GPF is under the Ministry of Finance. Board appointments in these four countries are made by the relevant Minister (or the President). Given the political economy of these countries, it has been a major challenge to find Board members who are both competent and independent minded. In these countries, the requirement that the Board members must give high priority towards fiduciary responsibilities to members is fairly weak.

The monocentric power structure and treatment of even routine socio-economic data as a strategic resource rather than a public good are dominant characteristics of Singapore's political economy. The governance structure of the CPF, including its Board composition (and investment policies), reflects these characteristics. In the Philippines, the leadership and policies of the SSS and the GSIS have been closely tied to the prevailing political power structure (Templo 2002). Thailand's SSS and GPF operate within the structure of the government. GPF aspires to be a professional organization with good governance practices. But its autonomy is constrained by governmental goals and objectives. In Malaysia, the investment panel of the EPF is separate from the Board and reports directly to the Minister of Finance. While this permits introduction of outside expertise in investment decisions, it also dilutes the Board's authority and autonomy (Thillainathan 2005).

In none of the four countries is there an independent regulator for provident and pension funds. This impedes the required emphasis that is needed on fiduciary responsibilities and the professional development of these organizations. Actuarial studies by the SSS of the Philippines estimate that at current rates of contribution, benefits and investment income, the SSS will become insolvent by 2015.[17] Yet, there is no requirement for authorities, whether Congress, the President's office, the SSS Board, or any other agency, to act on this publicly available information. In any social insurance scheme, matching assets and liabilities is an essential part of good governance. Thai law does not indicate what the fiduciary duties of the Provident Fund Committee are. It also does not have a Trust Law. The lack of independent regulators also hampers a system-wide perspective of the social security systems in these countries.

There is also considerable room for improvement in the timeliness and accessibility of data concerning the operations of the provident and pension funds in these countries. Transparency and accountability levels, therefore, need to be improved. A regulator would be better able to enforce guidelines on these aspects of governance. The transparency and accountability of the civil service schemes are especially low in all the four countries (Asher 2000). It is strongly suggested that the civil service schemes in these countries be subjected to frequent actuarial evaluation and that these be made publicly available to all the stakeholders. At a future date, these schemes should also come under the purview of a pension regulator. It should be stressed that in developing countries, pension regulators also need to play a developmental role. This involves enhancing pension economics literacy among policymakers as well as the general public, and facilitating the orderly development of different components of the pensions industry. Coordination between the pension regulator, the insurance industry regulator, and the stock market regulator is also essential.

CONCLUDING REMARKS

There are several themes that emerge from this chapter's comparative analysis of social security systems in Southeast Asia. Not all themes are applicable to the same degree in each country as local contexts, and political, demographic, and other conditions will differ. However, each country will certainly need to address the limitations of its own system in relation to each of the themes outlined below.

The first theme concerns the need for a multi-tier social security system. This is particularly relevant for Malaysia and Singapore, and, to a lesser extent, for the Philippines. Thailand and the Philippines need to strengthen the zero-pillar of social assistance or flat universal pensions financed from the budget. Indonesia needs to consider carefully how to translate ambitious goals incorporated in its 2004 social security law into effective outcomes.

The second theme concerns the need for professionalism in designing and managing provident and pension funds organizations and schemes. As in other areas of public policy, such as tax reforms, it is the professional attention to details of design and implementation that are crucial. It is important to keep in mind that the primary objective of any provident or pension fund is to provide retirement income security for members. Too complex an objective function for these organizations is, therefore, likely to be counterproductive. This is particularly the case in Singapore, and to a lesser extent, in Malaysia. The governance structure, and in particular, the fiduciary responsibilities, become important elements of a professional approach to provident and pension fund design and management. The importance of maintaining high levels of administrative and compliance efficiency in managing provident and pension funds should not be minimized either.

Provident and pension funds also need to perform their investment role, utilizing modern portfolio management principles and practices. The investment function will become increasingly complex, and appropriate strategies, including international diversification, may need to be considered. For Singapore, the main task should be to ensure that the investment returns ultimately obtained by government holding companies are actually credited to CPF members.

Another aspect of professionalism concerns transparency, accountability, and timeliness of information provision to stakeholders. In all four countries, substantial improvements in these areas are needed, particularly with respect to the civil service and armed forces schemes. A professionally managed organization is also adept at using outside expertise, whether on its Board or as outside consultants or service providers. The emphasis, however, should not be on the form, but the substance of the arrangements. It may be useful for the provident and pension fund organizations in these countries to consider appointing outside advisory committees. Their role will be to convey current knowledge and relevant market realities to the Board, thus improving policy making and practices. The committees may be particularly helpful in facilitating the investment function of these organizations.

The third theme concerns the need for a system-wide perspective. As these countries progress towards a multi-pillar system, it will be essential to ensure that all the different elements of the system are compatible with one another. As the financial entities involved in the accumulation phase and the payout phase may be different, there is a need to coordinate among the different agencies supervising or regulating them. Currently, different rules and standards apply to private sector schemes on the one hand, and the civil service scheme, on the other. Often the same provident or pension fund organization acts as a service provider, as well as supervisor or regulator of the exempted provident and pension fund plans. The responsibility for different elements of the social security system tends to be diffused with little coordination.

There is, therefore, a strong case for considering establishing a regulator for the pension sector. The regulator should not only require professionalism from all provident and pension fund organizations, whether public or private, but also ensure that the progress towards a multi-pillar system proceeds in a rational and sustainable manner. This will not be an easy task and the political economy considerations will undoubtedly play an important role. However, without a strong and independent regulator, it is also difficult to envisage how the challenges of social security will be met in the four countries.

Fourth, it is worth stressing that there is an urgent need to develop indigenous research capabilities in the area of social security. In none of the Southeast Asian countries do any of the universities offer specializations in this area. To make progress in this area, however, the authorities will need to regard socio-economic information in general, and information concerning operations of provident and pension funds, in particular, as a public good rather than as a strategic resource to be used for tactical purposes. Much of social security research is contextual and institutional, specific to a particular society. It is only through genuine cooperation and desire to improve social protection for those in the informal sector and for the elderly poor that innovative, but locally relevant, policies and programmes can be designed and implemented.

Our final point is that development of appropriate social security systems should be regarded as an essential aspect of competitiveness and of managing globalization, rather than being regarded as conflicting with the goals of attaining international competitiveness.

Notes

1. This has been earlier confined to capital and finance, but strong logic requires that movement of natural persons (human resources) should also be liberalized, albeit in a socially and politically sustainable manner. It is recognized that economic liberalization which is not undertaken at the global level through the World Trade Organization (WTO) could hinder the emergence of truly multilateral trade and investment regimes.

2. The total fertility rate, defined in terms of children per woman, in the 2000–2005 period (medium variant) was higher than the replacement rate

of 2.15 in countries such as Indonesia (2.37), Malaysia (2.93), and the Philippines (3.22), and below the replacement rate in Singapore (1.35) and Thailand (1.93) (United Nations 2005). Individual ageing refers to increased life expectancy. In 2000–2005, life expectancy at birth for males (females) averaged 64.5 (68.6) years in Indonesia; 70.8 (75.5) years in Malaysia; 68.1 (72.4) years in the Philippines; 66.0 (73.7) years in Thailand; and 76.7 (80.5) years in Singapore (United Nations 2005). Population ageing on the other hand, refers to the proportion of the total population which has aged, that is, over 60/65 years. In 2005, the population over 60 years was low in countries such as the Philippines (6.2 per cent), Malaysia (7 per cent), but relatively high in Indonesia (8.4 per cent), Thailand (10.25 per cent), and Singapore (12.2 per cent) (United Nations 2005). As women live longer than men on average, but usually have lower exposure in the labour force and earn less than men on average, the gender issue is an intimate part of social security issues and needs to be addressed.

3. In this chapter the terms social security, retirement financing, and pensions are used interchangeably.

4. Longevity risks relate to the probability that accumulated savings and retirement benefits may be inadequate to last until death. Inflation risk relates to the probability that the value of the retirement benefit may not be protected against inflation during the retirement period.

5. Pension experts generally recommend a replacement rate, i.e. ratio of retirement income to pre-retirement income of between 66 to 75 per cent, adjusted for both longevity and inflation risks. Some countries index wages to enable retirees to participate in the increased productivity of the nation.

6. It is particularly important not to compare the existing imperfect systems with reform options based on implicit assumptions about perfect implementation, no political compromises on design and governance, and a benign domestic and international economic environment (Diamond 2004).

7. In particular, it should be emphasized that there is no distinct East Asian (or Asian) welfare state model. Standard analytical concepts and discussions can explain widely varying practices in social security systems in these countries. Those who espouse distinctness or exceptionalism for East Asia (or Asia) are advancing ideological positions, which have no empirical support.

8. Under the Defined Benefit (DB) method, benefits to be provided to members are defined, and contributions, therefore, are left undefined. The pension plan sponsor (employer, government, etc.) bears investment and other risks. DB-type voluntary occupational pension plans are usually not portable (for example, when a person changes jobs), thereby impacting labour mobility. This is also the case with the civil service DB pensions. In mandated social insurance systems, society as a whole bears the risks, and the portability issue

is not relevant. Under the Defined Contribution (DC) method, contributions are defined, but benefits are not. It is the individual members who bear investment and other risks, and not the plan sponsor.

9. The informal sector covers a substantial proportion of the economy in the Southeast Asian countries. In 2000, over half of the labour force was engaged in the informal sector in Thailand (52.6 per cent), while in Malaysia and the Philippines it was relatively lower at 31.1 per cent and 43.4 per cent respectively. Singapore's informal sector is small, and, therefore, only 13.1 per cent of the labour force was engaged in the informal sector in the same period (Asher 2002).

10. It is, however, costly to address the inflation risk fully on a universal basis. Public policies, therefore, should be directed towards addressing the inflation risk as far as it is fiscally and economically prudent to do so. But these should not be used as an excuse to escape responsibility.

11. However, in both Malaysia and Singapore, the real rate of return credited to members is less than the real rate of growth of wages, or its proxy GDP. This implies that the replacement rate will be low. Thus, in Singapore, during the 1987–2004 period, real wages grew at an annual rate of 5.9 per cent, but the real rate of return to CPF members was only 1.2 per cent (Asher 2004). Asher's calculations suggest that the real annual rate of return of 3.39 per cent in Malaysia for the 1990–2004 period was much lower than the corresponding real GDP growth of 6.25 per cent, which is taken as a proxy for real wages. The replacement rate in Malaysia is also expected to be low. It is instructive to note that neither provident fund has felt it appropriate to provide the expected replacement rate that members at different income groups can actually expect.

12. The market capitalization of the Kuala Lumpur Stock Exchange is around RM450 billion, but the EPF alone has balances of nearly RM250 billion. The EPF balances are expected to grow more rapidly than stock market capitalization.

13. The income, wealth, inheritance, and other applicable taxes for provident and pension funds deserve much more emphasis than they have received in this period. This is usually a neglected area of research in the literature.

14. The Philippine government may consider making actuarial evaluation of the GSIS public to enhance credibility and generate more informed debate. The SSS should also be required to take similar steps.

15. With appropriate adjustments for local conditions and context, the administrative efficiency indicators of these two countries, especially Malaysia, could be used as benchmarks by other countries in Asia.

16. For the January–September 2003 period, operating expenses of the SSS were 11.3 per cent of contributions and 2 per cent of assets <http://www.sss.gov.ph>. A partial reason for the higher ratios in Philippines is the comprehensive set of social protection provided by the SSS.

17. This was stated in a speech titled "Why SSS is Fighting Its Own Retirement" by the Chief Actuary of the SSS <http://www.sss.gov.ph>.

References

Asher, M.G. "Reforming Civil Service Pensions in Selected Asian Countries". Paper prepared for the World Bank Social Security Workshop, World Bank, Washington, D.C., March 2000.

―――. "Southeast Asia's Social Security Systems: Need for a System-wide Perspective and Professionalism". *International Social Security Review* 55, no. 4 (2002): 71–88.

―――. "Retirement Financing Dilemmas: Experience of Singapore". *Economic and Political Weekly* XXXIX, no. 21 (2004): 2114–20.

Asher, M.G. and A. Nandy. "Governance and Regulation of Provident and Pension Schemes in Asia". In *De-regulation and its Discontents: Rewriting the Rules in the Asia Pacific*, edited by M. Ramesh and Michael Howlett. Cheltenham: Edward Elgar, 2006.

Diamond, P. "Social Security". *American Economic Review* 94, no. 1 (2004): 1–24.

Gill, Indermit S., Truman Packard, and Juan Yermo. *Keeping the Promise of Old Age Income Security in Latin America*. Washington, D.C.: World Bank, 2005.

Holzmann, Robert and Richard Hinz. *Old Age Income Support in the 21st Century*. Washington, D.C.: World Bank, 2005.

Kanjanaphoomin, N. "Pension Fund, Provident Fund and Social Security System in Thailand". In *Pensions in Asia: Incentives, Compliance and Their Role in Retirement*, edited by Noriyuki Takayama. Tokyo: Maruzen, 2005.

McCarthy, D., O.S. Mitchell, and J. Piggott. "Asset Rich and Cash Poor: Retirement Provision and Housing Policy in Singapore". Working Paper 2001–10. Pension Research Council, Wharton School, University of Pennsylvania, 2001.

Munnell A.H. and A. Sunden. *Coming Up Short: The Challenge of 401 (k) Plans*. Washington, D.C.: Brookings Institution Press, 2004.

Ramesh, M. with Mukul G. Asher. *Welfare Capitalism in Southeast Asia: Social Security, Health, and Education Policies*. London: Macmillan Press, 2000.

Ross, S.G. "Building Pension Institutions: Administrative Issues". In Proceedings of the Third APEC Regional Forum on Pension Fund Reform, Bangkok, 2000, pp. 129–48.

Templo, H. "Pension Reform: The Philippine Experience". *Hitotsubashi Journal of Economics* 43, no. 2 (2002): 135–50.

Thillainathan, R. "Malaysia: Pension and Financial Market Reforms and Key Issues on Governance". In *Pensions in Asia: Incentives, Compliance and Their Role in Retirement*, edited by Noriyuki Takayama. Tokyo: Maruzen, 2005.

United Nations. *World Population Prospects: The 2004 Revision.* Population Division of the Department of Economic and Social Affairs of the United Nations Secretariat, 2005. <http://esa.un.org/unpp>. Accessed 13 January 2006.

World Bank. *Averting the Old Age Crisis: Policies to Protect the Old and Promote Growth.* New York: Oxford University Press, 1994.

———. *East Asia: Recovery and Beyond.* Washington, D.C.: World Bank, 2000.

9

CORPORATE SOCIAL RESPONSIBILITY IN SOUTHEAST ASIA

Bala Ramasamy

INTRODUCTION

The concept of being "good" is changing in many societies. In the past, being good implied observance of laws and simply not hurting others. This might be acceptable in a society where its constituents have very little contact with one another. Visualize an environment where a farmer works his plot of land and where his nearest neighbour is a good two hours' walk away. His trip to the nearest village occurs weekly or perhaps even less frequently. Under such conditions, not causing any harm can be defined as being good. However, being good cannot have a similar meaning today when contact with our fellow human beings occurs on a daily basis. *Being* good today means *doing* good, that is, being an active protagonist in society. Similarly, a good company is not just one that makes profits, but also one that contributes to society.

In 1975, Sethi developed a three-tier model to describe the social responsibilities of firms. In Svendsen et al. (nd), this model is visualized in the form depicted in Figure 9.1. The first stage involves compliance, that is, when social obligations include responding to legal and market constraints. The second stage relates to responsiveness, which involves meeting the demands of various stakeholders in ways that are compatible with societal norms. Stage 3 moves into the engagement stage where firms adapt, anticipate, and

FIGURE 9.1
Three Stages of Social Responsibility

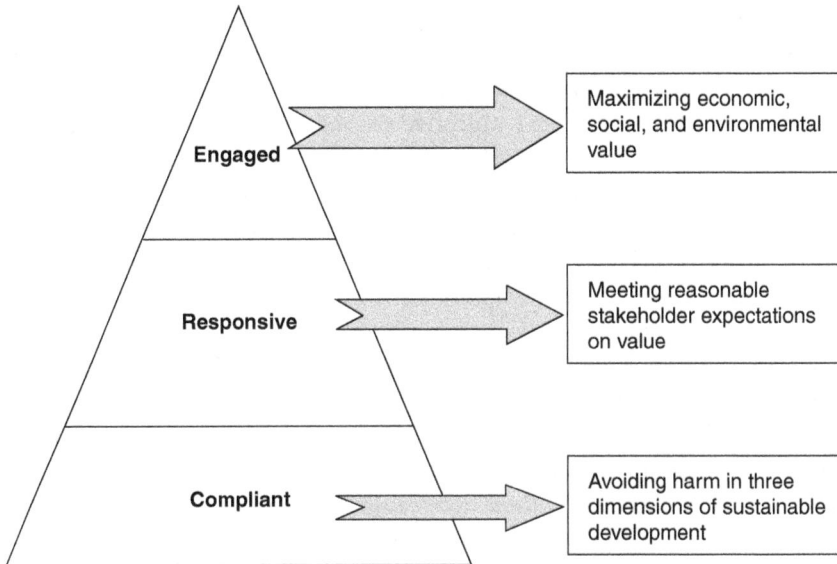

Source: Svendsen et al. (nd).

prevent the degradation of society and its wealth, which in turn leads to the maximization of value in the economic, social, and environmental spheres. Thus, one could argue that Milton Friedman's view that "the business of business is business" is losing support and in its place is the stakeholder theory of Ed Freeman and the social contract view (Davis 2005).

Three arguments can be put forth as to why companies should be socially responsible: gratitude, citizenship, and responsibilities to power (Bowie 1991). Society provides the company with its resources — human capital, legal systems, infrastructure, health facilities, and so on. In many cases, the tax that they pay does not match the benefits they get from the resources offered to them. As a matter of gratitude, a company needs to share its bounties with the rest of society. Even if it pays a considerable amount of corporate tax, it is duty bound to play its role as a corporate citizen since it is a legal entity within the community. After all, "business and organizations have a privilege denied to ordinary mortals ... they don't have to die ... this makes them especially responsible." (Handy 1999). Finally, companies are larger than individuals, possessing greater access to resources and power which they wield in the community. With power come responsibilities. In this regard, companies act as stewards of world resources, utilizing them in a way that would benefit both the present and later generations.

But the criticisms against corporate social responsibility (CSR) practices have not subsided. David Henderson, British economist and author of *The Role of Business in the Modern World* makes a scathing attack on CSR, arguing that shifting a firm's objective to non-economic goals will harm society and its stakeholders because CSR increases the cost of doing business and reduces the competitiveness of companies. However, rather than looking at CSR as merely a cost, we should perhaps see it as an investment. Philanthropic activities increase goodwill among consumers, daycare, and exercise facilities for company personnel improve productivity and retention rates, while compliance with safety regulations reduces legal sanctions (Martin 2002). This would imply that CSR can make business sense if seen from a long-term perspective. However, when the business case for CSR is the dominating motive behind its practice, then innovating and providing solutions to mitigate social and environmental problems are only undertaken when there are reasonable profits to be made. Under such conditions, CSR is undertaken to: (a) manage risk and reputation; (b) protect human capital assets; (c) respond to consumer demands; and (d) avoid regulation (Doane 2005). Given these intentions, businesses justify their actions under the pretext of engaging in CSR while ignoring the major issues facing society.[1]

A related debate among CSR advocates is whether the practice of CSR should be voluntary or regulated. Supporters of the voluntary approach highlight the need for flexibility, allowing companies to "blend profit pressures with non-financial pressures into coherent business activity and response" (Organization for Economic Cooperation and Development [OECD] 2001). Regulators, on the other hand, claim that the market system does not reward CSR active companies (referred to as "minnows" by Doane 2005) and so governments must regulate with CSR reporting made mandatory (OECD 2001).

To avoid being dragged into a debate as to whether CSR is necessary or not, and whether it should be regulated or otherwise, a broad definition of CSR is required. For the purpose of this chapter, we use the definition articulated by Business for Social Responsibility (BSR) as "achieving commercial success in ways that honour ethical values and respect people, communities, and the natural environment".[2] It is viewed as "a comprehensive set of policies, practices and programs that are integrated into business operations, supply chains, and decision-making processes throughout the company — wherever the company does business — and includes responsibility for current and past actions as well as future impacts".[3]

GLOBALIZATION AND CSR

Evidence to support the positive role of globalization on the social and economic development of the masses in the developing world is readily available from international institutions such as the World Bank and the United Nations. The link that is commonly used is as follows: trade is good for growth and growth is good for the poor. Among the poor, increasing economic growth raises their incomes proportionately higher compared with the population as a whole (Dollar and Kraay 2001). Countries that have participated in the globalization process have also raised their standards of living. Since 1960, life expectancy in India has risen by more than twenty years while illiteracy in Korea has decreased from about 30 per cent to nearly zero (Aninat 2002). While one could argue that globalization was not the sole reason for these improvements, one cannot deny the vital role it played.

In describing the good and evils of globalization, Thomas Friedman (2000) wrote

> [Globalization] can be incredibly empowering and incredibly coercive. It can democratize opportunity and democratize panic. It makes the whales bigger and the minnows stronger. It leaves you behind faster and faster, and it catches up to you faster and faster. While it is homogenizing cultures, it is also enabling people to share their unique individuality farther and wider.

Similarly, the link between CSR and globalization has two facets. On the one hand, globalization can lead to a convergence of the value systems and beliefs of various communities, thereby allowing a universal code of ethics to be promulgated. This would ensure that companies are good everywhere, not just in their home countries. This is especially true when multinational firms globalize their production networks and engage in productive activities in developing countries. The pressure by consumers of developed countries for companies to go beyond their commercial responsibilities could assist in the spread of CSR practices worldwide (Manakkathil and Rudolf 1995). The OECD Guidelines for multinational enterprises (MNEs) is an example of the globalization of business practices. The Guidelines calls on MNEs, among other things:

- Not to offer, nor give in to demands to bribe public officials.
- To apply precautionary principles in their operations with a view to avoiding potential risks to the environment.
- To respond promptly, efficiently and transparently in the event of any serious threats to public health and safety arising out of the consumption or use of their products.
- To promote research and development as a catalyst for change in host countries and as a stimulus for sustainable development.

In the same way, as MNEs from developing countries invest abroad, particularly in industrialized markets, the environmental, social, and quality standards imposed on them are brought back to the home base, resulting in the "race to the top".

On the other hand, the globalization phenomenon has been accused of ravaging the environment and exploiting labour in developing countries. In a recent work on Foreign Direct Investments (FDI) and pollution, we provide empirical evidence to support the pollution haven hypothesis among poorer developing countries (Hoffman et al. 2005). In particular, we show that low income countries use lax environmental legislations to attract FDI in the absence of other investment attracting features. We also show, using regression analysis, that among the middle income countries, FDI *granger* causes CO_2 emissions due to the scale effect.[4] Case study evidence involving, for instance, Union Carbide's chemical plant catastrophe in Bhopal, Shell's attempt to sink a 1,600-tonne oil rig in the North Sea, and the accusation against Nike that it operates sweatshop production in Southeast Asia, add further to the list of harm caused by the globalization process. Nevertheless, these same incidents have served as catalysts for the CSR movement to gain momentum.

An accusation that has direct relevance to Southeast Asian economies is that CSR reduces the competitive advantage in global markets by adding to the cost of production vis-à-vis newer players such as China and India. As explained earlier, CSR involves costs. If the government and society demand too much CSR, then MNEs would find other locations where such demands are lacking, that is, engage in the race to the bottom. In this view, CSR reduces the competitiveness of the Southeast Asian countries and would drive MNEs away to other low CSR locations.

Martin's (2002) Virtue Matrix can be employed to understand the above charge. The matrix, as shown in Figure 9.2, describes the various forces that generate CSR. The bottom quadrants, termed the civil foundation, comprise norms, customs, and laws that influence corporate behaviour. There are

FIGURE 9.2
The Virtue Matrix

Frontier

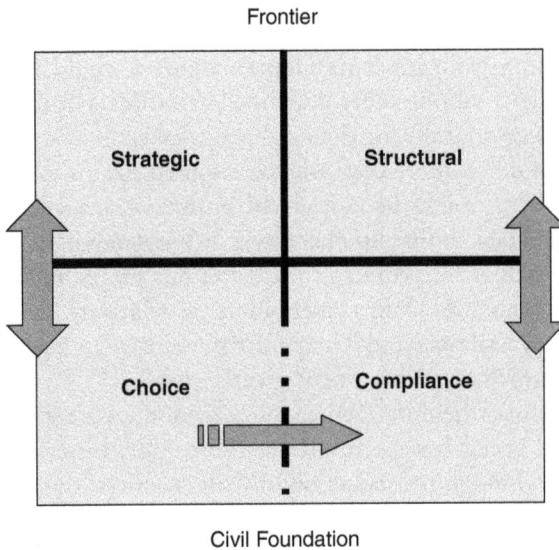

Civil Foundation

Source: Adapted from Martin (2002), p. 9.

laws and regulations which a company follows (compliance), and there are norms and customs that it observes by choice. A firm's behaviour based on compliance and choice fulfills society's baseline expectations. Health benefits for employees, abstinence from bribery, promoting product quality, among other things, are examples of the civil foundation. The line that separates the two bottom quadrants is porous in that actions which were taken by choice in the past could move to compliance when such activities become mandated by law. Pension funds and safety procedures are examples.

The top quadrants are termed the frontier, referring to activities which go beyond the normal responsibilities of a firm. The left-hand, strategic quadrant includes activities that add to shareholder value and generate positive reactions from the various stakeholders of the firm. Firms that emphasize environmentally friendly products, for instance, could attract loyal customers and employees. The right-hand, structural quadrant refers to activities that may reduce shareholder value as the benefits of such activities accrue to society rather than the firm. Firms that continued to pay employees who had been unable to continue working due to Hurricane Katrina in New Orleans come within the structural quadrant.

The line that separates the bottom civil foundation from the top frontier quadrants explains the debate on diminishing competitiveness highlighted above. This line is not fixed, but varies according to the country in question. CSR activities that are considered to be strategic (that is, in the frontier category) in lesser developed countries could fall in the civil foundation category among more developed countries. For instance, MNEs that provide transportation for their factory workers in Vietnam might be considered to be doing more than what is required from a CSR perspective, but the same action might be considered business as usual in a developed country setting. Thus, setting up operations in Vietnam might result in more value added as such actions could attract better human resource and establish goodwill. The demands from stakeholders in relatively more developed countries such as Malaysia and Thailand will tend to go beyond providing such facilities, which, therefore, incur greater costs.

The greater issue here is whether these economies are willing to accept a lower level of social benefit to attract more FDI. Instead of increasing competitiveness through the reduction of CSR practices, the countries stuck in the middle should emphasize productivity and innovation. This would attract higher value added FDI and MNEs that have CSR embedded in both their vision and operations. This view is supported by a recent World Bank-funded study on how CSR influences the investment decisions of MNEs (World Bank 2003). The survey conducted among 107 MNEs from around the world finds that more than 80 per cent of the respondents consider the CSR performance of potential partners and locations before deciding on a new venture. A majority of respondents also considers CSR at least as influential as traditional investment factors such as cost, quality, and delivery in assessing their new venture. The CSR consideration is more influential now than it was five years ago. Promoting CSR among domestic companies and insisting that foreign investors are equally committed to the cause would add to the attractiveness of Southeast Asian countries in the game of attracting FDI.

In fact, Chambers et al. (2003) go further to claim that MNEs are leading CSR in Asia and reject the claim that globalization undermines the social agenda. Their website survey of fifty firms each in seven Asian countries finds that international companies are associated with higher levels of CSR penetration compared with their domestic counterparts (Table 9.1). The rationale here is that international firms have a broader range of stakeholders and it would be in the interest of such firms to engage in CSR activities that meet the demands of these stakeholders.

At the firm level, there are accusations that MNEs impose CSR standards on small- and medium-sized enterprises (SMEs) in developing countries that

TABLE 9.1
CSR Penetration in Asian Domestic Companies and MNEs

	Domestic Companies (%)	MNEs (%)
India	60	72.5
South Korea	50	50
Thailand	60	48
Singapore	0	40
Malaysia	27	33
Philippines	29	43
Indonesia	20	23
Seven-Country Mean	33	45

Source: Chambers et al. (2003).

form part of their supply chains (Utting 2003). These imposed environmental and social standards are in addition to the tight price and delivery schedules to which the SMEs are supposed to adhere. When SMEs are unable to meet these demands, the contract is transferred to larger firms. There are several questions that arise here. First, are MNEs unreasonable in asking SMEs to meet such standards? The assistance provided by MNEs to SMEs in raising their CSR standards should be seen as a social responsibility in itself. For instance, Starbucks instituted a ten-cent per pound premium above world market prices for suppliers that met its CSR standards (Raynard and Forstater 2002). Such action is laudable and should be encouraged. Second, to what extent are SMEs capable of engaging in CSR? Our recent study provides an approach towards dealing with CSR among companies from developing countries (Hung, Ramasamy, and Lee 2004). Using a logit model, we identified management systems employed by a company to be the most potent source of CSR engagement. In other words, companies that comply with some international management standards such as the ISO series or OHSAS, tend to be CSR active. In fact, the World Bank (2003) study identified the ISO 14000 to be the most influential standard on CSR practice even among the MNEs. The third question in the context of CSR and SMEs is the extent to which such compliance affects financial performance. There is enough empirical evidence to show that environmental management systems, for instance, can be justified on purely financial grounds (Feldman, Soyka, and Ameer 1996). Given these answers, suffice it to say that the imposition of CSR standards is beneficial as it could raise the performance of SMEs, although MNEs should be generous in their assistance and guidance.

TABLE 9.2
CSR and Social Development

Country	CSR Penetration (%)	Life Expectancy at Birth (years) 2001	Adult Literacy (%) 2001	HDI 2001
India	72	63.3	58.0	0.590
South Korea	52	75.2	97.9	0.879
Thailand	42	68.9	95.7	0.768
Singapore	38	77.8	92.5	0.884
Malaysia	32	72.8	87.9	0.790
Philippines	30	69.5	95.1	0.751
Indonesia	24	66.2	87.3	0.682

Note: HDI refers to the Human Development Index.
Source: Chambers et al. (2003) and Human Development Index 2003.

From a social development perspective, we are unable to conclude if CSR makes any positive contribution. There are no extensive studies to show any causalities because the measurement of CSR is plagued by problems and criticisms. On the other hand, the definition of CSR and its wide implications are relatively new and may differ from country to country. The empirical evidence available that links CSR and social development cannot be statistically proven. Chambers et al. (2003) find no significant relationships between CSR and two proxies of social development — life expectancy and adult literacy — and the general Human Development Index (Table 9.2).

CSR IN SOUTHEAST ASIA

We have established thus far that globalization promotes CSR and that the social agenda is increasingly becoming a determining factor in the internationalization of firms. While no direct link with social development is evident, the balanced development (or the triple bottom line) promoted in CSR practices would support the social and economic development of a country. We now turn to Southeast Asia and examine the extent to which CSR is practised among the relevant stakeholders.

The 2003 study by Chambers and associates is among the few that analyse the level of CSR among Asian countries. As seen in Table 9.2, CSR practices differ from country to country, with India showing the highest rate of penetration. Among Southeast Asian countries, Thailand ranks the highest, and Indonesia, the lowest. The authors were unable to find any significant reasons for these different penetration rates. Economic wealth, level of economic development, strength of civil society, degree of governance, and democratic practices did not explain the differences in these penetration rates. They propose that CSR practices are a product of specific norms and cultures prevalent in the respective countries. This conclusion is further supported by Welford (2004), to be described below.

The low levels of CSR are further supported by comparative country studies between Malaysia and Singapore. If CSR reporting reflects CSR activity, then only 14 per cent of companies in Singapore went out of their way to consider the environment. Even among those companies reporting, an average of 143 words were used (about half a page) to describe their environmental commitment. This is based on the Association of Certified Chartered Accountants' (ACCA) State of Corporate Environmental Reporting in Singapore in 2000. The report considers 160 companies listed on the Singapore Stock Exchange. A similar report on Malaysia indicates that 7.7 per cent of companies listed on the Bursa Malaysia (Malaysian Stock Exchange) engaged in some form of environmental reporting. About 40 per cent of these companies were devoting more than a page to environmental information.

In an earlier study, Ramasamy and Hung (2004) asked employees of companies in these two countries if their own firms undertook CSR activities. Although Singaporean companies were reported to be more CSR active than their Malaysian counterparts, the level of CSR awareness was still low. For instance, although nearly 85 per cent of the Singaporean respondents stated that there were some CSR activities within their companies, only about 56 per cent of these companies had specified their CSR stand in their company objectives. Less than 50 per cent had any form of review or evaluation of their CSR agenda. Among Malaysian companies, 63 per cent reported having CSR activities, with less than 60 per cent specifying them in their company objectives, and 12 per cent carrying out reviews of their CSR activities. The general attitude towards CSR is, however, more positive among Singaporean companies than their Malaysian counterparts.

Welford (2004) compares CSR practices among companies in Asia and Europe. He asked 120 companies from twelve countries if these companies had any written statements on a range of CSR related issues.[5] Based on the responses, he concludes that Asian companies are doing less than European companies. Figure 9.3, which summarizes the results, shows more European companies having CSR policies on a wide range of issues, some of which are internal to the firm while others relate to the external environment and stakeholders in society. On issues such as corruption and bribery, responding to stakeholders, local community protection, and labour standards, Asian companies surpass the European mark or are very close to it. On the other hand, on issues such as human rights, protection of indigenous rights, and fair trade, Asian companies fare miserably. Welford concludes that Asian companies tend to pay more attention to issues that are important in their respective societies and culture, for instance, bribery and labour standards. Nevertheless, as development becomes more rampant, more CSR issues would have to be considered as part of the CSR agenda of firms. This may include issues relating to the CSR practices of their suppliers and human rights.

We now turn to the various themes[6] in CSR and examine aspects of CSR that are popular in the Southeast Asian countries. Moon (2002) and Chambers et al. (2003) consider three themes of CSR: community involvement; socially responsible production processes; and socially responsible employee relations. Table 9.3 reveals the extent to which these three themes are reported among companies considered CSR active.[7] The mean of the seven countries shows community involvement as the main theme. This result is not specific to Asian countries per se, but is rather a worldwide observation (Moon 2002). However, particularly in Asia, one could expect corporate philanthropy to be an extension of individual social obligation that is emphasized in Asian religions and culture. Surprisingly, employee relations is the least popular theme, which led Welford (2004) to claim that in Asia, employees are considered as factors of production rather than human capital.

To a certain extent, our comparative analysis of Malaysia and Singapore shows slightly different results (Ramasamy and Hung 2004). We asked employees the extent to which CSR terms are used in community activities, in core product/services, and the way the company is run (which includes

TABLE 9.3
Themes of CSR in Asia

	Community Involvement (%)	Production Processes (%)	Employee Relations (%)
India	66.7	58.3	30.6
South Korea	42.3	53.8	11.5
Thailand	71.4	19.0	9.5
Singapore	47.4	10.5	21.1
Malaysia	68.8	50.0	18.8
Philippines	71.4	28.6	0.0
Indonesia	27.3	27.3	27.3
Mean	59.0	38.9	18.1

Source: Chambers et al. (2003).

FIGURE 9.3
CSR in Asian and European Companies

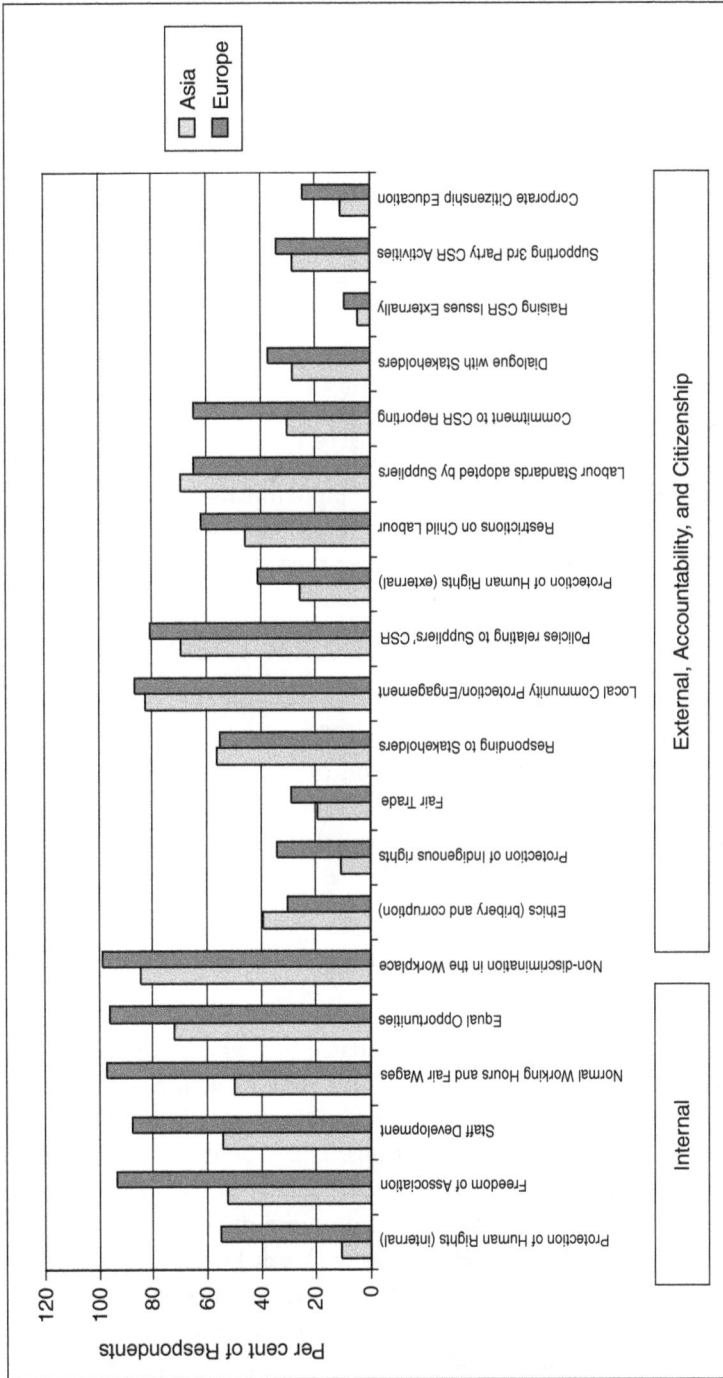

Source: Welford (2004).

TABLE 9.4
CSR Themes in Malaysia and Singapore

	Malaysia	Singapore
Terms are used in community activities	2.55	2.98
Terms are used in core products/services	1.92	3.23
Terms used in the way the company is run	2.12	3.00

Note: Scores were between 1 and 6; 1 — not at all, to 6 — all the time.
Source: Ramasamy and Hung (2004).

employee relations). Results, as shown in Table 9.4, indicate that indeed, in Malaysia, community involvement is the most popular form of CSR engagement. However, CSR in production processes do not score as highly. In Singapore, CSR practices are more predominant in the production process compared with other areas. However, one should note that the degree to which CSR terms are used in all three themes is low.

DRIVERS OF CSR IN SOUTHEAST ASIA

The results discussed thus far reveal that the level of CSR penetration among the Southeast Asian countries is low. We now identify five main drivers of CSR and discuss how they could contribute to the CSR movement. These drivers are: government and regulations; multinational enterprises; non-governmental groups and international institutions; CEO/Managers; and consumers.

Government and Regulations

As described earlier, there is a long standing debate as to whether social responsibility of firms should be mandated by laws and regulations. Supporters of this view reckon that the effects of corporate action on the environment and society are severe enough to warrant the imposition of laws that would internalize the cost of business actions. That would ensure that firms become more responsible for their actions, particularly in the area of environmental protection. Other less radical views promote the incentive system, whereby governments offer incentives (such as tax breaks) to firms that are CSR active. Defenders of voluntary action argue that regulations would only set minimum targets for social responsibilities. In developing countries where enforcement is lacking, regulations would result in aversion and corruption.

In Southeast Asia, CSR is largely voluntary in nature. In Malaysia, except for some basic requirements on occupational safety and health, and control of major industrial accidents, there is no statutory requirement for firms to disclose information pertaining to their CSR activities (ACCA 2003). However, listing requirements by Bursa Malaysia does require disclosure of information that has direct influence on the financial performance of a company. The Malaysian Accounting Standards Board encourages companies to report on their environmental activities if these help users in their economic decisions. In Singapore, the government sees itself as an enabler of CSR, stepping into social and business policies only if these adversely affect the business environment and the country's future (Haley, Low, and Toh 1996).

A combination of regulations and encouragement is clearly necessary for Southeast Asia. Regulation pertaining to basic responsibilities is required. This may include banning activities that degrade the environment, exploit labour, and voliate basic human rights. On the other hand, actions that address community issues and human resource development could be voluntary in nature, but supported by the public sector.

Multinational Enterprises

In a region where international economic relationships form an important component of the economy, the role of multinationals in driving the CSR agenda in Southeast Asia is obviously important, particularly with trade forming a large portion of the GDP of these countries. In Malaysia and Singapore, for instance, trade is two and three times larger than their GDP respectively. FDI is also a major driving force for economic growth. In countries such as Thailand and Indonesia, the size of FDI as a proportion of gross fixed capital formation is also sizeable. By setting high CSR standards in the business environment, multinationals engaged in trading and investment activities involving local firms could be instrumental in promoting CSR practices in the region. This is particularly true as Southeast Asian countries become "factories" and "service centres" for MNEs from more advanced countries. MNEs would want to impose high CSR standards on their suppliers as a condition for outsourced contracts because customers and other stakeholders do not differentiate between a company and its suppliers. MNEs could be branded unethical due to the actions of their suppliers.

In a study involving fifty-two "green" companies from the ASEAN-5, Rao (2002) finds that choosing suppliers based on environmental criteria is the most likely approach towards establishing a supply chain environmental management (SCEM) system. In a related study, Rao (2004) shows the importance of integrating suppliers within a company's clean production system, and the role of workers in supporting such a system. However, one should note the discussion earlier pointing out that passing the cost of CSR down the supply chain would result in efforts to pay lip service to CSR, with no benefit to anyone as a consequence. Rather, a partnership between the MNE and the local counterpart is called for. For instance, by assisting local firms to meet international codes such as the ISO14000, ISO9000, and the SA8000, the MNE is able to improve both quality and social responsibility targets. The green companies in Rao's (2002, 2004) studies, for instance, hold seminars to increase awareness among suppliers and guide them in their efforts to establish their own environmental programmes. Among the MNEs active in increasing their supplier awareness are Ford in the Philippines, Hitachi in Malaysia, Bitratex Industries in Indonesia, Seagate in Thailand, and Philips in Singapore.

Non-governmental Groups and International Institutions

The high level of CSR awareness in many industrialized countries can be attributed largely to the increasing number of non-governmental groups established to promote the social responsibility agenda. In the United Kingdom, for example, the Institute for Social and Ethical Accountability (AccountAbility) and Business in the Community (BITC) are dedicated to the promotion of social, ethical, and overall organizational accountability as an essential part of business excellence. At the global level, the United Nations-initiated Global Compact recognizes MNEs that adhere to its basic principles such as human rights and democracy.

In Southeast Asia, the number of similar organizations is small. For Malaysia, the Consumer Association of Penang (CAP), the Federation of Malaysia Consumers Association (FOMCA), and Worldwide Fund for Nature (WWF) Malaysia are the dominant institutions contributing to CSR awareness. In the Philippines, the Philippine Business for Social Progress (PBSP) is a foundation that promotes a sustainable approach towards poverty reduction. The Singapore Environmental Council (a government initiated body) claims that since its inception, companies have been proactive in learning more about environmental management. Another strategy to promote awareness has been through an award system. In Malaysia for instance, the ACCA honours companies that have reported on their social and environmental activities. The Malaysian Environmental and Social Reporting Award (MESRA) was launched in 2000 and has seen an increasing number

TABLE 9.5
ISO 9001 and ISO 14001 Certifications in Southeast Asia

Country	ISO 9001				ISO 14001			
	2001	2002	2003	2004	2001	2002	2003	2004
Brunei	4	13	36	46	4	3	3	4
Cambodia		5	5	5			1	1
Indonesia	161	308	1,318	3,134	199	229	297	373
Malaysia	257	1,119	3,076	4,337	367	367	370	566
Philippines	43	270	456	1,108	120	124	174	261
Singapore	333	1,953	3,341	3,964	298	441	523	616
Thailand	89	938	1,675	5,955	483	671	736	966
Vietnam	33	354	1,237	1,598	33	33	56	85

Source: The ISO Survey of Certifications 2004 available at <www.iso.org/iso/en/prods-services/otherpubs/pdf/survey2004.pdf> (accessed 11 October 2005).

of participants with better quality reporting (Ramasamy and Hung 2005).

If international management systems and standards are a gauge of CSR awareness and activity, the increase in the number of certificates issued by the ISO to companies in Southeast Asia is encouraging. Table 9.5 shows a marked increase in the number of ISO 9001 certificates issued in 2004 compared with previous years. However, in the case of ISO 14001 certificates, although the number of issued certificates is increasing, it is relatively small. However, this seems to be global phenomenon.[8] For many developing countries in Southeast Asia, the impetus provided by international agencies such as the ISO towards raising the CSR awareness through quality systems is accepted and, in fact, encouraged by the relevant governments. However, when the international agencies raise issues that are "political" in nature, the support that is given is lukewarm. The Global Compact is a case in point. By including human rights and democracy within its goals, the popularity of the initiative in several Southeast Asian countries is low as the definition of these concepts is ambiguous in these nations.

CEO/Managers

One could argue that the degree to which CSR is practised by a firm depends on the person(s) at the helm. As Wood (1991, p. 690) observes, "a company's social responsibilities are not met by some abstract organizational actor;

they are met by individual human actors who constantly make decisions and choices, some big and some small, some minor and others of great consequence". In particular, it is the chief executive of an organization — who often makes important decisions about its future direction — who plays an important role in determining the way an organization chooses to fulfil its moral obligations and social responsibilities (Thomas and Simerly 1994). There is also sufficient research to conclude that within the upper echelons of a firm, many CEOs and board members acknowledge that they have certain responsibilities towards the welfare of their stakeholders (Ford and McLaughlin 1980; Frederick 1983; Ibrahim, Howard, and Angelidis 2003).

In other words, the extent to which CSR permeates the philosophy of senior management could become an important contributing factor towards corporate social awareness (Teoh and Thong 1986). Taking this thought further, several studies show the personal and environmental factors that influence the attitude of managers towards CSR. Evidence from several studies undertaken in Asia points to family training and upbringing, traditional beliefs, and customs as key attributes (Gilles and Leinbach 1983). A study of Malaysian managers reveals that family upbringing, religious training, conduct of superiors, and traditional beliefs and customs are the most important factors that affect attitudes towards CSR (Abdul Rashid and Ibrahim 2002).

One study on Malaysian companies in which this author was involved noted that firms with ethnic Malay chief executives were more CSR active than companies with ethnic Chinese CEOs (Ramasamy, Ng, and Hung 2007). The study, which was based on content analysis, suggests that voluntary disclosure of CSR practices was significantly greater among companies with a Malay CEO at the helm. A cursory review of the CSR disclosure on a thematic basis revealed that companies with Malay chief executives rank environmental issues as more important when compared with companies with Chinese chief executives. In contrast, the latter companies seem to rank product themes higher on their agenda, followed by the environmental theme. This appears to agree with the general contention that ethnic Chinese are more business orientated and focus on investment with more visible returns. From this study, it is possible to conclude that apart from age and educational background, the ethnicity (and in the case of Malaysia, religion) of chief executives may play a role in formulating and implementing socially responsible policies and programmes of organizations. While there may be little that can be done if ethnicity and religion are drivers of CSR, previous studies do support the view that the promotion of CSR values should be instilled among the young at schools and universities.

Consumers

In a free market economy, a firm acts as an agency that is designed to fulfill the needs and wants of consumers. In such an environment, the degree to which firms are CSR active depends on the degree to which consumers demand that such agendas be embedded within the product and services they purchase. Studies by Brown and Dacin (1997), Handelman and Arnold (1999), and Maignan (2001) suggest that firms with greater CSR association tend to receive greater support from customers in industrialized countries such as the United States, France, and Germany. A survey of European consumers by CSR Europe in 2000 found that seven in ten consumers consider a company's CSR commitment to be important when making buying decisions (Business in the Community, Ireland 2002). However, Globescan's 2005 Corporate Social Responsibility Monitor suggests that while expectations amongst the public have grown across the world, CSR performance among companies is consistently decreasing. Figure 9.4, which describes the expectations and performance of CSR, is based on a survey of respondents from twenty-one countries. When respondents were asked

FIGURE 9.4
Societal Expectations of CSR vs Industry CSR Performance Ratings

Average of 21 Countries, 2001–05

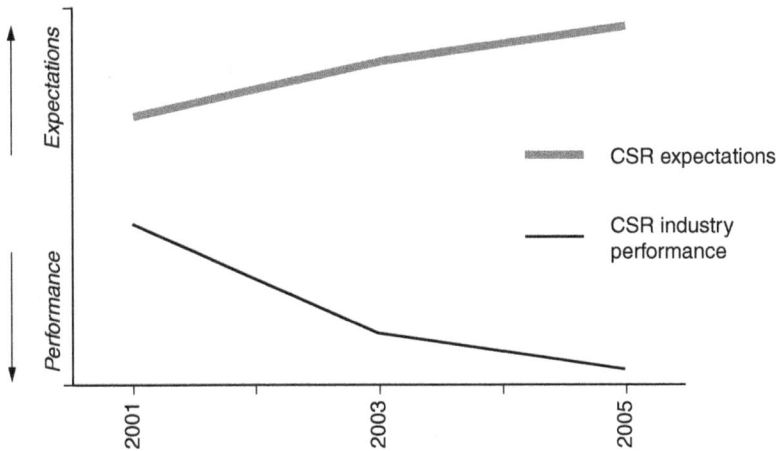

Source: Globescan, *2005 Corporate Social Responsibility Monitor*, available at <www.globescan.com> (accessed 13 October 2005).

FIGURE 9.5
CSR Aspects Most Looked for in a Company

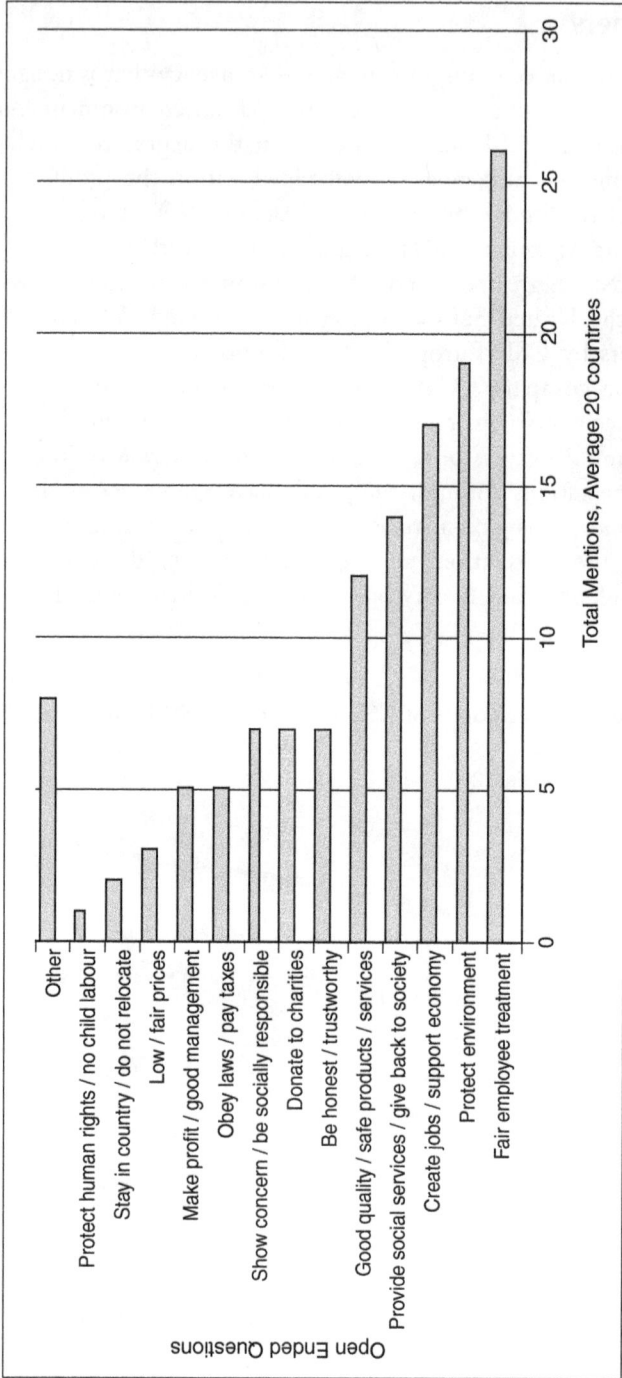

Source: Globescan, *2005 Corporate Social Responsibility Monitor*, available at <www.globescan.com> (accessed 13 October 2005).

what they consider to be the most socially responsible acts of firms, treating employees fairly and protecting the environment were the most common responses (Figure 9.5).

Studies and surveys that examine the role of consumer pressure and buying behaviour vis-à-vis CSR in Asia are sorely lacking. An attempt to consider the perception of Malaysian consumers on CSR is Ahmad (2004), who finds that while consumers are not willing to pay a premium for CSR, they are prepared to penalize those companies that are known to be CSR violaters. More research on Asian consumer perception of CSR and further aspects of CSR that are of importance is necessary. If such findings reveal the lacklustre nature of Asian consumers towards CSR, consumer associations should be empowered to create awareness of CSR and highlight the benefits to the individual consumer as well as to society of supporting CSR active firms.

CONCLUSION

Irrespective of whether CSR is a passing fad or a movement that will gain momentum, profit maximization as the sole objective of firms is no longer a sustainable option. Firms act as agencies that fulfil the demands of their respective stakeholders. Stakeholders, however, are not just dictating *what* they want, but increasingly *how* goods and services should be produced as well. This implies that firms need to adapt and design their production systems in order to fulfill both these requirements. In a globalized world, where access to information allows international comparisons among firms to be made more easily, and the media hounds every wrongdoing of businesses, there is little option for firms, but to meet these twin demands. Businesses in Southeast Asia, a region known for its economic openness, will not be spared either. Consumers in the region, with increasing per capita incomes and education levels, as well as MNEs that act as clients to various local suppliers, are likely to continue to raise their demands for firms to be socially responsible. To base competitiveness on low production costs is not a sustainable option.

Previous studies have shown low, albeit increasing, awareness of CSR among stakeholders in Southeast Asia. Efforts at further extending the CSR agenda have to focus on the main drivers of social responsibility. In this regard, consumers have to be educated to be more demanding, MNEs have to develop a more encouraging attitude towards their suppliers, CEOs have to take a more proactive attitude towards CSR, and international and non-governmental agencies have to offer a more systematic process for adopting and reporting on CSR initiatives. Finally, governments need to promulgate regulations to enforce minimum standards in this area, and to provide incentives to encourage firms to be socially responsible participants in society.

Notes

1. Doane (2005), for instance, cites an example of how BP, Tesco, and Cadbury highlight their CSR activities and dialogue, but sidestep the adverse effects of their business decisions.
2. BSR, Overview of Corporate Social Responsibility, www document, <http://www.bsr.org> (accessed 2 September 2005).
3. Ibid.
4. Granger causality, an economic term, implies a causal than a correlational relationship between the variables concerned.
5. The Asian companies were from Hong Kong, Singapore, Japan, Korea, Malaysia, and Thailand.
6. Also referred to as waves of CSR by the Chambers et al. study as well as Moon (2002).
7. Active companies are those that have more than three pages devoted to CSR. Totals may not add up to 100 per cent because other themes may be covered, or totals may come up to more than 100 per cent due to overlaps between the themes.
8. In 2004, the number of ISO 9001 certificates worldwide was 670,399 compared with 90,569 ISO 14001 certificates.

References

Abdul Rashid, M.Z. and S. Ibrahim."Executive and Management Attitude towards Corporate Social Responsibility in Malaysia". *Corporate Governance* 2, no. 4 (2002): 10–16.

ACCA. *The State of Corporate Environmental Reporting in Malaysia*. Kuala Lumpur: ACCA, 2003 <www.accaglobal.com/sustainability>.

―――. *The State of Corporate Environmental Reporting in Singapore*. Singapore: ACCA, 2003*a* <www.accaglobal.com/sustainability>.

Ahmed, M. "A Study on the Influence of CSR Activities of Firms on Consumer Purchasing Decisions in Malaysia". MBA Dissertation, University of Nottingham, 2003.

Aninat, E. "Surmounting the Challenges of Globalization". *Finance and Development*, 39, no. 1 (2002).

Bowie, N.E. "New Directions in Corporate Social Responsibility". *Business Horizons* 34 (July/August 1991): 56–65.

Brown, T.J. and P.A. Dacin. "The Company and the Product: Corporate Associations and Consumer Product Responses". *Journal of Marketing* 61 (January 1977): 68–84.

Business in the Community Ireland. *Consumer Attitudes in Ireland towards Corporate Responsibility.* 2002 <www.csreurope.org/uploadstore/cms/docs/CSRE_Pub_BITC_Ireland_booklet.pdf>. Accessed 13 October 2005.

BSR. *Overview of Corporate Social Responsibility*, Business for Social Responsibility, <www.bsr.org>. Accessed 2 September 2005.

Chambers, E., W. Chapple, J. Moon, and M. Sullivan. "CSR in Asia: A Seven Country Study of CSR Website Reporting". ICCSR Research Paper Series, No. 09-2003, University of Nottingham, 2003.

Davis, I. "The Biggest Contract". *The Economist*, 28 May 2005, pp. 69–71.

Doane, D. "Beyond Corporate Social Responsibility: Minnows, Mammoths and Markets". *Futures* 37 (2005): 215–29.

Dollar, D. and A. Kraay. "Trade, Growth, and Poverty". World Bank Policy Research Working Paper, No. 199, Washington, D.C.: World Bank, 2001.

Feldman, S., P. Soyka, and P. Ameer. "Does Improving a Firm's Environmental Management System and Environmental Performance Result in a Higher Stock Price?". ICF Kaiser International Inc., 1996 <www.icfconsulting.com/Publications/doc_files/resp_pays.pdf>. Accessed 23 September 2005.

Ford, R. and F. McLaughlin. "Perceptions of Social Responsible Activities and Attitudes: A Comparison of Business School Deans and Corporate Chief Executives". *Academy of Management Journal* 27 (1980): 658–76.

Frederick, W. "Corporate Social Responsibility in the Reagan Era and Beyond". *California Management Review* 25 (1983): 145–56.

Friedman, T. *The Lexus and the Olive Tree: Understanding Globalization* 1 (Anchor Edition), 2000.

Gilles, R.W.T. and L.J. Leinbach. "Corporate Social Responsibility in Hong Kong". *California Management Review* 25, no. 2 (1983): 107–23.

Haley, U.C.V., L. Low, and M.H. Toh. "Singapore Incorporated: Reinterpreting Singapore's Business Environment through a Corporate Metaphor". *Management Decision* 34, no. 9 (1996): 17–28.

Handelman, J.M. and S.J. Arnold. "The Role of Marketing Actions with a Social Dimension: Appeals to the Institutional Environment". *Journal of Marketing* 63 (July 1999): 33–48.

Handy, C. *The Hungry Spirit*. Doubleday Broadway Books, 1999.

Henderson, D. "10 Questions with David Henderson on the Role of Business Today: Does it Include Corporate Social Responsibility". *Voices, Journal of Financial Planning* (August 2005).

Hoffmann, R., C.G. Lee, B. Ramasamy, and M. Yeung. "FDI and Pollution: A Granger Causality Test Using Panel Data". *Journal of International Development* 17 (2005): 311–17.

Hung, W.T., B. Ramasamy, and C.G. Lee. "Building CSR Capacity Among Firms in Developing Countries: A Resource-based View". Paper presented at the International Business Research Conference, Victoria University of Technology, Melbourne, Australia, 15–16 November 2004.

Ibrahim, N., D. Howard, and J. Angelidis. "Board Members in the Service Industry: An Empirical Examination of the Relationship Between Corporate Social Responsibility Orientation and Directorial Type". *Journal of Business Ethics* 47, no. 4 (2003).

Maignan, I. "Consumers' Perceptions of Corporate Social Responsibilities: A Cross Cultural Comparison". *Journal of Business Ethics* 30, no. 1 (2001): 57–72.

Manakkalathil, J. and E. Rudolf. "Corporate Social Responsibility in a Globalizing Market". *SAM Advanced Management Journal* (Winter 1995): 29–32.

Martin, R.L. "The Virtue Matrix: Calculating the Return on Corporate Responsibility". *Harvard Business Review* (March 2002): 5–11.

Moon, J. "Corporate Social Responsibility: An Overview". *International Directory of Corporate Philanthropy*. London: Europe, 2002.

OECD. "Private Initiatives for Corporate Responsibility: An Analysis". Working Papers on International Investment, No. 2001/1, 2001.

Ramasamy, B. and W.T. Hung. "A Comparative Analysis of Corporate Social Responsibility Awareness: Malaysian and Singaporean Firms". *Journal of Corporate Citizenship* 13 (2004): 109–23.

Ramasamy, B. and W.T. Hung. "Communicating CSR to Stakeholders: The Case of Malaysia". *Corporate Environmental Strategy: International Journal for Sustainable Business* 12, nos 3–4 (2005): 117–28.

Ramasamy, B., Ng H.L., and Hung W.T. "Corporate Social Performance and Ethnicity: A Comparison between Malay and Chinese Chief Executives in Malaysia". *International Journal of Cross Cultural Management* 7, no. 1 (2007): 29–45.

Rao, P. "Greening the Supply Chain: A New Initiative in Southeast Asia". *International Journal of Operations & Production Management* 22, no. 6 (2002): 632–55.

————. "Greening Production: Southeast Asian Experience". *International Journal of Operations & Production Management* 24, no. 3 (2004): 289–320.

Raynard, P. and M. Forstater. *Corporate Social Responsibility: Implications for Small and Medium Enterprises in Developing Countries*. Vienna: UNIDO, 2002.

Sethi, S.P. "Dimensions of Corporate Social Performance: An Analytical Framework". *California Management Review* 17 (1975): 58–64.

Svendsen, A.C., R.G. Boutilier, R.M. Abbot, and D. Wheeler. *Measuring the Business Value of Stakeholder Relationships*, Part One. The Centre for Innovation in Management, Simon Fraser University, n.d.

Teoh, H.Y. and G. Thong. "Another Look at Corporate Social Responsibility and Reporting: An Empirical Study in a Developing Country". *Malaysian Management Review* 21, no. 3 (1986): 36–51.

Thomas, A.S. and R.L. Simerly. "The CEO and Corporate Social Performance: An Interdisciplinary Examination. *Journal of Business Ethics* 13, no. 12 (1994): 959–68.

Utting, P. "Profits and Loss? Corporations and Development". *Global Future*, Third Quarter 2003.

Welford, R. "Corporate Social Responsibility in Europe and Asia". *Journal of Corporate Citizenship* 13 (2004): 31–47.

Wood, D.J. Corporate Social Performance Revisited. *Academy of Management Review*, 16, no. 4 (1991): 691–718.

World Bank. *Race to the Top: Attracting and Enabling Global Sustainable Business.* NY: World Bank, 2003.

INDEX